# THE SCOUT MINDSET

*Why Some People*
*See Things Clearly*
*and Others Don't*

## Julia Galef

PIATKUS

PIATKUS

First published in the US in 2021 by Portfolio, an imprint of
Penguin Random House LLC
First published in Great Britain in 2021 by Piatkus

13 5 7 9 10 8 6 4 2

A CIP catalogue record for this book
is available from the British Library.

ISBN 978-0-349-42764-5

Printed and bound in Great Britain by Clays Ltd, Elcograf S.p.A.

Papers used by Piatkus are from well-managed forests
and other responsible sources.

Piatkus
An imprint of
Little, Brown Book Group
Carmelite House
50 Victoria Embankment
London EC4Y 0DZ

An Hachette UK Company
www.hachette.co.uk

www.littlebrown.co.uk

*To Luke, the best scout I've ever met*

# CONTENTS

# INTRODUCTION

WHEN YOU THINK of someone with excellent judgment, what traits come to mind? Maybe you think of things like intelligence, cleverness, courage, or patience. Those are all admirable virtues, but there's one trait that belongs at the top of the list that is so overlooked, it doesn't even have an official name.

So I've given it one. I call it *scout mindset: the motivation to see things as they are, not as you wish they were.*

Scout mindset is what allows you to recognize when you are wrong, to seek out your blind spots, to test your assumptions and change course. It's what prompts you to honestly ask yourself questions like "Was I at fault in that argument?" or "Is this risk worth it?" or "How would I react if someone from the other political party did the same thing?" As the late physicist Richard Feynman once said, "The first principle is that you must not fool yourself—and you are the easiest person to fool."

Our capacity to fool ourselves was a hot topic throughout the 2000s and 2010s. Popular media and bestselling books like *How We Know What Isn't So, Predictably Irrational, Why People Believe Weird Things, Mistakes Were Made (But Not by Me), You Are Not So Smart,*

*Denialism, Why Everyone (Else) Is a Hypocrite,* and *Thinking, Fast and Slow* painted an unflattering picture of a human brain hardwired for self-deception: We rationalize away our flaws and mistakes. We indulge in wishful thinking. We cherry-pick evidence that confirms our prejudices and supports our political tribe.

That picture isn't wrong, but it is missing something.

Yes, we often rationalize away our mistakes—but we sometimes acknowledge them, too. We change our minds less often than we should but more often than we could. We're complex creatures who sometimes hide the truth from ourselves and sometimes confront it. This book is about the less explored side of that coin, the times we succeed in *not* fooling ourselves, and what we can learn from those successes.

MY PATH TO this book began in 2009, after I quit graduate school and threw myself into a passion project that became a new career: helping people reason out tough questions in their personal and professional lives. At first, I imagined that this would involve teaching people about things like probability, logic, and cognitive biases, and showing them how those subjects applied to everyday life. But after several years of running workshops, reading studies, doing consulting, and interviewing people, I finally came to accept that *knowing how to reason* wasn't the cure-all I thought it was.

Knowing that you should test your assumptions doesn't automatically improve your judgment, any more than knowing you should exercise automatically improves your health. Being able to rattle off a list of biases and fallacies doesn't help you unless you're willing to acknowledge those biases and fallacies in your own thinking. The biggest lesson I learned is something that's since been corroborated by researchers, as we'll see in this book: our judgment isn't limited by knowledge nearly as much as it's limited by attitude.

None of which is to say that I'm a perfect exemplar of scout mindset, by the way. I rationalize away mistakes; I avoid thinking about problems; I get defensive in response to criticism. More than once during my research for this book, I realized I had essentially wasted an interview because I spent it trying to convince my interviewee that my thesis was correct, instead of trying to understand their point of view. (The irony of my being closed-minded during an interview about open-mindedness is not lost on me.)

But I'm better than I used to be, and you can be, too—that's the aim of this book. My approach has three prongs.

# 1. REALIZE THAT TRUTH ISN'T IN CONFLICT WITH YOUR OTHER GOALS

Many people actively resist viewing reality accurately because they believe that accuracy is a hindrance to their goals—that if they want to be happy, successful, and influential, it's better to view themselves and the world through a distorted lens.

Part of my goal in writing this book was to set the record straight. There are a lot of myths out there about self-deception, some of which have even been promoted by prestigious scientists. For example, maybe you've seen one of the many articles and books claiming that "studies show" that self-deception is part of mental health, and that seeing the world realistically only leads to depression. In chapter 7, we'll examine the questionable research behind those claims, and discover how psychologists fooled themselves about the benefits of positive thinking.

Or maybe you hold the common belief that when you're doing something hard, like starting a company, you need to be delusionally overconfident. You might be surprised to learn that some of the world's most famous entrepreneurs expected their companies to fail.

Jeff Bezos put Amazon's probability of success at about 30 percent. Elon Musk estimated a 10 percent chance of success for each of his companies, Tesla and SpaceX. In chapter 8, we'll come to understand their reasoning and why it's valuable to have a clear-eyed picture of the odds you're facing.

Or perhaps you share this widespread sentiment: "Sure, being objective is a good thing if you're a scientist or a judge. But if you're an activist trying to change the world, you don't need objectivity—you need passion." In fact, as we'll see in chapter 14, scout mindset complements passion. We'll travel back to the height of the AIDS crisis in the 1990s, and discover why scout mindset was so crucial to activists' success in stopping the epidemic.

## 2. LEARN TOOLS THAT MAKE IT EASIER TO SEE CLEARLY

I've packed this book with concrete tools you can use to get better at scout mindset. For example, how can you tell when your own reasoning is biased? It's not as simple as just asking yourself, "Am I biased?" In chapter 5, we'll learn thought experiments like the outsider test, the selective skeptic test, and the conformity test to examine your reasoning about what you believe and what you want.

How do you decide how certain you are about a particular belief? In chapter 6, we'll practice some introspection techniques that will help you pin down your level of certainty from 0 to 100 percent, and train you to recognize what it feels like when you're making a claim you don't really believe.

Do you ever try to listen to the "other side" of an issue, and find yourself getting frustrated or angry? That might be because you're approaching it the wrong way. In chapter 12, I'll share some pointers that make it much easier to learn from opposing perspectives.

## 3. APPRECIATE THE EMOTIONAL REWARDS OF SCOUT MINDSET

Concrete tools are important, but I'm also hoping to leave you with something more. Facing reality with all its uncertainty and disappointments might seem bleak. But as you peruse this book's examples of "scouts" (my term for people who are especially good at some aspects of scout mindset, even though nobody is perfect), you'll notice that they don't seem depressed. For the most part, they're calm, cheerful, playful, and resolute.

That's because even though it may not be obvious from the outside, scout mindset is emotionally rewarding. It's empowering to be able to resist the temptation to self-deceive, and to know that you can face reality even when it's unpleasant. There's an equanimity that results from understanding risk and coming to terms with the odds you're facing. And there's a refreshing lightness in the feeling of being free to explore ideas and follow the evidence wherever it leads, unconstrained by what you're "supposed to" think.

Learning to appreciate these emotional rewards is what makes scout mindset stick. To that end, I've woven into this book some of my favorite inspiring examples of scouts who have helped me and others cultivate scout mindset over the years.

OUR JOURNEY WILL take us through the worlds of science, business, activism, politics, sports, cryptocurrency, and survivalism. We'll dip our toes in the Culture Wars, the Mommy Wars, and the Probability Wars. Along the way, we'll unlock the answers to puzzles such as: Why did the sight of a peacock's tail make Charles Darwin sick? What made a professional climate change skeptic switch sides? Why do some victims of cultlike pyramid schemes manage to extract themselves while others stay stuck?

This book is not a rant about how irrational people are. Nor is it an attempt to scold you into thinking "correctly." It's a tour of a different way of being, one that's rooted in an appetite for truth, and one that's both useful and fulfilling—and, in my opinion, woefully underappreciated. I'm excited to share it with you.

# PART I

# The Case for Scout Mindset

*Chapter 1*

# Two Types of Thinking

I N 1894, a cleaning lady in the German embassy in France found something in a wastebasket that would throw the entire country into chaos. It was a torn-up memorandum—and the cleaning lady was a French spy.[1] She passed the memo on to senior staff in the French army, who read it and realized with alarm that someone in their ranks had been selling valuable military secrets to Germany.

The memo was unsigned, but suspicion quickly fell on an officer named Alfred Dreyfus, the only Jewish member of the army's general staff. Dreyfus was one of a small number of officers who was of high enough rank to have access to the sensitive information mentioned in the memo. He was not well liked. His fellow officers considered him cold, arrogant, and boastful.

As the army investigated Dreyfus, suspicious anecdotes began to pile up. One man reported seeing Dreyfus loitering somewhere, asking probing questions. Another reported having heard Dreyfus praising the German Empire.[2] Dreyfus had been spotted at least once in a gambling establishment. Rumor had it that he kept mistresses, despite being married. Hardly signs of a trustworthy character!

Feeling increasingly confident that Dreyfus was the spy, French army officers managed to obtain a sample of his handwriting to compare with the memo. It was a match! Well, at least it looked similar. There were admittedly a few inconsistencies, but surely it couldn't be a coincidence that the handwriting was so much alike. They wanted to make sure, so they sent the memorandum and the sample of Dreyfus's writing to two experts for evaluation.

Expert Number 1 declared it to be a match! The officers felt vindicated. Expert Number 2, however, was not convinced. It was quite possible that the two writing samples came from different sources, he told the officers.

A mixed verdict wasn't what the officers were hoping for. But then they remembered that Expert Number 2 worked with the Bank of France. The world of finance was full of powerful Jewish men. And Dreyfus was Jewish. How could they trust the judgment of someone with such conflicts of interest? The officers made up their minds. Dreyfus was their man.

Dreyfus insisted he was innocent, but to no avail. He was arrested, and a military court found him guilty of treason on December 22, 1894. He was sentenced to solitary confinement for life on the aptly named Devil's Island, a former leper colony off the coast of French Guiana, far across the Atlantic Ocean.

When Dreyfus heard the decision, he was in shock. After being dragged back to prison, he considered suicide, but eventually decided that such an act would only prove his guilt.

The final ritual before sending Dreyfus away was to strip him of his army insignia in public, an event dubbed "the degradation of Dreyfus." As an army captain tore the braid from Dreyfus's uniform, one officer cracked an anti-Semitic joke: "He's a Jew, remember. He's probably calculating the value of that gold braid."

As Dreyfus was paraded past his fellow troops, journalists, and crowds of onlookers, he shouted, "I am innocent!" The crowd, meanwhile, spat insults and yelled, "Death to Jews!"

Once he arrived on Devil's Island, he was kept in a small stone hut with no human contact except for his guards, who refused to speak to him. At night, he was shackled to his bed. During the day, he wrote letters begging the government to reopen his case. But as far as France was concerned, the matter was settled.

## "CAN I BELIEVE IT?" VS. "MUST I BELIEVE IT?"

It might not look this way, but the officers who arrested Dreyfus had not set out to frame an innocent man. From their perspective, they were conducting an objective investigation of the evidence, and the evidence pointed to Dreyfus.*

But although their investigation felt objective to them, it was clearly colored by their motives. They were under pressure to find the spy quickly, and they were already inclined to distrust Dreyfus. Then, once the wheels of the investigation had been set in motion, another motive was born: they had to prove themselves right or risk losing face, and potentially their jobs as well.

The investigation of Dreyfus is an example of an aspect of human psychology called directionally motivated reasoning—or, more often, just motivated reasoning—in which our unconscious motives affect the conclusions we draw.[3] The best description of motivated reasoning I've ever seen comes from psychologist Tom Gilovich. When we want something to be true, he said, we ask ourselves, "Can I believe this?," searching for an excuse to accept it. When we don't want

---

* It's worth noting that Dreyfus's prosecutors put a finger on the scales of justice by slipping the judge a dossier of faked letters that incriminated Dreyfus. Nevertheless, historians don't believe that the officers who arrested Dreyfus set out to intentionally frame him from the beginning; rather, they became convinced of his guilt and were willing to play dirty to secure his conviction.

something to be true, we instead ask ourselves, "Must I believe this?," searching for an excuse to reject it.[4]

When the officers first began investigating Dreyfus, they evaluated rumors and circumstantial evidence through the lens of "Can I accept this as evidence of guilt?," erring more on the side of credulity than they would have if they weren't already motivated to suspect him.

When Expert Number 2 told them that Dreyfus's handwriting didn't match the memo, the officers asked themselves, "Must I believe it?" and came up with a reason not to: Expert Number 2's supposed conflict of interest due to his Jewish faith.

The officers had even searched Dreyfus's home for incriminating evidence and failed to find any. So they asked themselves, "Can we still believe Dreyfus is guilty?" and were able to come up with a reason to: "He probably got rid of the evidence before we got here!"

Even if you've never heard the phrase *motivated reasoning*, I'm sure you're already familiar with the phenomenon. It's all around you under different names—denial, wishful thinking, confirmation bias, rationalization, tribalism, self-justification, overconfidence, delusion. Motivated reasoning is so fundamental to the way our minds work that it's almost strange to have a special name for it; perhaps it should just be called *reasoning*.

You can see it in the way people happily share news stories that support their narratives about America or capitalism or "kids today," while ignoring stories that don't. You can see it in the way we rationalize away red flags in an exciting new relationship, and always think we're doing more than our fair share of the work. When a coworker screws up, it's because they're incompetent, but when we screw up, it's because we were under a lot of pressure. When a politician from the rival party breaks the law, it proves how corrupt that whole party is, but when one of our politicians breaks the law, he's just a corrupt individual.

Even two thousand years ago, Greek historian Thucydides described the motivated reasoning of the cities that believed they could overthrow their Athenian rulers: "[Their] judgment was based more upon blind wishing than upon any sound prediction; for it is a habit of mankind . . . to use sovereign reason to thrust aside what they do not desire."[5] Thucydides's is the earliest account of the phenomenon I've found so far. But I have no doubt humans have been irritated and amused by each other's motivated reasoning for many thousands of years before that. Perhaps if our Paleolithic ancestors had developed a written language, we would have found a complaint scrawled on the cave walls of Lascaux: "Og crazy if he think he best mammoth hunter."

## REASONING AS DEFENSIVE COMBAT

The tricky thing about motivated reasoning is that even though it's easy to spot in other people, it doesn't *feel* like motivated reasoning from the inside. When we reason, it feels like we're being objective. Fair-minded. Dispassionately evaluating the facts.

Beneath the surface of our conscious awareness, however, it's as if we're soldiers, defending our beliefs against threatening evidence. In fact, the metaphor of reasoning as a kind of defensive combat is baked right into the English language, so much so that it's difficult to speak about reasoning at all without using militaristic language.[6]

We talk about our beliefs as if they're military positions, or even fortresses, built to resist attack. Beliefs can be *deep-rooted, well-grounded, built on fact*, and *backed up* by arguments. They *rest on solid foundations*. We might hold a *firm* conviction or a *strong* opinion, be *secure* in our beliefs or have *unshakeable* faith in something.

Arguments are either forms of attack or forms of defense. If we're not careful, someone might *poke holes in* our logic or *shoot down* our ideas. We might encounter a *knock-down* argument against something we believe. Our positions might get *challenged, destroyed, undermined,* or *weakened.* So we look for evidence to *support, bolster,* or *buttress* our position. Over time, our views become *reinforced, fortified,* and *cemented.* And we become *entrenched* in our beliefs, like soldiers holed up in a trench, safe from the enemy's volleys.

And if we do change our minds? That's surrender. If a fact is *inescapable,* we might *admit, grant,* or *allow* it, as if we're letting it inside our walls. If we realize our position is *indefensible,* we might *abandon* it, *give it up,* or *concede* a point, as if we're ceding ground in a battle.*

Throughout the next few chapters, we'll learn more about motivated reasoning, or as I call it, *soldier mindset*—Why are our minds built this way? Does motivated reasoning help us or hurt us?—but first, I'm happy to inform you that this isn't the end of the line for poor Dreyfus. His story continues, as a new character steps onto the scene.

## PICQUART REOPENS THE CASE

Meet Colonel Georges Picquart: by all appearances, a conventional man, not the sort you'd expect to rock the boat.

Picquart was born in 1854 in Strasbourg, France, to a family of government officers and soldiers, and rose to a position of prominence in the French army at a young age. Like most of his countrymen, he was patriotic. Like most of his countrymen, he was Catholic. And—again, like most of his countrymen—Picquart was anti-Semitic. Not

---

* Even words that don't seem to have any connection to the defensive combat metaphor often reveal one when you dig into their origins. To *rebut* a claim is to argue that it's untrue, but the word originally referred to repelling an attack. Have you heard of someone being a *staunch believer*? A staunch is a solidly constructed wall. Or perhaps you've heard of someone being *adamant* in their beliefs, a word that once referred to a mythical unbreakable stone.

aggressively so, mind you. He was a refined man and considered propaganda against Jews, such as the tirades being printed in France's nationalistic newspapers, to be in bad taste. But anti-Semitism was in the air he breathed, and he grew up with a reflexively disdainful attitude toward Jewish people.

Therefore, Picquart had no difficulty believing it when, in 1894, he was told that the only Jewish member of the French general staff had turned out to be a spy. When Dreyfus professed his innocence during his trial, Picquart observed him closely and concluded that it was an act. And during the "degradation," as Dreyfus's insignia was stripped away, it was Picquart who cracked that anti-Semitic joke ("He's a Jew, remember. He's probably calculating the value of that gold braid").

Shortly after Dreyfus was shipped off to Devil's Island, Colonel Picquart was promoted and put in charge of the counterespionage department that had led the investigation of Dreyfus. He was tasked with accumulating additional evidence against Dreyfus, in case the conviction was questioned. Picquart began searching, but failed to find anything.

However, a more urgent matter soon took precedence—there was another spy! More torn-up letters to the Germans had been discovered. This time, the culprit seemed to be a French officer named Ferdinand Walsin Esterhazy. Esterhazy had a drinking problem and a gambling problem and was deeply in debt, thus giving him ample motive to sell information to Germany.

But as Picquart studied Esterhazy's letters, he started to notice something. The precise, slanted handwriting was uncannily familiar . . . It reminded him of the original memo attributed to Dreyfus. Was he imagining things? Picquart retrieved the original memo and set it next to Esterhazy's. His heart jumped into his throat. The handwriting was identical.

Picquart showed Esterhazy's letters to the army's in-house handwriting analyst, the one who had testified that Dreyfus's handwriting was a match for the original memo. "Yes, these letters match the memo," the analyst agreed.

"And what if I told you these letters were written quite recently?" Picquart asked. The analyst shrugged. In that case, he said, the Jews must have trained the new spy to imitate Dreyfus's handwriting. Picquart did not find this argument plausible. Increasingly, with dread, he began to face the inevitable conclusion that they had convicted an innocent man.

He had one last hope: the sealed file of evidence used in Dreyfus's trial. His fellow officers had assured him that he need only consult it to be convinced of Dreyfus's guilt. So Picquart retrieved it and scoured its contents. But he was disappointed once again. As far as he could tell, the file he had been led to believe was so damning contained no hard evidence, only speculation.

Picquart was indignant at his fellow officers' rationalizations and their disinterest in the question of whether they had condemned an innocent man to rot in prison. He pressed on with his investigation, even as the resistance he met from the army grew into outright enmity. His superiors sent him off on a dangerous mission in hopes that he would never come back. When that ploy failed, they had him arrested on charges of leaking sensitive information.

But after ten years, a stint in jail, and multiple additional trials, Picquart succeeded. Dreyfus was fully pardoned and reinstated in the army.

Dreyfus lived for another thirty years after his reinstatement. His family remembers him as being stoic about the whole ordeal, although his health was never the same after his years on Devil's Island. The real spy, Esterhazy, fled the country and died in poverty. And Picquart continued to be harassed by the enemies he had made in the army, but in 1906 was appointed minister of war by the French prime minister, Georges Clemenceau, who had admired Picquart's work during what came to be known as the "Dreyfus affair."

Whenever anyone asked Picquart why he'd done it—why he had worked so tirelessly to uncover the truth that exonerated Dreyfus, risking his own career and his freedom in the process—his response was simple, and always the same: "Because it was my duty."

## "IS IT TRUE?"

The Dreyfus affair polarized a nation and stunned the world. But to me, its most intriguing aspect is the psychology of its unlikely hero, Colonel Picquart. Like his colleagues, Picquart had plenty of motives to believe Dreyfus was guilty. He didn't trust Jews, and he disliked Dreyfus as a person. Plus, he knew that if he discovered Dreyfus was innocent, it would have significant costs: a massive scandal for the army and a blow to his own career for causing that scandal. But unlike in the case of his colleagues, those motives didn't distort Picquart's ability to discern true from false, plausible from implausible.

Picquart's process of coming to realize that Dreyfus was innocent is a striking example of what cognitive scientists sometimes call accuracy motivated reasoning. In contrast to directionally motivated reasoning, which evaluates ideas through the lenses of "Can I believe it?" and "Must I believe it?," accuracy motivated reasoning evaluates ideas through the lens of "Is it true?"

When Picquart went searching for additional evidence against Dreyfus, expecting and hoping to discover it, he couldn't find anything that seemed convincing. When he examined Esterhazy's handwriting, he was able to recognize its resemblance to the memo supposedly written by Dreyfus. When he was offered a convenient excuse to explain away the new evidence ("The new spy was probably just trained to imitate Dreyfus's handwriting"), he was unable to find it plausible enough to accept. And when he studied the folder of evidence against

Dreyfus, which he had always assumed was damning, he was able to see that it was not damning at all.

If directionally motivated reasoning is like being a soldier fighting off threatening evidence, accuracy motivated reasoning is like being a scout forming a map of the strategic landscape. What's beyond that next hill? Is that a bridge over the river or are my eyes deceiving me? Where are the dangers, the shortcuts, the opportunities? What areas do I need more information about? How reliable is my intel?

The scout isn't indifferent. A scout might hope to learn that the path is safe, that the other side is weak, or that there's a bridge conveniently located where his forces need to cross the river. But above all, he wants to learn what's really there, not fool himself into drawing a bridge on his map where there isn't one in real life. Being in scout mindset means wanting your "map"—your perception of yourself and the world—to be as accurate as possible.

Of course, all maps are imperfect simplifications of reality, as a scout well knows. Striving for an accurate map means being aware of the limits of your understanding, keeping track of the regions of your map that are especially sketchy or possibly wrong. And it means always being open to changing your mind in response to new information. In scout mindset, there's no such thing as a "threat" to your beliefs. If you find out you were wrong about something, great—you've improved your map, and that can only help you.

## YOUR MINDSET CAN MAKE OR BREAK YOUR JUDGMENT

Life is made up of judgment calls, and the more you can avoid distorting your perception of reality, the better your judgment will be.

Scout mindset is what keeps you from fooling yourself on tough questions that people tend to rationalize about, such as: Do I need to get tested for that medical condition? Is it time to cut my losses or would that be giving up too early? Is this relationship ever going to get better? How likely is it that my partner will change their mind about wanting children?

At work, those tough questions might include: Do I really have to fire that employee? How much do I need to prepare for that presentation tomorrow? Is it best for my company to raise a lot of funding now or am I just tempted by the instant validation that raising funds would give me? Do I really need to keep improving this product before releasing it or am I just looking for reasons to put off taking the plunge?

Scout mindset is what prompts us to question our assumptions and stress-test our plans. Whether you're proposing a new product feature or a military maneuver, asking yourself, "What are the most likely ways this could fail?" allows you to strengthen your plan against those possibilities in advance. If you're a doctor, that means considering alternate diagnoses before settling on your initial guess. As one master clinician used to ask himself—if he suspected a patient had pneumonia, for example—"If this could not be pneumonia, what else would it be?"[7]

Even jobs that don't seem to depend on scout mindset usually do once you look closer. Most people associate being a lawyer with arguing for a side, which sounds like soldier mindset. But when a lawyer is choosing cases and preparing for trial, they need to be able to form an accurate picture of the strengths and weaknesses of their case. Overestimate your own side and you're setting yourself up for a rude awakening in the courtroom. That's why experienced lawyers often cite objectivity and self-skepticism as among the most important skills they had to learn over their career. As one leading lawyer says: "When you're young, you want to help your client so badly you tell yourself, 'There's really not an elephant in the room, there's really not a big gray elephant over there with a pink ribbon on it . . .'"[8]

In our relationships with other people, we construct self-contained narratives that feel, from the inside, as if they're simply objective fact. One person's "My partner is coldly ignoring me" can be another person's "I'm respectfully giving him space." One person's "authentic" can be another person's "rude." To be willing to consider other interpretations—to even believe that there *could* be other reasonable interpretations besides your own—requires scout mindset.

Being the kind of person who welcomes the truth, even if it's painful, is what makes other people willing to be honest with you. You can *say* that you want your partner to tell you about any problems in your relationship, or that you want your employees to tell you about any problems in the company, but if you get defensive or combative when you hear the truth, you're not likely to hear it very often. No one wants to be the messenger that gets shot.

| Soldier Mindset | Scout Mindset |
| --- | --- |
| Reasoning is like defensive combat. | Reasoning is like mapmaking. |
| Decide what to believe by asking either "Can I believe this?" or "Must I believe this?" depending on your motives. | Decide what to believe by asking, "Is this true?" |
| Finding out you're wrong means suffering a defeat. | Finding out you're wrong means revising your map. |
| Seek out evidence to fortify and defend your beliefs. | Seek out evidence that will make your map more accurate. |
| Related concepts: Directionally motivated reasoning, rationalizing, denial, self-deception, wishful thinking | Related concepts: Accuracy motivated reasoning, truth-seeking, discovery, objectivity, intellectual honesty |

THE SCOUT AND the soldier are archetypes. In reality, nobody is a perfect scout, just as nobody is a pure soldier. We fluctuate between mindsets from day to day, and from one context to the next.

A trader might be especially scoutlike at work, happy to test their own assumptions and discover they were wrong about the market . . . and then come home and be a soldier in their personal life, unwilling to acknowledge problems in their marriage or consider the possibility that they might be wrong. An entrepreneur could be in scout mindset while talking to a friend about her company, wondering aloud whether her current plan is a mistake . . . and then shift into soldier mindset the next day at the office, defending her plan reflexively when her cofounder criticizes it.

We're all a mixture of scout and soldier. But some people, in some contexts, are better scouts than most. Like Picquart, they're more genuinely desirous of the truth, even if it's not what they were hoping for, and less willing to accept bad arguments that happen to be convenient. They're more motivated to go out, test their theories, and discover their mistakes. They're more conscious of the possibility that their map of reality could be wrong, and more open to changing their mind. This book is about what those people are doing right, and what we can learn from them to help us move from soldier to scout ourselves.

First, we have to start by taking the soldier seriously. Why is soldier mindset so often our default? What makes it so tenacious? Or, put differently, if scout mindset is so great, why isn't everyone already using it all the time? That's the subject of the next chapter: What the Soldier Is Protecting.

*Chapter 2*

# What the Soldier
# Is Protecting

I TRY TO ABIDE by the rule that when you advocate changing something, you should make sure you understand why it is the way it is in the first place.

This rule is known as Chesterton's fence, after G. K. Chesterton, the British writer who proposed it in an essay in 1929.[1] Imagine you discover a road that has a fence built across it for no particular reason you can see. You say to yourself, "Why would someone build a fence here? This seems unnecessary and stupid, let's tear it down." But if you don't understand why the fence is there, Chesterton argued, you can't be confident that it's okay to tear it down.

Long-standing customs or institutions are like those fences, he said. Naive reformers look at them and say, "I don't see the use of this; let's clear it away." But more thoughtful reformers reply, "If you don't see the use of it, I certainly won't let you clear it away. Go away and think. Then, when you can come back and tell me that you do see the use of it, I may allow you to destroy it."[2]

In this book, I'm proposing a kind of reform. I'm arguing that in many, if not all, situations, we would be better off abandoning our default setting of soldier mindset and learning to be in scout mindset instead. And I'd like to be a thoughtful reformer, not a naive one. No matter how strong a case there seems to be for the benefits of scout mindset, the argument is incomplete until we know what soldier mindset is doing there in the first place. Does motivated reasoning benefit us in important ways? What might we lose if we give it up?

EXPERTS IN MANY fields have explored motivated reasoning in different ways, from psychologists to behavioral economists to evolutionary psychologists to philosophers. By now there's a sprawling body of literature on the question "What function does motivated reasoning serve?" I've broken it down into six overlapping categories: comfort, self-esteem, morale, persuasion, image, and belonging.

## COMFORT: AVOIDING UNPLEASANT EMOTIONS

There was a certain cartoon that was everywhere on the internet in 2016, thanks to the way it seemed to capture the global mood at the time. It depicts a dog wearing a hat and sitting at a desk. All around him, the room is in flames. The dog forces a smile and insists, "This is fine."

Soldier mindset helps us avoid negative emotions like fear, stress, and regret. Sometimes we do that with denial, like the "This is fine" dog. Other times, we reach for comforting narratives about the world, and opt not to scrutinize them too closely. *Everything happens for the best. People get what's coming to them. The darker the night, the brighter the stars.*

In Aesop's fable "The Fox and the Grapes," a fox spots a bunch of juicy grapes, high up on a branch he can't reach, and concludes that the grapes were sour anyway. We use similar "sour grapes" reasoning when we don't get something we want. When someone we had a great first date with doesn't return our calls, we may decide they were a bore anyway. When a job offer slips through our fingers, we conclude, "It's for the best; the hours would have been brutal."

A close cousin to the sour grape is the sweet lemon: when it doesn't seem feasible to fix a problem, we may try to convince ourselves that our "problem" is actually a blessing, and that we wouldn't change it even if we could. Until very recently in human history, excruciating pain was an unavoidable part of childbirth. Since there was nothing we could do about that, many doctors and clergy argued that pain was a *good* thing, because it promoted spiritual growth and strength of character. Labor pains were allotted by God, "and most wisely we cannot doubt," one obstetrician assured people in 1856.[3]

Now that we have access to epidural anesthesia, we no longer insist on the sweetness of that particular lemon. But we still say similar things about aging and death—that they're beautiful, and they give meaning to life. "Perhaps mortality is not simply an evil, perhaps it is even a blessing," argued Leon Kass, who chaired the President's Council on Bioethics under George W. Bush. Maybe, he suggests, our ability to feel love depends on our awareness of the finitude of our lives.[4]

To add a wrinkle to this story, the comforting thing to believe isn't always optimistic. Sometimes it's the opposite: that there's no hope, so you might as well not worry about it. If you're struggling to keep your head above water in a difficult class, it can be tempting to conclude "This is pointless, I'm never going to do well enough to bring my grade up." The moment of giving up offers a rush of sweet relief. Or you might decide that there's no point in preparing for a potential future disaster like an earthquake or tsunami, so you don't have to think about it. "Most people throw up their hands and say, 'It's fate, it's out of my control,'" says Eric Klinenberg, a professor of sociology at New York University who studies the psychology of disaster preparation.[5]

## SELF-ESTEEM: FEELING GOOD ABOUT OURSELVES

In the movie *Election*, the character Tracy Flick is ambitious and hardworking, but struggles to make friends. "That's okay," she tells herself. "I've come to accept that very few people are truly destined to be special, and we're solo fliers . . . if you're gonna be great, you've got to be lonely."[6] Like Tracy, we often use soldier mindset to protect our egos by finding flattering narratives for unflattering facts. *I may not be wealthy, but that's because I have integrity. The reason I don't have a lot of friends is because people are intimidated by me.*

All sorts of beliefs can get drafted into service defending our egos because they relate in some way to our strengths or weaknesses. If your desk is constantly covered in piles of books and papers, you might be especially receptive to the claim "Messiness is a sign of creativity." If you have the time and disposable income to travel a lot, you might believe "You can't be a truly well-rounded person without having seen the world." If you did poorly on the SATs, you might be especially sympathetic to arguments like, "Standardized tests don't measure how smart you are, only how good you are at taking tests."

Over time, our beliefs about the world adjust to accommodate our track record. One study in the late 1990s followed students throughout four years of college, tracking the GPA they expected to achieve, the GPA they actually achieved, and their beliefs about the importance of grades. Students who consistently underperformed their own expectations increasingly began to conclude that "Grades aren't that important after all."[7]

Your self-image shapes even your most fundamental beliefs about how the world works. Poorer people are more likely to believe that luck plays a big role in life, while wealthier people tend to credit hard work and talent alone. When economist Robert Frank wrote in a *New York Times* column that luck was an important (though not sufficient) ingredient in success, Fox business commentator Stuart Varney bristled. "Do you know how insulting that was, when I read that?" he asked Frank. "I came to America with nothing thirty-five years ago. I've made something of myself, I think through hard work, talent, and risk-taking, and you're going to write in the *New York Times* that this is luck."[8]

Again, there's a wrinkle in this story: Motivated reasoning for the sake of self-esteem doesn't always mean believing that you're brilliant and talented and everyone likes you. Psychologists make a distinction between *self-enhancement*, which means boosting your ego with positive beliefs, and *self-protection*, which means avoiding blows to your ego. For the sake of self-protection, you might err on the side of assuming the worst about yourself. In a popular video, YouTuber Natalie Wynn calls it "masochistic epistemology"—*whatever hurts is true*. The term resonated with a lot of people. As one viewer commented, "It feels safer to assume that people think I'm unattractive rather than getting my hopes up that someone thinks I'm pretty when they really don't."[9]

# MORALE: MOTIVATING OURSELVES TO DO HARD THINGS

I wrote this book while living in San Francisco, the city where everyone and their Uber driver has a vision for the next billion-dollar tech company. Out here, it's common wisdom that irrational optimism is a good thing—it's what motivates you to launch yourself into daunting challenges, ignore the naysayers, and persevere when things get tough. Small wonder then that in one survey of entrepreneurs, almost everyone estimated their company's probability of success to be at least 7 out of 10, with a third giving themselves an eyebrow-raising 10 out of 10 chance, despite the fact that the baseline rate of start-up success is closer to 1 in 10.[10]

One strategy we use to justify such high confidence is downplaying the relevance of the baseline odds and telling ourselves that success is purely a matter of trying hard enough. As one motivational blogger promised, "[You] have 100% chance of being successful at doing what you love if you commit yourself to it and get off your ass and do it every day."[11]

Another mental move is to selectively focus on the features of a situation that justify optimism, while ignoring those that justify pessimism. When I was starting an organization, I was aware that most organizations fail, but I reassured myself with the thought, "We're in a better position than most because we already have a network of backers." This was true, and a reason for optimism. But I could instead have observed, "Our organization is in a worse position than most because all of us are young and inexperienced," which was also true.

We need morale to make tough decisions and act on them with conviction. That's why decision-makers often avoid considering alternative plans or downsides to their current plan. A sociologist named Nils Brunsson spent time embedded in a Swedish company in the 1970s and observed that when they held meetings to "decide" on a project to work on, they actually spent very little time comparing options. Instead, they quickly anchored on one option and spent most of the meeting raising points in favor of it. "This helped them to build up enthusiasm for projects—an enthusiasm that they deemed necessary to overcome difficulties," Brunsson concluded.[12]


COMFORT, SELF-ESTEEM, AND morale are *emotional* benefits, meaning that the ultimate target of our deception is ourselves. The next three benefits of soldier mindset are a little different. Persuasion, image, and belonging are *social* benefits—in these cases, the ultimate target of our deception is other people, by way of ourselves.[13]

## PERSUASION: CONVINCING OURSELVES SO WE CAN CONVINCE OTHERS

When Lyndon B. Johnson was a senator, he had a ritual his friends and aides called "working up." When he needed to be able to convince people of something, he would practice arguing that position, with passion, over and over, willing himself to believe it. Eventually he would be able to defend it with utter certainty—because by that point, he *was* certain, regardless of what his views had been at the start. "It was not an act," said George Reedy, Johnson's press secretary. "He had a fantastic capacity to persuade himself that the 'truth' which was convenient for the present was the truth and anything that conflicted with it was the prevarication of enemies."[14]

Johnson's capacity for intentional self-deception was unusual. But we all do this to some extent, just less intentionally: When we need to persuade other people of something, we become motivated to believe it ourselves, and seek out arguments and evidence we could use in its defense.

When law students prepare to argue for either the plaintiff or defendant in a moot court, they come to believe that their side of the case is both morally and legally in the right—even when the sides were randomly assigned.[15] As an entrepreneur, if you can talk with sincere enthusiasm about how your company is "totally killing it right now," other people might believe it, too. Lobbyists, salespeople, and fundraisers might play up the strengths and play down the flaws in their cause or product to make it easier for them to sell it to other people.

A professor might convince herself that her theory is more original than it really is so that she can claim as much in her public speaking and writing. Even if a few people who are closely familiar with her field realize she's overstating her case, she may still be able to get away with the exaggeration with most people. This often requires her to "accidentally" misunderstand other people's theses and fail to notice that she's attacking a straw man argument no one is actually making.

Even those of us who aren't professional persuaders have plenty of things we might like our friends, family, and coworkers to believe: *I'm a good person. I deserve your sympathy. I'm trying my hardest. I'm a valuable employee. My career is really taking off.* The more we can get ourselves to genuinely believe those claims, and the more evidence and arguments we can collect to support them, the easier it will be for us to persuade other people of them (or so the logic goes).

As Johnson used to say: "What convinces is conviction."[16]

## IMAGE: CHOOSING BELIEFS THAT MAKE US LOOK GOOD

When we're picking out clothing to wear, deciding between suits or jeans, leather or hemp, high heels or high-tops, we implicitly ask ourselves: "What kind of person would wear this? Someone sophisticated, free-spirited, unconventional, down to earth? Is that how I want other people to see me?"

We choose beliefs in a similar way.* Psychologists call it impression management, and evolutionary psychologists call it signaling: When considering a claim, we implicitly ask ourselves, "What kind of person would believe a claim like this, and is that how I want other people to see me?"

---

\* I owe this analogy between beliefs and clothing to Robin Hanson, "Are Beliefs Like Clothes?" at http://mason.gmu.edu/~rhanson/belieflikeclothes.html.

Different people like to present themselves differently with their clothing, and the same is true with beliefs. One person might be drawn to nihilism because it makes him seem edgy, while another might be drawn to optimism because it makes him likeable. Still another might gravitate toward moderate positions on controversial issues in order to seem mature. Note that the goal here isn't to get other people to share your beliefs, the way it is in the case of "Persuasion." The nihilist isn't trying to get other people to believe in nihilism. He's trying to get them to believe that *he* believes in nihilism.

Just as there are fashions in clothing, so, too, are there fashions in ideas. When an idea like "socialism is better than capitalism" or "machine learning is going to change the world" begins to gain currency in your social circles, you might be motivated to adopt it as well in order to remain fashionable. That is, unless being contrarian is part of your image, in which case an idea's growing popularity might make you *less* receptive to it, not more.

Despite all the variety, some preferences about self-presentation are near universal. Almost no one prefers to go around in dirty or stained clothing. Analogously, almost no one wants to hold beliefs that make them look crazy or selfish. So for the sake of our image, we reach for defensible explanations for our behavior, such as "The reason I'm opposed to new construction in my neighborhood is because I'm worried about its impact on the environment. It's certainly not because I want to keep my own property values high!"

Here again, the inability to understand something can be helpful. I remember sitting with a group of classmates in high school, discussing how someone we knew was bitter about their friend's recent success. A girl in our group named Dana expressed puzzlement: "Why would someone be jealous of a friend?"

"Aww . . . Dana is so pure she can't even comprehend the concept of jealousy!" someone said fondly.

"You guys, I really don't get it!" Dana protested over the chorus of *awwww*s. "Why wouldn't you be happy that your friend is happy?"

# BELONGING: FITTING IN TO YOUR SOCIAL GROUPS

In some religious communities, losing your faith can mean losing your marriage, family, and entire social support system along with it. That's an extreme case, but all social groups have some beliefs and values that members are implicitly expected to share, such as "Climate change is a serious problem," or "Republicans are better than Democrats," or "Our group is fighting for a worthy cause," or "Children are a blessing." Dissent may not get you literally kicked out of the group, but it can still alienate you from the other members.

To be clear, deferring to a consensus isn't inherently a sign of soldier mindset. In the web comic *XKCD*, a parent asks their child that age-old rhetorical question: "If all your friends jumped off a bridge, would you jump, too?" The correct answer is presumed to be a grudging "No, of course not." But the child replies, "Probably," because after all, which is more likely—that his friends all went crazy at the same time or that the bridge is on fire?[17] The kid's got a point. Deferring to the consensus is often a wise heuristic, since you can't investigate everything for yourself, and other people know things you don't.

What makes it motivated reasoning is when you wouldn't even want to find out if the consensus was wrong. A friend of mine named Katja grew up in what she describes as a small "hippie" town where everyone held strong environmentalist views, including her. But once she got to high school, Katja began to encounter arguments online or in her economics textbooks that some environmentalist policies are ineffective and that logging companies aren't as harmful as people think.

She would hunt for flaws in the logic. But sometimes, to her alarm, the arguments just seemed . . . correct. In those moments, her stomach would drop. "I just felt sick when I got the 'wrong answer,'" she told me, "like when there was some argument for forestry that I didn't immediately have a good counterargument to."

Fitting in isn't only about conforming to the group consensus. It also means demonstrating your loyalty to the group by rejecting any evidence that threatens its figurative honor. People who identify strongly as "gamers" (i.e., they endorse statements like "When somebody criticizes gamers, it feels like a personal insult") are more skeptical of studies that show violent video games are harmful.[18] People who identify strongly as Catholics (i.e., they endorse statements like "I feel solidarity with Catholic people") are more skeptical when a Catholic priest is accused of sexual abuse.[19]

And in some groups, fitting in comes with restrictions on what you're allowed to want or to believe about yourself. It's been called tall poppy syndrome: anyone who seems like they're trying to be a "tall poppy," showing too much self-regard or ambition, is cut down to size. If you want to fit in to such a culture, you might acquire the habit of downplaying your achievements and goals—even in the privacy of your own mind.

WHEN YOU THINK about all of the things we use soldier mindset for, it becomes obvious why the frequently proposed fixes for it are futile. Such fixes typically involve words like "teaching" or "training," as in:

*We need to teach students about cognitive biases.*
*We need to train people in critical thinking.*
*We need to educate people in reason and logic.*

None of these approaches have shown much promise in changing people's thinking in the long run or outside of the classroom. And that should not surprise us. We use motivated reasoning not because we don't know any better, but because we're trying to protect things that are vitally important to us—our ability to feel good about our lives and ourselves, our motivation to try hard things and stick with them, our ability to look good and persuade, and our acceptance in our communities.

However, the fact that soldier mindset is often our default strategy for getting what we want doesn't necessarily mean it's a *good* strategy. For one thing, it can backfire. In "Persuasion," we saw that law students who are randomly assigned to one side of a moot court case become confident, after reading the case materials, that their side is morally and legally in the right. But that confidence doesn't help them persuade the judge. On the contrary, law students who are more confident in the merits of their own side are significantly *less* likely to win the case—perhaps because they fail to consider and prepare for the rebuttals to their arguments.[20]

Even when soldier mindset doesn't completely backfire, it's still not obvious that it's our best option. Rather than boosting your self-esteem by denying your flaws, you could instead boost your self-esteem by noticing and fixing those flaws. Rather than pursuing social acceptance by suppressing your disagreements with your community, you could instead decide to leave and find a different community you fit in to better.

This chapter began with the question of Chesterton's fence: What purpose is soldier mindset meant to serve, and can we be confident that it's okay to tear it down? So far, we've addressed the first half of that question. To answer the second, we need to determine whether we can get the things we value just as effectively, or even more so, without soldier mindset. That's what the next chapter is about.

*Chapter 3*

# Why Truth Is More Valuable Than We Realize

L ET'S RECAP. IN soldier mindset, our thinking is guided by the question *"Can* I believe it?" about things we want to accept, and *"Must* I believe it?" about things we want to reject. We use soldier mindset to help us maintain beliefs that boost our self-esteem, give us comfort, preserve our morale, persuade other people, cultivate an attractive image, and help us fit in to our social groups.

In scout mindset, our thinking is guided by the question "Is it true?" We use it to help us see things clearly for the sake of our judgment, so that we can fix problems, notice opportunities, figure out which risks are worth taking, decide how we want to spend our lives, and, sometimes, better understand the world we live in for the sake of sheer curiosity.

## THE FUNCTIONS OF SCOUT MINDSET
## AND SOLDIER MINDSET

| We use soldier mindset to *adopt and defend* beliefs that give us . . . | We use scout mindset to *see things clearly* so we can . . . |
| --- | --- |
| **Emotional benefits:**<br>Comfort: Coping with disappointment, anxiety, regret, envy<br>Self-esteem: Feeling good about ourselves<br>Morale: Tackling challenges and not getting discouraged | **Make good judgment calls** about which problems are worth fixing, which risks are worth taking, how to pursue our goals, who to trust, what kind of life we want to live, and how to improve our judgment over time |
| **Social benefits:**<br>Persuasion: Convincing other people of things that benefit us<br>Image: Appearing smart, sophisticated, compassionate, virtuous<br>Belonging: Fitting in to our social groups | |

# WE MAKE UNCONSCIOUS TRADE-OFFS

This is one of the paradoxes of being human: that our beliefs serve such different purposes all at once. Invariably, we end up making trade-offs.

We trade off between judgment and belonging. If you live in a tight-knit community, it might be easier to fit in if you use soldier mindset to fight off any doubts you have about your community's core beliefs and values. On the other hand, if you *do* allow yourself to entertain those doubts, you might realize you're better off rejecting your community's views on morality, religion, or gender roles, and deciding to live a less traditional life.

We trade off between judgment and persuasion. A friend of mine used to work at a well-known charity and marveled at how its president was able to convince himself that every dollar in the budget was well spent, so that he could make that case to potential donors. On the other hand, the president's self-deception also made him unwilling to cut failing programs—because in his mind, they *weren't* failing. "You would have a real debate on your hands trying to prove to him something that was so obvious," my friend recalled. In this case, soldier mindset made the president better at persuading people to give him money, but worse at deciding how to use that money.

We trade off between judgment and morale. When you come up with a plan, focusing only on its positives ("This is such a great idea!") can help you work up enthusiasm and motivation to carry it out. On the other hand, if you scrutinize your plan for flaws ("What are the downsides? How might this fail?"), you're more likely to notice if there's a better plan you should switch to instead.

We make these trade-offs, and many more, all the time, usually without even realizing we're doing so. After all, the whole point of self-deception is that it's occurring beneath our conscious awareness. If you were to find yourself thinking, explicitly, "Should I admit to myself that I screwed up?" the issue would already be moot. So it's left up to our unconscious minds to choose, on a case-by-case basis, which goals to prioritize. Sometimes we choose soldier mindset, furthering our emotional or social goals at the expense of accuracy. Sometimes we choose scout mindset, seeking out the truth even if it turns out not to be what we were hoping for.

And sometimes our unconscious minds attempt to have it both ways. When I used to teach educational workshops, I made a point of checking in with my students to find out how things were going for them. I knew that if a student was confused or unhappy, it was better to find out sooner rather than later, so I could try to fix the problem. Seeking out feedback has never been easy for me, so I was proud of myself for doing the virtuous thing this time.

At least, I *was* proud, until I realized something I was doing that had previously escaped my notice. Whenever I asked a student, "So, are you enjoying the workshop?" I would begin nodding, with an encouraging smile on my face, as if to say, *The answer is yes, right? Please say yes.* Clearly, my desire to protect my self-esteem and happiness was in competition with my desire to learn about problems so that I could fix them. That memory of myself requesting honest feedback while nodding encouragingly and asking leading questions is now imprinted on my brain—the tension between the soldier and scout in a single image.

## ARE WE RATIONALLY IRRATIONAL?

Since we're constantly making these unconscious trade-offs between scout and soldier mindsets, it's worth asking: Are we any good at it? Are we good at intuitively weighing the costs and benefits of knowing the truth, in a given situation, against the costs and benefits of believing a lie?

The hypothesis that the human mind evolved the ability to make these trade-offs well is called the *rational irrationality* hypothesis, coined by economist Bryan Caplan.[1] If the name sounds like a paradox, that's because it's using two different senses of the word *rational*: epistemic rationality means holding beliefs that are well justified, while instrumental rationality means acting effectively to achieve your goals.

Being rationally irrational, therefore, would mean that we're good at unconsciously choosing *just enough* epistemic irrationality to achieve our social and emotional goals, without impairing our judgment too much. A rationally irrational person would deny problems only when the comfort of denial is sufficiently high and their chance of fixing the problem is sufficiently low. A rationally irrational CEO would inflate his perception of his company's health only when the positive impact on his ability to persuade investors was large enough to outweigh the negative impact on his strategic decision-making.

So, are we rationally irrational?

If we were, there wouldn't be much left for me to say in this book. I could appeal to your sense of altruism and encourage you to choose scout mindset more for the sake of being a good citizen. Or I could appeal to your innate love of truth for its own sake. But I couldn't claim that additional scout mindset would make you personally better off if you were already striking an optimal balance between scout and soldier.

The fact that this book is in your hands is a bit of a spoiler for my answer: No, we're far from rationally irrational. There are several major biases in our decision-making, several ways in which we systematically misjudge the costs and benefits of truth. In the rest of this chapter, we'll explore how those biases cause us to *overvalue* soldier mindset, choosing it more often than we should, and *undervalue* scout mindset, choosing it less often than we should.

# WE OVERVALUE THE IMMEDIATE REWARDS OF SOLDIER MINDSET

One of the most frustrating aspects of being human is our knack for undermining our own goals. We pay for gym memberships, then rarely use them. We start diets, then break them. We procrastinate on writing a paper until it's the night before the deadline and we're cursing our past self for putting us in this predicament.

The source of this self-sabotage is *present bias*, a feature of our intuitive decision-making in which we care too much about short-term consequences and too little about long-term consequences. In other words, we're impatient, and we get more impatient as the potential rewards grow closer.[2]

When you contemplate a gym membership, the trade-off seems well worth it, in theory. Spend a few hours per week exercising, in exchange for looking and feeling a lot better? Sign me up! But on any given morning, when you're faced with the choice between "Turn off my alarm and sink blissfully back into sleep" or "Head to the gym and make an imperceptible amount of progress toward my fitness goals," it's a much tougher call. The rewards of choosing to sleep in are immediate; the rewards of choosing to exercise are diffuse and delayed. What difference will one exercise session make to your long-term fitness goals, anyway?

It's widely known that present bias shapes our choices about how to act. What's much less appreciated is that it also shapes our choices about how to think. Just like sleeping in, breaking your diet, or procrastinating on your work, we reap the rewards of thinking in soldier mindset right away, while the costs don't come due until later. If you're worried about a mistake you made and you convince yourself that "It wasn't my fault," you're rewarded with a hit of instant emotional relief. The cost is that you miss out on learning from your mistake, which means you're less able to prevent it from happening again. But that won't affect you until some unknown point in the future.

Overestimating your positive traits is most effective in the early days of a relationship (romantic, professional, or otherwise). When someone first meets you, they have very little information about your quality as an employee or a mate, so they're forced to rely more on proxies like "How confident does he seem in his own quality?" But the longer a person spends with you, the more information they get about your actual strengths and weaknesses, and the less they need to use your confidence as a proxy.

Being overly optimistic about your chance of success gives you a burst of motivation right away. But those motivational benefits dwindle over time, or even backfire, when success takes longer than you predicted. As Francis Bacon said, "Hope is a good breakfast, but a bad supper."

## WE UNDERESTIMATE THE VALUE OF BUILDING SCOUT HABITS

When you wake up in the morning and head to the gym, the benefit of that choice isn't just in the calories you burn or the muscle tone you develop that day. The benefit also lies in the fact that you're reinforcing valuable skills and habits. That includes the habit of going to the gym, obviously, but also the broader skill of doing hard things, and the broader habit of following through on your promises to yourself.

We know this in the abstract. But it can be hard to appreciate those benefits viscerally, especially when your alarm goes off at six a.m. and your bed is cozy and warm. Any single day, on its own, doesn't make much difference to your overall habits and skills. "I can just go tomorrow," you think as you turn off the alarm. Which is true—but of course, you'll think the same thing tomorrow.

Analogously, the benefit of an act of scout mindset isn't just about making your map of reality a bit more accurate. The benefit is in the habits and skills you're reinforcing. Even when you're reasoning about something like foreign politics that doesn't impact your life directly, the way you think still impacts you *indirectly*, because you're reinforcing general habits of thought. Every time you say, "Oh, that's a good point, I hadn't thought of that," it gets a little bit easier for you to acknowledge good points in general. Every time you opt to check a fact before citing it, you become a little bit more likely to remember to check your facts in general. Every time you're willing to say, "I was wrong," it gets a little bit easier to be wrong in general.

These and other valuable scout habits build up over time. But in any particular instance, it's hard for the "Incrementally improve my thinking habits" benefit to compete with the vivid and immediate rewards of soldier mindset.

## WE UNDERESTIMATE THE RIPPLE EFFECTS OF SELF-DECEPTION

A trope often milked for comedy on sitcoms is "deception begets more deception." You've seen it before—the protagonist commits some minor misdeed, such as forgetting to buy his wife a Christmas present. To cover it up, he tells a small lie. For example, he gives her the gift he had originally bought for his father, pretending he bought it for her. But then he needs to tell another lie to cover the first lie: "It's a necktie . . . uh, right, I've been wanting to tell you I think you look sexy in neckties!" . . . and by the end of the episode, he's stuck with his wife wearing neckties every day.

The trope is exaggerated for comic effect, but it's based on a real phenomenon: when you tell a lie, it's hard to predict exactly what you've committed your future self to.

Just like the lies we tell others, the lies we tell ourselves have ripple effects. Suppose you tend to rationalize away your own mistakes, and consequently you see yourself as more perfect than you really are. This has a ripple effect on your views of other people: Now, when your friends and family screw up, you might not be very sympathetic. After all, *you* never make such mistakes. *Why can't they just be better? It's not that hard.*

Or suppose that for the sake of your self-esteem, you view yourself through rose-colored glasses, judging yourself to be more charming, interesting, and impressive than you actually appear to other people. Here's one possible ripple effect: How do you explain the fact that women don't seem to be interested in dating you, given what a great catch you are? Well, maybe they're all shallow.

But that conclusion sets off a ripple effect of its own. How do you explain why your parents, friends, or internet commenters keep trying to convince you that most women aren't as shallow as you think? Well, I guess you can't trust people to tell it like it is—people just say what they think they're supposed to say, don't they? That conclusion, in turn, sends still more ripples through your map of reality.

These are examples for the sake of illustration, and not necessarily representative ones. It's hard to know exactly how the ripple effect of a particular act of self-deception will hurt you in the future, or if it will at all. Perhaps in many instances the harm is negligible. But the fact that the harm is delayed and unpredictable should ring an alarm bell. This is exactly the kind of cost we tend to neglect when we're intuitively weighing costs and benefits. Ripple effects are yet more reason to suspect that we underestimate the cost of deceiving ourselves—and are therefore choosing soldier mindset too often and scout mindset not often enough.

## WE OVERESTIMATE SOCIAL COSTS

Have you ever lied to your doctor? If so, you're not alone. In two recent surveys, 81 percent and 61 percent of patients, respectively, admitted to withholding information from their doctor about important things such as whether they were regularly taking their medication or whether they understood their doctor's instructions.[3] The most common reasons patients gave for this behavior? Embarrassment and a fear of being judged. "Most people want their doctor to think highly of them," the study's lead author said.[4]

Think about how perverse that trade-off is. First of all, your doctor almost certainly doesn't judge you as harshly as you fear she will. She's seen hundreds of patients with similar embarrassing ailments or bad habits. More important, your doctor's opinion of you *doesn't matter*—it has close to zero impact on your life, or career, or happiness. Rationally, it makes a lot more sense to be fully honest with your doctor so you can get the best possible medical advice.

This is another way in which our intuition about costs and benefits is skewed—we overestimate the importance of how we come across to other people. Social costs like looking weird or making a fool out of ourselves *feel* a lot more significant than they actually are. In reality, other people aren't thinking about you nearly as much as you intuitively think they are, and their opinions of you don't have nearly as much impact on your life as it feels like they do.

As a result, we end up making tragic trade-offs, sacrificing a lot of potential happiness to avoid relatively small social costs. If you ask someone out on a date and they say no, that isn't the end of the world—but it can feel like it is. The prospect of rejection is so stressful that we often come up with rationalizations to justify not doing it, convincing ourselves that we're not interested in a relationship, or that we don't have time to date right now, or that no one would want to date us anyway, so it's not even worth trying.

In chapter 2, in the section on belonging, I described tall poppy syndrome, in which people who are perceived as being too ambitious get cut down to size. It's a real phenomenon, but we overreact to it. Economist Julie Fry studies attitudes about ambition in New Zealand, where tall poppy syndrome has historically been common. One day she got back in touch with a woman she had interviewed two years earlier, to renew the permission to publish her recording.

In the original interview, the woman had claimed she found the idea of ambition unappealing, and preferred to stay put in her career. But now she was happily leading a team at her company. She told Fry that their conversation about ambition two years earlier had caused her to go from thinking, "This is not for me, I'm not interested" to "Well, I don't have to be brash and grabby, but maybe it's okay for me to reach out and pick something."[5]

When we allow ourselves to reflect on a social cost we've been avoiding (or when someone else prompts us to reflect on it, like in the case of this New Zealander), we often realize, "Hey, this isn't such a big deal after all. I can decide to take on a little more responsibility at work, and it'll be fine. No one's going to hate me for that." But when we leave the decision up to our instincts, even a hint of potential social risk prompts a reflexive "Avoid at all costs!" reaction.

We'll even risk death to avoid looking foolish in front of strangers. In *Big Weather: Chasing Tornadoes in the Heart of America,* writer Mark Svenvold describes being in a motel in El Reno, Oklahoma, as a tornado approached. The motel television blared an alarm, and a warning from the National Weather Service scrolled across the bottom of the screen: "TAKE COVER IMMEDIATELY." Svenvold wondered if his last hours alive were really going to be spent in a cheap motel.

Yet he hesitated to act. Two local men were drinking beers outside the motel, leaning nonchalantly against their truck, apparently unperturbed by the tornado bearing down upon them. Was he being naive? The motel desk clerk also seemed calm. Svenvold asked her if the motel had a basement where he could take cover. "No, we don't have a basement," she replied, with a touch of what he took to be contempt.

As Svenvold later recalled, "The sneer of the motel clerk, a local, shaming me, an unschooled visitor, into denial" and the two men outside "implacably sipping their beer" paralyzed him with indecision. After thirty minutes of second-guessing his own judgment, he noticed the men outside were gone, and only then did he finally feel permitted to flee.[6]

WE'RE OVERLY TEMPTED by immediate payoffs, even when they come at a steep cost later on. We underestimate the cumulative harm of false beliefs, and the cumulative benefit of practicing scout habits. We overestimate how much other people judge us, and how much impact their judgments have on our lives. As a result of all these tendencies, we end up being far too willing to sacrifice our ability to see clearly in exchange for short-term emotional and social rewards. That doesn't mean scout mindset is always the better choice—but it does mean we have a bias in favor of the soldier, *even when the scout is a better choice.*

Finding out that our brains have these built-in deviations from optimal decision-making might feel like bad news. But it's actually good news. It means there's room for improvement, untapped opportunities to make our lives better, if we can learn to rely less on soldier mindset and more on scout mindset instead.

WE WOULD BE BETTER OFF CHOOSING SOLDIER MINDSET LESS OFTEN, AND
SCOUT MINDSET MORE OFTEN, THAN OUR INSTINCTS TELL US TO

## AN ACCURATE MAP IS MORE USEFUL NOW

If you were born fifty thousand years ago, you were more or less stuck with the tribe and family you were born into. There wasn't much in the way of career choice, either. You could hunt, forage, or have children, depending on your role in the tribe. If you didn't like it, well, that was too bad.

We have far more options now. Especially if you live in a relatively developed country, you have the freedom to choose where to live, what career to pursue, who to marry, whether to start or end a relationship, whether to have children, how much to borrow, where to invest, how to manage your physical and mental health, and much more. Whether your choices make your life better or worse depends on your judgment, and your judgment depends on your mindset.

Living in the modern world also means we have many more opportunities to fix things we don't like about our lives. If you're bad at something, you can take classes, read a *For Dummies* book, watch a YouTube tutorial, get a tutor, or hire someone to do it for you. If you're chafing under the constrictive social mores of your town, you can find kindred spirits online or move to a big city. If your family is abusive, you can cut ties with them.

If you're unhappy in general, you can visit a therapist, get more exercise, change your diet, try antidepressants, peruse self-help or philosophy books, meditate, volunteer to help other people, or move to a place that gets more sunlight throughout the year.

Not all of these solutions are equally effective for everyone, and not all of them are worth the effort or cost. Deciding which solutions are worth trying is a matter of judgment. Deciding which problems in your life are worth trying to solve at all, versus simply learning to live with, is a matter of judgment, too.

This abundance of opportunity makes scout mindset far more useful than it would have been for our ancestors. After all, what's the point of admitting your problems exist if you can't fix them? What's the point of noticing your disagreements with your community if you can't leave? Having an accurate map doesn't help you very much when you're allowed to travel only one path.

So if our instincts undervalue truth, that's not surprising—our instincts evolved in a different world, one better suited to the soldier. Increasingly, our world is becoming one that rewards the ability to see clearly, especially in the long run; a world in which your happiness isn't nearly as dependent on your ability to accommodate yourself to whatever life, skills, and social groups you happened to be born into.

More and more, it's a scout's world now.

# PART II

# Developing
# Self-Awareness

## Chapter 4

# Signs of a Scout

O NE OF MY guilty reading pleasures is a forum on Reddit called "Am I the Asshole?" in which people describe a recent conflict in their lives and ask others to weigh in on who was in the right.

In a post from 2018, someone on the forum described the following dilemma.[1] He's been dating a girl for a year and wants her to live with him. The problem is that she owns a cat, and he finds cats annoying. Therefore, he would like his girlfriend to give away her cat before moving in. But even though he has explained his position to her "very calmly and rationally," as he put it, his girlfriend is refusing to budge. She and her cat are a package deal, she says. He thinks she's being unreasonable, and he appeals to Reddit to back him up.

They do not back him up. Instead, they inform him that although he may not like cats, people's pets are extremely important to them, and you can't just ask someone to give away their cat because you find it annoying. The verdict in this case was far more unanimous than usual: "Yes, you're the asshole."

A KEY FACTOR preventing us from being in scout mindset more frequently is our conviction that we're already in it. In this chapter, we'll examine a few things that make us feel like scouts even when we're not—followed by a few more genuine indicators of scout mindset.

# FEELING OBJECTIVE DOESN'T MAKE YOU A SCOUT

That phrase I pulled from the Redditor's post—"very calmly and rationally"—is a telling one. We think of ourselves as objective because we *feel* objective. We scrutinize our own logic and it seems sound. We don't detect any signs of bias in ourselves. We feel unemotional, dispassionate.

But the fact that you feel calm doesn't mean you're being fair, as this Redditor inadvertently proved. And being able to explain a position "rationally," as he put it—by which people usually mean that they can make a compelling argument in favor of their position—doesn't mean the position is fair. Of *course* your argument seems compelling to you; everyone's argument seems compelling to them. That's how motivated reasoning works.

In fact, viewing yourself as rational can backfire. The more objective you think you are, the more you trust your own intuitions and opinions as accurate representations of reality, and the less inclined you are to question them. "I'm an objective person, so my views on gun control must be correct, unlike the views of all those irrational people who disagree with me," we think. Or "I'm unbiased, so if this job applicant seems better to me, he must really be better."

In 2008, the financier Jeffrey Epstein was convicted of soliciting sex from underage girls. Several years later, a journalist brought up the case in an interview with physicist Lawrence Krauss, a close friend of Epstein's. Krauss dismissed the accusations, saying:

As a scientist I always judge things on empirical evidence and he always has women ages 19 to 23 around him, but I've never seen anything else, so as a scientist, my presumption is that whatever the problems were I would believe him over other people.[2]

This is a very dubious appeal to empiricism. Being a good scientist doesn't mean refusing to believe anything until you see it with your own two eyes. I would argue Krauss simply trusts his friend more than he trusts the women who accused his friend or the investigators who confirmed those accusations. Objective science, that is not. When you start from the premise that you're an objective thinker, you lend your conclusions an air of unimpeachability they usually don't deserve.

## BEING SMART AND KNOWLEDGEABLE DOESN'T MAKE YOU A SCOUT

"What an idiot," we exclaim when someone shares an exceptionally wrongheaded opinion on Facebook. "I guess people don't care about facts and evidence anymore," we sigh when we read about some trendy pseudoscientific belief. Journalists write somber essays about the public's "cult of ignorance"[3] and "anti-intellectualism," and publish books with titles like *Just How Stupid Are We? Facing the Truth About the American Voter.*[4]

Language like this seems to imply that the problem with our discourse—the reason so many people have the "wrong" views on controversial topics—is a lack of knowledge and reasoning ability. If only people were smarter and more well-informed, they would realize their errors!

But is that true? Yale law professor Dan Kahan surveyed Americans about their political views and their beliefs about climate change.

As you would expect, those two things were highly correlated. Liberal Democrats were much more likely than conservative Republicans to agree with the statement "There is solid evidence of recent global warming due mostly to human activity such as burning fossil fuels."*

So far, not surprising. The twist is that Kahan also measured his respondents' "science intelligence" with a collection of different questions: Some were puzzles designed to test reasoning ability, such as "If it takes 5 machines 5 minutes to make 5 widgets, how long would it take 100 machines to make 100 widgets?" Other questions were tests of basic scientific knowledge, such as "Lasers work by focusing sound waves—true or false?" and "Which gas makes up most of the earth's atmosphere: Hydrogen, nitrogen, carbon dioxide, or oxygen?"

If knowledge and intelligence protect you from motivated reasoning, then we would expect to find that the more people know about science, the more they agree with each other about scientific questions. Kahan found the opposite. At the lowest levels of scientific intelligence, there's no polarization at all—roughly 33 percent of both liberals and conservatives believe in human-caused global warming. But as scientific intelligence increases, liberal and conservative opinions diverge. By the time you get to the highest percentile of scientific intelligence, liberal belief in human-caused global warming has risen to nearly 100 percent, while conservative belief in it has fallen to 20 percent.[5]

The same funnel-shaped pattern shows up when you ask people for their opinions on other ideologically charged scientific issues: Should the government fund stem cell research? How did the universe begin? Did humans evolve from lower animal species? On all these questions, the people with the highest levels of scientific intelligence were also the most politically polarized in their opinions.[6]

---

* This pattern doesn't imply that liberals and conservatives engage in motivated reasoning about climate change to the same extent, just that people in general engage in motivated reasoning about this issue.

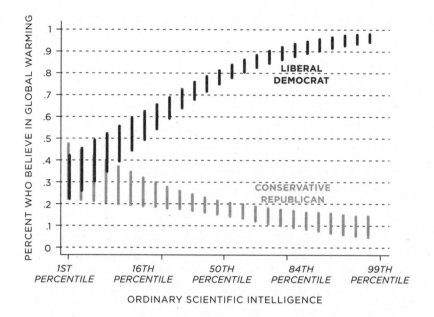

AS SCIENCE INTELLIGENCE INCREASES, LIBERALS AND CONSERVATIVES
DIVERGE OVER WHETHER THERE IS "SOLID EVIDENCE" OF HUMAN-CAUSED
GLOBAL WARMING. ADAPTED FROM KAHAN (2017), FIGURE 8, PAGE 1012.

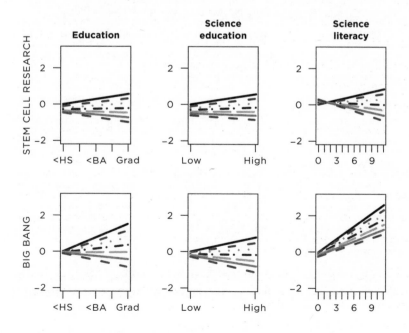

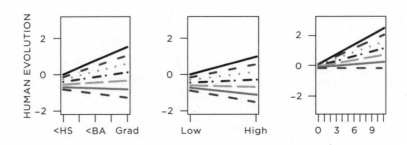

ON IDEOLOGICALLY CHARGED SCIENTIFIC ISSUES—STEM CELL RESEARCH, THE BIG BANG, AND HUMAN EVOLUTION—MORE KNOWLEDGEABLE PEOPLE ARE MORE POLITICALLY POLARIZED. ADAPTED FROM DRUMMOND & FISCHHOFF (2017), FIGURE 1, PAGE 4.

From the way I'm talking about polarization, some readers might infer that I think the truth always lies in the center. I don't; that would be false balance. On any particular issue, the truth may lie close to the far left or the far right or anywhere else. The point is simply that as people become better informed, they should start to converge on the truth, *wherever it happens to be*. Instead, we see the opposite pattern—as people get better informed, they diverge.

This is a crucially important result, because being smart and being knowledgeable on a particular topic are two more things that give us a false sense of security in our own reasoning. A high IQ and an advanced degree might give you an advantage in ideologically neutral domains like solving math problems or figuring out where to invest your money. But they won't protect you from bias on ideologically charged questions.

Speaking of which . . . the question "Are some people more prone to bias than others?" is itself ideologically charged. And sure enough, researchers who study bias fall prey to the very phenomenon they're studying.

For decades, it's been common wisdom among psychologists that conservatives are *inherently* more prone to bias than liberals. It's called the "rigidity of the right" theory, that conservatism attracts people with certain innate personality traits: closed-mindedness, authoritarianism, dogmatism, fear of change and novelty. It's an irresistible theory if you're a liberal—which academic psychologists overwhelmingly are. A recent survey of social and personality psychologists found that the ratio of self-identified liberals to conservatives was almost 14 to 1.[7]

Perhaps that has something to do with why the field as a whole was so willing to accept the "rigidity of the right" theory even though the research behind it is dubious, to say the least. Check out some of the questions that are typically used to determine whether someone has a "rigid" personality:[8]

Do you agree that "homosexuals and feminists should be praised for being brave enough to defy 'traditional family values'"? If not, then you're rigid.

Do you favor the death penalty? If so, you're rigid.

Do you favor socialism? Legalized abortion? If not, then yup, you guessed it—you're rigid.

Hopefully, you'll be quicker to recognize the problem with this research than academic psychologists were. These questions are supposedly measuring rigidity, but they're actually measuring whether you hold conservative beliefs. Which means that the theory that conservatives have more rigid personalities than liberals isn't an empirical finding at all—it's a tautology.

Intelligence and knowledge are just tools. You can use those tools to help you see the world clearly, if that's what you're motivated to do. Or you can use them to defend a particular viewpoint, if you're motivated to do that instead. But there's nothing inherent to the tools that makes you a scout.

# ACTUALLY PRACTICING SCOUT MINDSET MAKES YOU A SCOUT

One evening at a party, I was talking about how hard it is to have productive disagreements, in which people actually change their minds, on Twitter. A man in the group chimed in: "I don't find it difficult at all."

"Wow, what's your secret?" I asked.

He shrugged. "There's no secret. You just bring up the facts."

My brow furrowed in confusion. "And that . . . works? You bring up facts, and people change their minds?"

"Yeah, all the time," he said.

The next day, I perused his Twitter feed to figure out what I was missing. I read through months of tweets, but I couldn't find a single instance that matched the description he'd given me at the party. Whenever someone disagreed with something he said in a tweet, he either ignored them, mocked them, or simply informed them that they were wrong and considered the discussion closed.

It's easy to *think*, "Of course I change my mind in response to evidence," or "Of course I apply my principles consistently," or "Of course I'm fair-minded," whether or not those things are true. The test of scout mindset isn't whether you see yourself as the kind of person who does these things. It's whether you can point to concrete cases in which you did, in fact, do these things.

Feeling reasonable, being smart and knowledgeable, being aware of motivated reasoning—all these things *seem* like they should be indicators of scout mindset, yet they have surprisingly little to do with it. The only real sign of a scout is whether you act like one. In the rest of this chapter, we'll explore five signs of scout mindset, behavioral cues that someone cares about truth and will seek it out even when they're not forced to, and even when the truth isn't favorable to them.

## 1. Do you tell other people when you realize they were right?

In the American Civil War, the city of Vicksburg was of the utmost importance. It was strategically situated on the Mississippi River, which meant that whoever controlled it could control the movement of troops and supplies up and down the country. As Confederate president Jefferson Davis put it, "Vicksburg is the nailhead that holds the South's two halves together."[9]

The head of the Union army, General Ulysses S. Grant, had tried unsuccessfully to capture Vicksburg for months. Finally, in May 1863, he settled on a daring plan to approach the city from an unexpected direction, while using subterfuge to hide his troops' progress from the Confederates. President Abraham Lincoln was worried—the plan struck him as far too risky. But two months later, on Independence Day, Grant's army stood victorious in the center of Vicksburg.

Lincoln had never met Grant in person, but decided to write him a letter after hearing of the victory. "My dear General," it began. After expressing his gratitude, Lincoln continued:

> I wish to say a word further. . . . I thought you should go down the river and join General Banks; and when you turned northward, east of the Big Black, I thought it was a mistake. I now wish to make the personal acknowledgment that you were right and I was wrong.[10]

The letter was "perfectly in character" for Lincoln, a colleague of his commented later upon reading it. The president never had any difficulty telling other people their judgment was superior.[11]

Technically, scout mindset only requires you to be able to acknowledge to yourself that you were wrong, not to other people. Still, a willingness to say "I was wrong" to someone else is a strong sign of a person who prizes the truth over their own ego. Can you think of cases in which you've done the same?

## 2. How do you react to personal criticism?

Maybe you've had a boss or a friend who insisted, "I respect honesty! I just want people to be straight with me," only to react poorly when someone took them up on that. They got offended or defensive or lashed out at the feedback-giver in retaliation. Or perhaps they politely thanked that person for their honesty and then gave them the cold shoulder from then on.

It's a lot easier to *say* you welcome criticism than it is to actually welcome it. But in so many domains, getting honest feedback is essential to improvement. Could your public speaking skill be improved? Do your customers have complaints? Are there things you're doing as a boss, employee, friend, or romantic partner that are frustrating to other people?

To gauge your comfort with criticism, it's not enough just to ask yourself, "Am I open to criticism?" Instead, examine your track record. Are there examples of criticism you've acted upon? Have you rewarded a critic (for example, by promoting him)? Do you go out of your way to make it easier for other people to criticize you?

A friend of mine named Spencer runs a start-up incubator and manages several teams of people. Twice a year, he invites all his employees to fill out a survey on how he's doing as a manager. The survey is anonymous, to make it easier for people to be candid. He's also learned to phrase his feedback requests in multiple ways to more effectively coax criticism out of people. For example, in addition to asking "What are my weaknesses as a manager?" he asks, "If you had to pick one thing for me to improve on, what would it be?"

I don't score very well on this aspect of scout mindset, as you might recall from my story about approaching my students for "honest feedback" while asking them leading questions. I hate getting personal criticism and have to all but force myself to seek it out. The difference between me and Spencer on this score is sometimes very stark—such as the day when he approached me with this enthusiastic suggestion: "Hey, Julia, I just heard about this cool speed-dating event," he said. "You go on a five-minute 'date' with ten different people, and then each person tells you their impressions of you and how you could improve! Want to sign up with me?"

"Spencer," I replied sincerely, "I would rather saw off my own leg with a butter knife."

## 3. Do you ever prove yourself wrong?

One Monday morning, a journalist named Bethany Brookshire sat down at her desk and opened her email. She had received two replies from scientists she had emailed to request an interview. One was from a female scientist and began, "Dear Dr. Brookshire . . ." The other was from a male scientist and began, "Dear Ms. Brookshire . . ."

*How typical,* Brookshire thought. She went to Twitter, typed the following, and hit send:

Monday morning observation:

I have "PhD" in my email signature. I sign my emails with just my name, no "Dr." I email a lot of PhDs.

Their replies:

Men: "Dear Bethany." "Hi Ms. Brookshire."

Women: "Hi Dr. Brookshire."

It's not 100%, but it's a VERY clear division.[12]

Her tweet was liked over 2,300 times. "Not surprised," one woman commented. "For sure there is bias!" another wrote. "Totally my experience, too," said another.

As the supportive replies piled up, however, Brookshire began to squirm. Her claim was based on a rough impression, from memory, of how male and female scientists typically replied to her emails. But the actual data itself was sitting in her inbox. "Shouldn't I test my claim?" she thought to herself.

So she went through her old emails, ran the numbers—and discovered she had been wrong. Out of the male scientists, 8 percent called her "Dr.," and among female scientists, 6 percent called her "Dr." The data was sparse enough that no confident conclusions could be drawn from it, but it certainly did not support her initial observation. She followed up her original tweet one week later,[13] sharing the results of her investigation: "New post: I took the data on this. It turns out . . . I was wrong."

To be clear, the fact that Brookshire was wrong in this case doesn't mean there *isn't* gender bias in science. It just means that in this particular instance, her impression of bias was mistaken. "We all identified with something because it sounded like our reality," Brookshire wrote in a follow-up blog post. "In many cases, it may well be reality. But my observation about my emails was a mistake."[14]

Can you think of any examples in which you voluntarily proved yourself wrong? Perhaps you were about to voice an opinion online, but decided to search for counterarguments first, and ended up finding them compelling. Or perhaps at work you were advocating for a new strategy, but changed your mind after you ran the numbers more carefully and realized it wouldn't be feasible.

# 4. Do you take precautions to avoid fooling yourself?

A hotly debated question in twentieth-century physics was whether the expansion of our universe is speeding up or slowing down. That matters in part because it tells us what the far future will look like: If expansion is speeding up, then all the matter in existence will keep getting farther and farther apart for all eternity. If expansion is slowing down, then everything will eventually collapse into a single point, like the big bang in reverse. (It's actually called the "big crunch.")

In the 1990s, physicist Saul Perlmutter ran the Supernova Cosmology Project, a team of researchers who investigated the universe's changing speed of expansion by measuring the light given off by supernovae, or exploding stars. Personally, Perlmutter suspected the answer was going to turn out to be "expansion is speeding up." But he was worried about the potential for motivated reasoning tainting the research process. He knew that even the most well-intentioned scientists can fool themselves and end up finding what they hope or expect to find in their data.

So Perlmutter opted for a method called blind data analysis. He used a computer program to shift all the supernova data by a random amount, which remained hidden from the researchers as they did their analyses. Because they couldn't see the original data, they couldn't consciously or unconsciously tweak their analysis to get the answer they wanted. Only once all the analyses were finalized did the team get to see what the results looked like with the real data—and indeed, the "speeding up" theory was confirmed.

Perlmutter would go on to win the Nobel Prize for the finding in 2015. Blind data analysis is "a lot more work in some sense, but I think it leaves you feeling much safer as you do your analysis," he told a journalist.[15]

It's probably not every day that you find yourself testing a Nobel

Prize–worthy theory about the nature of reality, but the same principle applies to more ordinary situations as well. Do you try to avoid biasing the information you get? For example, when you ask your friend to weigh in on a fight you had with your partner, do you describe the disagreement without revealing which side you were on, so as to avoid influencing your friend's answer? When you launch a new project at work, do you decide ahead of time what will count as a success and what will count as a failure, so you're not tempted to move the goal-posts later?

## 5. Do you have any good critics?

When Charles Darwin published *On the Origin of Species* in 1859, he knew it was going to be a controversial bombshell. The book made his case for evolution by natural selection, a theory that was not just difficult for people to wrap their minds around, but verging on blasphemous, as it upended the traditional picture of man's God-given dominion over the animal kingdom. Arguing for evolution was "like confessing a murder," he told a fellow scientist.[16]

The book did indeed generate a firestorm of criticism, which Darwin found galling, even though he had known it was coming. His critics straw-manned his arguments, demanded an unrealistically high burden of proof, and raised flimsy objections. Darwin stayed polite in public but vented his frustrations in private letters. "Owen is indeed very spiteful. He misrepresents and alters what I say very unfairly," he fumed about one review.[17]

Of course, it's typical for the maverick with the fringe theory to feel unfairly dismissed by the mainstream. What made Darwin atypical was that he also recognized a handful of *good* critics in addition to the bad, people who he could tell had taken the trouble to really understand his theory and were raising intelligent objections to it.

One of the good critics was a scientist named François Jules Pictet de la Rive, who published a negative review of *On the Origin of Species* in a literary magazine called *The Athenaeum*. Darwin was so impressed with Pictet de la Rive's review that he wrote him a letter thanking him for having summarized the book's argument so accurately, and calling his criticisms perfectly fair. "I literally agree to every word you say," he told Pictet de la Rive. "I most fully admit that I by no means explain away all the vast difficulties. The only difference between us is that I attach much more weight to the explanation of facts, & somewhat less weight to the difficulties than you do."[18]

You can probably think of people who are critical of your deeply held beliefs and life choices. People who hold the opposite view on political issues such as gun control, capital punishment, or abortion. People who disagree with you on scientific questions such as climate change, nutrition, or vaccination. People who condemn the industry you work in, such as tech or the military.

It's tempting to view your critics as mean-spirited, ill-informed, or unreasonable. And it's likely that some of them are. But it's unlikely that *all* of them are. Can you name people who are critical of your beliefs, profession, or life choices who you consider thoughtful, even if you believe they're wrong? Or can you at least name reasons why someone might disagree with you that you would consider reasonable (even if you don't happen to know of specific people who hold those views)?

BEING ABLE TO name reasonable critics, being willing to say "The other side has a point this time," being willing to acknowledge when you were wrong—it's things like these that distinguish people who actually care about truth from people who only think they do.

But the biggest sign of scout mindset may be this: Can you point to occasions in which you were in soldier mindset? If that sounds backward, remember that motivated reasoning is our natural state. It's universal, hardwired into our brains. So if you never notice yourself doing it, what's more likely—that you happen to be wired differently from the rest of humanity or that you're simply not as self-aware as you could be?

Learning to spot your own biases, in the moment, is no easy feat. But it's not impossible, if you have the right tools. That's what the next two chapters are about.

*Chapter 5*

# Noticing Bias

To GRASP HOW insidious motivated reasoning is, it helps to know a little magic.

One of the essential tools in a magician's tool kit is a form of manipulation called forcing. In its simplest form, forcing works like this: The magician places two cards facedown in front of you. In order to make his trick succeed, he needs you to end up with the card on the left. He says: "Now we're going to remove one of these cards—please pick one."

If you point to the card on the left, he says, "Okay, that one's yours."

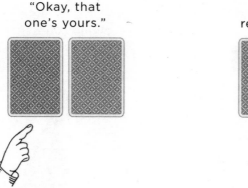

"Okay, that one's yours."

"Okay, we'll remove that one."

If you point to the card on the right, he says, "Okay, we'll remove that one." Either way, you end up holding the card on the left, feeling like you chose it of your own free will. If you could see both of those possible scenarios at once, the trick would be obvious. But because you end up in only one of those worlds, you never realize.

Forcing is what your brain is doing to get away with motivated reasoning while still making you feel like you're being objective. Suppose a Democratic politician gets caught cheating on his wife, but a Democratic voter doesn't consider that a reason not to vote for him: "What he does in his private life is his own business," she reasons. However, if the adulterous politician had been a Republican, she would instead have thought, "Adultery is a sign of poor character—that shows he's not fit to govern."

If the Democratic voter could see the way she would have reacted in that counterfactual world and compare it to her reaction in the actual world, the influence of her motivations would be obvious to her. But because she only ever sees one of those worlds, she never realizes that she's being anything less than dispassionate.

It's easiest for your brain to pull the "forcing" trick on topics you've never considered before, because you have no preexisting principles to get in the way of choosing whichever answer is convenient for you in the case at hand. You may have already formed opinions about

"Adultery is a sign of
poor character."

"His private life is his
own business."

how harshly to judge adultery, so how about this example instead: If you get sued and you win the case, should the person who sued you pay your legal costs? If you're like most people (85 percent, in one study[1]), your answer is yes. After all, if you're falsely accused of something, why should you be out thousands of dollars in lawyers' fees? That wouldn't be fair.

However, when the question in that study was slightly reworded—"If you sue someone and you lose the case, should you pay his costs?"—only 44 percent of people said yes. Imagining yourself in the role of the person who sued and lost brings to mind alternate arguments. For example, you might have lost simply because the other side is wealthy and can afford better lawyers. It's not fair to discourage victims from suing just because they can't afford to lose, right?

Both the arguments for and against the "loser pays" policy have at least some merit. But which one comes to mind will depend on whether you're the plaintiff or the defendant—and it will likely never occur to you that you could have thought of an opposing argument if you had been on the other side of the case.

## A THOUGHT EXPERIMENT IS A PEEK INTO THE COUNTERFACTUAL WORLD

You can't detect motivated reasoning in yourself just by scrutinizing your reasoning and concluding that it makes sense. You have to compare your reasoning to the way you *would have* reasoned in a counterfactual world, a world in which your motivations were different—would you judge that politician's actions differently if he was in the opposite party? Would you evaluate that advice differently if your friend had offered it instead of your spouse? Would you consider that study's methodology sound if its conclusions supported your side?

Of course, you can't know for sure how you would have reasoned if circumstances were different. You can't literally visit the counterfactual world. But you can do the next best thing—peek into it virtually, with a thought experiment.

Over the next few pages, we'll explore five different types of thought experiments: the double standard test, the outsider test, the conformity test, the selective skeptic test, and the status quo bias test. But before we start, here's an important tip to keep in mind when doing a thought experiment: Try to *actually imagine* the counterfactual scenario. To see why that matters, think of a six-year-old child who's just made fun of another child. His mother reprimands him and tries to show him why what he did was wrong by posing this age-old thought experiment: "Imagine you were in Billy's shoes and someone was making fun of you in front of your friends. How would you feel?"

Her son replies instantly: "I wouldn't mind!"

It's pretty obvious the child isn't really imagining himself in Billy's shoes, right? He's just saying what he knows to be the correct answer, the answer that means he hasn't done anything wrong. Thought experiments only work if you actually do them. So don't simply formulate a verbal question for yourself. Conjure up the counterfactual world, place yourself in it, and observe your reaction.

You might be surprised at what a difference that makes. A law student I knew a few years ago, whom I'll call Keisha, was unhappy in law school and unexcited about the idea of being a lawyer, but she always dismissed the idea of quitting. One of her friends asked, "Are you just staying in law school because you don't want to disappoint your parents? If you knew they didn't care, would that change your decision?"

"No, I wouldn't stay in law school just for their sake. That would be crazy," Keisha said firmly.

Her friend pushed her a little harder, this time making the question more vivid: "Okay, imagine that tomorrow, your parents call you up and say, 'You know what, Keisha, we've been talking about it and we're concerned that you aren't happy in law school. We just wanted to make sure you know that we don't care if you quit—we just want you to do something you enjoy.'"

And Keisha realized: *In that case, I would quit law school right away.*

## THE DOUBLE STANDARD TEST

As a young man, "Dan" (not his real name) attended a military high school with a very lopsided gender ratio. There were around 30 girls in his class and 250 boys. Because the girls had so much choice, they tended to go for guys who were especially attractive, athletic, or charming.[2] That did not describe Dan. He was socially awkward and awkward-looking, and he received none of the girls' scarce attention. Stung by their disinterest, he concluded that girls were all "stuck-up bitches."

But one day he did a thought experiment that changed his perception. He asked himself: "Can you honestly say that if the situation was reversed, you wouldn't be doing the exact same thing?" The answer was clear. "Yeah, if that were the case, I'd definitely be making time with all the hotties," he realized. That perspective shift didn't immediately net him a date, but it did make him feel more at peace with the situation at school, and it made it easier for him to connect with women when he was a little older.

What Dan did was a version of the "double standard test": "Am I judging other people's behavior by a standard I wouldn't apply to myself?" The double standard test can be applied to groups as well as individuals. In fact, you've probably already encountered this test in its most common form—hurled angrily across the political aisle: "Oh, come on, stop defending your candidate! How would you have reacted if someone from our party did the same thing?"

It's much rarer for someone to turn that question on themselves, but it happens occasionally. I was impressed to see the double standard test pop up in an online discussion in 2009 about the Democrats' intention to abolish the filibuster option. One commenter—a Democrat—expressed disapproval: "I'm just imagining how I would have reacted if I'd have heard that a similar tactic was used by [Republican president George W. Bush] about a war budget or something of that nature. I wouldn't like it one bit," he said.[3]

So far, these examples have involved judging other people or groups by an unfairly critical standard. But this test can also reveal the opposite double standard—that you're judging yourself more harshly than you would judge someone else in exactly the same situation. If you're kicking yourself for asking a stupid question in class or in a meeting, imagine someone else asking the same "stupid" question. What would your reaction be? How big a deal would it be?

## THE OUTSIDER TEST

The first half of 1985 was a "grim and frustrating" time for the tech company Intel, according to its cofounder Andy Grove. Intel had been doing a booming business specializing in memory chips. But by 1984, its Japanese competitors had figured out how to make memory chips that worked faster and better than Intel's.

As Intel executives watched Japan's market share soar and their own plummet, they talked endlessly about what to do. They were getting destroyed in the memory-chip market. Should they try to move into another market? But memory was Intel's identity. The thought of no longer being a "memory company" felt shocking, almost like the violation of a religious dogma.

In Grove's memoir, *Only the Paranoid Survive*, he describes the conversation he had with his cofounder, Gordon Moore, that ended up saving the company:

Our mood was downbeat. I looked out the window at the Ferris wheel of the Great America amusement park revolving in the distance, then I turned back to Gordon and I asked, "If we got kicked out and the board brought in a new CEO, what do you think he would do?"

Gordon answered without hesitation, "He would get us out of memories." I stared at him, numb, then said, "Why shouldn't you and I walk out the door, come back and do it ourselves?"[4]

Once they had acknowledged the fact that abandoning their once-celebrated memory-chip business was, from an external perspective, the obvious choice, the decision was almost as good as made. That's how Intel managed to rebound with vigor from its mid-eighties slump, shifting its focus from memory chips to what it's most known for today: microprocessors.

The thought experiment Grove and Moore did is called an outsider test: Imagine someone else stepped into your shoes—what do you expect they would do in your situation? When you're making a tough decision, the question of what to do can get tangled up with other, emotionally fraught questions like, "Is it my fault that I'm in this situation?" or "Are people going to judge me harshly if I change my mind?" The outsider test is designed to strip away those influences, leaving only your honest guess about the best way to handle a situation like the one you're in.

In a twist on the outsider test, you can also imagine that *you* are the outsider. Suppose you have about two years of graduate school left, but you're feeling increasingly unhappy about the field you've chosen. You've toyed with the possibility of quitting—but the thought that you might have wasted years of your life on this career track is so painful, you always find a reason to stick it out longer.

Try imagining that you've just magically teleported into the life of this person named [Your Name]. You have no attachment to their past decisions, no desire to look consistent or to prove them right. You just want to make the best of the situation you've suddenly found yourself in. It's as if you're hanging a sign around your neck: "Under New Management."[5] Now, which option do you feel more enthusiastic about: spending an additional two years in graduate school to finish [Your Name]'s degree, or quitting to do something else?*

## THE CONFORMITY TEST

When I was a kid, I idolized my cousin Shoshana, who was two years older than me and therefore impossibly sophisticated in my eyes. During a family camping trip one summer, she introduced me to a trendy band called New Kids On The Block. As we sat in her tent, listening to their latest album on her cassette player, Shoshana said, "Ooh, this next song is my favorite!"

After the song was over, she turned to me and asked me what I thought. I replied enthusiastically, "Yeah, it's so good! I think it's my favorite, too."

"Well, guess what?" she replied. "That's *not* my favorite song. It's my *least* favorite song. I just wanted to see if you would copy me."

I was embarrassed at the time. But in retrospect, it was an instructive experience. When I claimed that song was my favorite, I meant it—the song truly seemed better than the other songs. I didn't feel like I was just saying so to impress Shoshana. Then, after Shoshana revealed her trick, I could feel my attitude shift in real time. The song suddenly seemed corny. Lame. Boring. It was as if someone had just

---

* A more common version of this thought experiment is, "What would you say to a friend who was in this situation?" That can be useful, but comes with its own potential bias, that you might go too easy on a friend.

switched on a harsher light, and the song's flaws were thrown into sharp relief.*

Now I use Shoshana's trick as a thought experiment when I want to test how much of "my" opinion is actually my own. If I find myself agreeing with someone else's viewpoint, I do a conformity test: Imagine this person told me that they no longer held this view. Would I still hold it? Would I feel comfortable defending it to them?

For example, suppose you're in a strategic meeting and your colleague is making the case for hiring more people. You find yourself nodding along in agreement. "That's true, it would end up saving us money," you think. That feels like your own opinion—but to check, you can do a conformity test. Imagine your colleague suddenly said, "By the way, everyone, I'm just playing devil's advocate here. I don't necessarily believe we should hire right now."

Hearing that, do you still feel like you're in favor of hiring?

The conformity test can be used to interrogate your preferences as well as your beliefs. A woman I know in her late twenties was thinking about whether she wanted to have children someday. She had always assumed she would end up being a mother—but did she really want that or was she just going along with what most people do? She tried a conformity test: "Suppose having kids wasn't the majority choice, and instead only about 30 percent of people wanted to do it. Would I?" In that world, she realized, the idea of having children seemed much less appealing to her. The result highlighted for her that she was less inherently interested in parenthood than she had thought.

---

* It's possible my cousin Shoshana crossed paths with Barack Obama at some point, because he used a similar trick on his advisors when he was president. It was essentially a "yes man" test: If someone expressed agreement with a view of his, Obama would pretend he had changed his mind and no longer held that view. Then he would ask them to explain to him why they believed it to be true. "Every leader has strengths and weakness, and one of my strengths is a good B.S. detector," Obama said.[6]

# THE SELECTIVE SKEPTIC TEST

During my research for this book, I came across a paper claiming to show that soldier mindset makes people successful in life. "Oh, come on," I scoffed to myself, and checked its methodology section for flaws. Sure enough, it turned out to be a poorly designed study.

Then, somewhat grudgingly, I did a thought experiment: *What if this study had claimed that soldier mindset makes people unsuccessful in life?*

In that case, I realized, my reaction would have been: "Exactly as I suspected. I'll have to find a place for this study in my book!" That contrast between my reactions in the real and hypothetical worlds was a wake-up call for me, a warning that I needed to be a little less credulous of evidence that happened to support my side. It prompted me to go back through the studies I had been planning to cite in my favor, and scrutinize their methodology for flaws, just as I had done with the pro-soldier mindset study. (Sadly, this ended up disqualifying most of them.)

I call this type of thought experiment the selective skeptic test: Imagine this evidence supported the other side. How credible would you find it then?

Suppose someone criticizes a decision your company made, and your knee-jerk reaction is, "They don't know what they're talking about, because they don't have all the relevant details." *Selective skeptic test*: Imagine the person had praised your company's decision instead. Would you still think that only insiders are informed enough to have valid opinions?

Suppose you're a feminist and you read an article complaining about how feminists hate men. As evidence, the author offers a handful of tweets from people you've never heard of, which say something like, "All men need to die in a fire!!! #girlpower #feminism." You think to yourself: "Give me a break. Of *course* you can find examples of people being idiots or extremists, in any group, if you look hard enough for them. Cherry-picking like that doesn't prove anything about feminism."

*Selective skeptic test*: Imagine the article had been full of cherry-picked quotes from a group you dislike, such as conservatives.* How would you react? Would you reject the evidence on the same logic, that a few cherry-picked examples of people in a group being jerks don't prove anything about that group?

# THE STATUS QUO BIAS TEST

A friend of mine named David was living in his hometown with his college friends. He had a dream job opportunity in Silicon Valley, but he was torn about whether to take it. After all, he got along great with his college friends, most of whom lived nearby. Was it really worth giving that up for a better job?

So he tried a thought experiment: "Suppose I was already living in San Francisco, working at an exciting and well-paying job. Would I be tempted to quit and move back home to be closer to my college friends?

"No, I wouldn't," he realized.

David's thought experiment revealed that his attitude toward his options was likely being influenced by the "status quo bias," a motivation to defend whatever situation happens to be the status quo. A leading theory for why we're biased in favor of the status quo is that we're *loss averse*: the pain we feel from a loss outweighs the pleasure we feel from a similar-size gain. That makes us reluctant to change our

---

* Obviously, feel free to swap out "feminists" and "conservatives" for two other groups that make the example work better for you.

situation, because even if the change would make us better off overall, we fixate more on what we'll be losing than what we'll be gaining.

I call David's thought experiment the status quo bias test: Imagine your current situation was no longer the status quo. Would you then actively choose it? If not, that's a sign that your preference for your situation is less about its particular merits and more about a preference for the status quo.*

The status quo bias test works on policy choices as well as personal life choices. In 2016, when British citizens were voting on whether to leave or remain in the European Union, one British blogger was torn about how to vote. The question that finally decided things for her was a status quo bias test: "If we weren't already part of the European Union, would I think it was a good idea to vote to join?" she asked herself. For her, the answer was no.†

Whenever you reject some proposed change to society, that's an opportunity to test yourself for status bias. Consider life extension research. If scientists could figure out how to double the human life span, from roughly 85 years to 170 years, would that be a good thing? Not according to many people I've discussed this with. "If humans lived that long, progress would slow to a crawl," they argue. "We need older generations to die off and make room for younger generations with new ideas."

To do a status quo bias test, imagine the human life span was naturally 170 years. Now suppose that a genetic mutation reduced the human life span to 85 years. Would you be pleased? If not, then maybe you don't really think that shorter life spans are worth faster societal change.[7]

---

* Astute readers will have noticed that the status quo bias test isn't a perfectly clean thought experiment—by flipping the status quo, you're adding a transaction cost to the decision. But since it's a thought experiment, you can pretend the transaction cost is magically zero.

† You could argue that there's a difference between (1) choosing not to invite Europeans into the UK society and economy in the first place, and (2) choosing to rescind that invitation once it's already been extended. Indeed, that's another potential asymmetry in the status quo bias test. Still, it's useful to know whether that's your main objection, if it is.

## COMMON THOUGHT EXPERIMENTS

| | |
|---|---|
| The Double Standard Test | Are you judging one person (or group) by a different standard than you would use for another person (or group)? |
| The Outsider Test | How would you evaluate this situation if it wasn't *your* situation? |
| The Conformity Test | If other people no longer held this view, would you still hold it? |
| The Selective Skeptic Test | If this evidence supported the other side, how credible would you judge it to be? |
| The Status Quo Bias Test | If your current situation was not the status quo, would you actively choose it? |

THOUGHT EXPERIMENTS AREN'T oracles. They can't tell you what's true or fair or what decision you should make. If you notice that you would be more forgiving of adultery in a Democrat than a Republican, that reveals you have a double standard, but it doesn't tell you what your standard "should" be. If you notice that you're nervous about deviating from the status quo, that doesn't mean you can't decide to play it safe this time anyway.

What thought experiments do is simply reveal that your reasoning changes as your motivations change. That the principles you're inclined to invoke or the objections that spring to your mind depend on your motives: the motive to defend your image or your in-group's status; the motive to advocate for a self-serving policy; fear of change or rejection.

Catching your brain in the act of motivated reasoning—noticing when an experiment's previously invisible flaws jump out at you, or noticing that your preferences change as you switch around supposedly irrelevant details of a scenario—breaks down the illusion that your initial judgment is the objective truth. It convinces you, viscerally, that your reasoning is *contingent*; that your initial judgments are a starting point for exploration, not an end point.

In the metaphor of the scout, it's like peering through your binoculars at a far-off river and saying, "Well, it sure seems like the river is frozen. But let me find another vantage point—different angle, different lighting, different lens—and see if things look any different."

*Chapter 6*

# How Sure Are You?

I N A SCENE in the 2016 movie *Star Trek Beyond*, a spaceship careens across the sky.[1] It's being piloted by Captain Kirk, who is hot on the tail of three enemy ships headed straight for the center of a city, where they intend to detonate a superweapon. Kirk's right-hand man, Commander Spock, yells to him: "Captain, intercepting all three ships is an impossibility!"

*An impossibility.* The words sound so authoritative, so definitive. And yet less than sixty seconds later, Kirk has figured out how to maneuver in front of the enemy ships, stopping them with his own ship's hull before they can reach their destination.

If you've watched much *Star Trek* before, this won't surprise you. Spock doesn't have a great track record when it comes to making accurate predictions. "There's only a very slight chance this will work," Spock warns Kirk in one episode of the original TV show, right before their plan works.[2] The odds of survival are "less than seven thousand to one," Spock tells Kirk in another episode, shortly before they escape unharmed.[3] The chance of finding survivors is "absolutely none," Spock declares in yet another episode, right before they discover a large colony of survivors.[4]

# WE LIKE FEELING CERTAIN

Spock is *overconfident*, meaning that his confidence that he's right outstrips his actual accuracy. In that respect, Spock isn't all that different from most of us (except that he makes a much bigger deal about how his predictions are objective and "logical," which is why I've chosen to make an example of him). We very often speak as if there's no chance we could be mistaken—"There's no way he can make that shot from that distance!" or "I'll definitely have that done by Friday"—and yet we turn out to be wrong nonetheless.

To be fair, the certainty we express is partly just for simplicity's sake. Conversation would be unwieldy if we had to stop and assign a probability to every statement we made. But even when someone does prompt us to stop and reflect on our level of confidence, we often claim to be completely certain. You'll notice this if you search online for phrases like, "How certain are you that" or "How confident are you that." Here are a few examples I pulled from discussions on Quora, Yahoo! Answers, Reddit, and other forums:

- As a percentage, how certain are you that intelligent life exists outside of Earth? "I am 100% certain there's other intelligent life."[5]
- How confident are you that you are going to hit your 2017 sales goals? "I'm 100% confident."[6]
- Atheists, how confident are you that you won't convert to a religion like Christianity on your deathbed? "100% confident."[7]

Even professionals are frequently certain and wrong in their area of expertise. For example, many studies have found that doctors routinely overestimate their ability to diagnose patients. One study examined the autopsy results for patients who had been given diagnoses with "complete certainty," and found that in 40 percent of those cases, the diagnosis was incorrect.[8]

If we tend to be overly certain about our knowledge, that's even more the case when it comes to our opinions. We say things like, "There is *no question* that America needs a living wage," or "It's *obvious* that the internet has wrecked our attention spans," or "*Of course* that bill would be a disaster."

Not all overconfidence is due to motivated reasoning. Sometimes we simply don't realize how complicated a topic is, so we overestimate how easy it is to get the right answer. But a large portion of overconfidence stems from a desire to feel certain. Certainty is simple. Certainty is comfortable. Certainty makes us feel smart and competent.

Your strength as a scout is in your ability to resist that temptation, to push past your initial judgment, and to think in shades of gray instead of black and white. To distinguish the feeling of "95% sure" from "75% sure" from "55% sure." That's what we'll learn to do in this chapter.

But first, let's back up—what does it even mean to put a number on your degree of belief?

## QUANTIFYING YOUR UNCERTAINTY

Typically, when people think about how sure they are, they ask themselves something like: "Do I actively feel any doubt?" If the answer is no, as it often is, they declare themselves to be "100% certain."

That's an understandable way to think about certainty, but it's not the way a scout thinks about it. A scout treats their degree of certainty as a prediction of their likelihood of being right. Imagine sorting all of your beliefs into buckets based on how sure you are that you're right about each one. This would include quotidian predictions ("I will enjoy this restaurant"), beliefs about your life ("My partner is faithful to me"), beliefs about how the world works ("Smoking causes cancer"), core premises ("Magic isn't real"), and so on. Putting a belief into the "70% sure" bucket is like saying, "This is the kind of thing I expect to get right roughly 70 percent of the time."

What you're implicitly aiming for when you tag your beliefs with various confidence levels is *perfect calibration*. That means your "50% sure" claims are in fact correct 50 percent of the time, your "60% sure" claims are correct 60 percent of the time, your "70% sure" claims are correct 70 percent of the time, and so on.

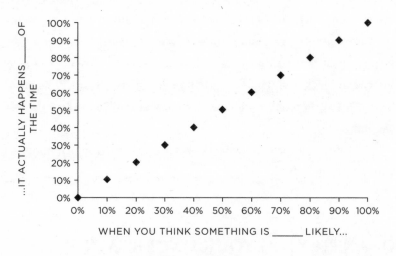

PERFECT CALIBRATION

Perfect calibration is an abstract ideal, not something that's possible to achieve in reality. Still, it's a useful benchmark against which to compare yourself. To get a hang of the concept, let's continue picking on Spock and see how his calibration measures up against perfection.

I went through all of Spock's appearances in *Star Trek: The Original Series*, *Star Trek: The Animated Series*, and the *Star Trek* movies, searching for the words *probability, percent, odds, chance, possible, im-*

*possible, likely, unlikely, probable,* and *improbable.* In total, I found twenty-three instances in which Spock made a prediction with a corresponding confidence level, and in which the prediction was proven either true or false. You can read the full details of Spock's predictions and how I categorized them in Appendix A, but here's the headline summary:

When Spock thinks something is *impossible,* it happens 83 percent of the time.

When Spock thinks something is *very unlikely,* it happens 50 percent of the time.

When Spock thinks something is *unlikely,* it happens 50 percent of the time.

When Spock thinks something is *likely,* it happens 80 percent of the time.

When Spock thinks something is *more than 99.5 percent likely,* it happens 17 percent of the time.[9]

As you can see, he's not doing great. The only confidence level at which he seems to be well calibrated is when he judges something to be "likely"; those predictions actually do come true at a rate that

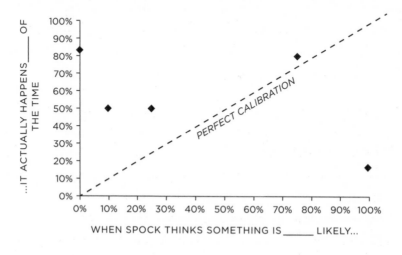

SPOCK'S CALIBRATION (N = 23)

matches his confidence level. Other than that, Spock's predictions are anti-correlated with reality—the less likely he thinks something is, the more likely it is to happen, and the *more* likely he thinks something is, the *less* likely it is to happen.

Want to see if you can do better than Spock? You can test your own calibration, and practice feeling the difference between different levels of certainty, by answering a few rounds of trivia questions. Below are forty questions for you to practice on. You don't need to answer all of them, but the more you answer, the more informative your results will be.

For each question, circle an answer and then indicate how sure you are by circling a confidence level. Since these questions have only two possible answers, your confidence level could range from 50 percent if you truly have no clue (i.e., you might as well be guessing the outcome of a coin flip) to 100 percent if you think there is no chance you could be wrong. For the sake of simplicity, I've listed five confidence levels between those extremes: 55%, 65%, 75%, 85%, and 95%. Just circle the one that best represents how sure you are.

As you go through the list, you should notice your level of certainty fluctuating. Some questions might feel easy, and you'll be near certain of the answer. Others may prompt you to throw up your hands and say, "I have no idea!" That's perfectly fine. Remember, the goal isn't to know as much as possible. It's to *know how much you know*.

## CALIBRATION PRACTICE: CIRCLE YOUR ANSWERS.

| Round 1: Are these animal facts true or false? | How sure are you? |
| --- | --- |
| 1. The elephant is the world's largest mammal. (T / F) | 55% 65% 75% 85% 95% |
| 2. Sea otters sometimes hold hands while they sleep. (T / F) | 55% 65% 75% 85% 95% |

| | |
|---|---|
| 3. Centipedes have more legs than any other animal. (T / F) | 55% 65% 75% 85% 95% |
| 4. Mammals and dinosaurs coexisted. (T / F) | 55% 65% 75% 85% 95% |
| 5. Bears can't climb trees. (T / F) | 55% 65% 75% 85% 95% |
| 6. Camels store water in their humps. (T / F) | 55% 65% 75% 85% 95% |
| 7. Flamingos are pink because they eat shrimp. (T / F) | 55% 65% 75% 85% 95% |
| 8. The giant panda eats mostly bamboo. (T / F) | 55% 65% 75% 85% 95% |
| 9. The platypus is the only mammal that lays eggs. (T / F) | 55% 65% 75% 85% 95% |
| 10. A mule is a cross between a male donkey and a female horse. (T / F) | 55% 65% 75% 85% 95% |
| **Round 2: Which historical figure was born first?** | **How sure are you?** |
| 11. Julius Caesar or Confucius? | 55% 65% 75% 85% 95% |
| 12. Fidel Castro or Mahatma Gandhi? | 55% 65% 75% 85% 95% |
| 13. Nelson Mandela or Anne Frank? | 55% 65% 75% 85% 95% |
| 14. Cleopatra or Muhammad? | 55% 65% 75% 85% 95% |
| 15. William Shakespeare or Joan of Arc? | 55% 65% 75% 85% 95% |
| 16. George Washington or Sun Tzu? | 55% 65% 75% 85% 95% |
| 17. Genghis Khan or Leonardo da Vinci? | 55% 65% 75% 85% 95% |
| 18. Queen Victoria or Karl Marx? | 55% 65% 75% 85% 95% |
| 19. Saddam Hussein or Marilyn Monroe? | 55% 65% 75% 85% 95% |
| 20. Albert Einstein or Mao Zedong? | 55% 65% 75% 85% 95% |
| **Round 3: Which country had more people in 2019?** | **How sure are you?** |
| 21. Germany or France? | 55% 65% 75% 85% 95% |
| 22. Japan or South Korea? | 55% 65% 75% 85% 95% |
| 23. Brazil or Argentina? | 55% 65% 75% 85% 95% |
| 24. Egypt or Botswana? | 55% 65% 75% 85% 95% |
| 25. Mexico or Guatemala? | 55% 65% 75% 85% 95% |
| 26. Panama or Belize? | 55% 65% 75% 85% 95% |

| 27. Jamaica or Haiti? | 55% 65% 75% 85% 95% |
|---|---|
| 28. Greece or Norway? | 55% 65% 75% 85% 95% |
| 29. China or India? | 55% 65% 75% 85% 95% |
| 30. Iraq or Iran? | 55% 65% 75% 85% 95% |
| **Round 4: Are these science facts true or false?** | **How sure are you?** |
| 31. Mars has one moon, just like Earth. (T / F) | 55% 65% 75% 85% 95% |
| 32. Scurvy is caused by a deficit of vitamin C. (T / F) | 55% 65% 75% 85% 95% |
| 33. Brass is made from iron and copper. (T / F) | 55% 65% 75% 85% 95% |
| 34. One tablespoon of oil has more calories than one tablespoon of butter. (T / F) | 55% 65% 75% 85% 95% |
| 35. Helium is the lightest element. (T / F) | 55% 65% 75% 85% 95% |
| 36. The common cold is caused by bacteria. (T / F) | 55% 65% 75% 85% 95% |
| 37. The deepest place on Earth is in the Pacific Ocean. (T / F) | 55% 65% 75% 85% 95% |
| 38. Seasons are caused by the earth orbiting the sun in an elliptical path. (T / F) | 55% 65% 75% 85% 95% |
| 39. Jupiter is the largest planet in our solar system. (T / F) | 55% 65% 75% 85% 95% |
| 40. The atoms in a solid are more densely packed than the atoms in a gas. (T / F) | 55% 65% 75% 85% 95% |

Once you've finished, or answered as many questions as you want to, it's time to score yourself. Check the answers on page 239 to find out which you got right and which you got wrong.

Next, go through *only* the questions about which you were "55% sure" and calculate the percentage of those questions you actually got right. For example, if there were 10 questions for which you said you were 55 percent sure of your answer, and you got 6 of those questions right, then your total percentage right at this confidence level would be 6 / 10 = 60 percent.

## YOUR RESULTS:

|  | Column A: Number of times you were right | Column B: Number of times you were wrong | % of the time you're right at this confidence level = A / (A + B) |
|---|---|---|---|
| 55% sure |  |  |  |
| 65% sure |  |  |  |
| 75% sure |  |  |  |
| 85% sure |  |  |  |
| 95% sure |  |  |  |

Then do the same for the other confidence levels (65% sure, 75% sure, 85% sure, 95% sure). You can get a visual picture of your calibration by plotting those five results on this graph—the closer your points are to the dotted line, the more well-calibrated you are.

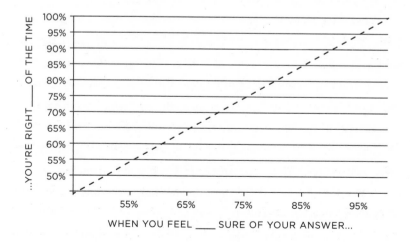

PLOT YOUR CALIBRATION

Happily, calibration is a skill with a quick learning curve. A couple of hours of practice is all it takes for most people to become very well calibrated—at least within a single domain, like trivia questions.[10] (Your calibration skill in one domain will carry over partially, but not completely, to other domains.)

## A BET CAN REVEAL HOW SURE YOU *REALLY* ARE

Imagine you're talking with a friend who's struggling to get her new catering business off the ground. You reassure her, "You're amazing at this stuff! The only reason business is slow is because you're just starting out. Everyone has trouble getting clients at first!"

She replies, "Thanks! I'm so glad you feel that way. Could you recommend me to your coworkers?"

Suddenly you feel hesitant. You recall her telling you about backing out of a job at the last minute . . . and you realize that you've never actually tasted her cooking . . . and you can't help but ask yourself, "How sure am I, really, that she'll do a decent job?"

When you were reassuring your friend a moment earlier, you weren't lying. You just weren't thinking about what you actually believed, because it didn't seem to matter. But once there are actual stakes, and your reputation could take a hit if you guess wrong about your friend's catering skill, your brain switches over from the goal "be supportive" to the goal "actually try to get the right answer."

Evolutionary psychologist Robert Kurzban has an analogy for these two modes.[11] In a company, there's a board of directors whose role is to make the crucial decisions for the company—how to spend its budget, which risks to take, when to change strategies, and so on. Then there's a press secretary whose role is to give statements about the company's values, its mission, and the reasoning behind its decisions.

If a competitor starts gaining market share, the company's press secretary might assure the public, "We're not worried. Our brand has been America's favorite for thirty years, and that's not going to change." However, if you were to sit in on a board meeting, you might find that behind the scenes, the board is taking the risk seriously and looking for ways to cut costs.

Imagine that the company sells toothpaste. The press secretary might assert confidently, "Our toothpaste whitens teeth better than any other brand on the market." But suppose the board is approached by a dental school professor who says, "I'd like to do a study. I'll assign groups of people to use one of the leading brands of toothpaste, without telling them which brand it is, and then I'll measure how much whiter their teeth are. I'll publish whatever results I get."

If the board was truly confident that their toothpaste worked best, they would say, "Great—a chance to prove to the public that we're the best!" But despite the press secretary's assurances, the board might decide that they're not confident enough they would win such a contest, and it's not worth risking the embarrassment of losing.

The press secretary isn't thinking about what's true. He's thinking about what he can get away with saying, what will present the company in the best light while still being at least sort of plausible. But the board is incentivized to form their best guess about the truth, because the company will thrive if they guess right and suffer if they're wrong. The press secretary makes *claims*; the board makes *bets*.

The word *bet* might conjure up horse races and blackjack tables, but its meaning is far more general. A bet is any decision in which you stand to gain or lose something of value, based on the outcome. That could include money, health, time—or reputation, as in the case of your catering friend who wants your endorsement. So when you're thinking about how sure you are, your answer will be more honest if you switch from thinking in terms of "What can I get away with claiming to myself?" to "How would I bet, if there was something at stake?"

Sometimes a project I'm working on seems hopeless. For example— just to pull a random, hypothetical situation out of thin air: "The book I'm writing is terrible and I should give up." But how sure am I that I'm not just in a temporary funk? *I'm 100% sure,* my press secretary insists—but let's ignore him, and pose a question to the board instead: "Suppose you would win $1,000 for correctly guessing whether you will still feel this way about your book a week from now. How would you bet?"

Now that there's money on the line, I hesitate. I recall that I have felt pessimistic about my book, or some other project, many times in the past, and the dark cloud usually goes away in a day or two. It feels like a better bet to pick "Yes, I probably will feel better." Going through that exercise doesn't magically get rid of my bad mood, but it does take the edge off it. It's useful to have proven to myself that I wouldn't be willing to bet on this mood lasting, even though it *feels* like it will last forever.

A tip when you're imagining betting on your beliefs: You may need to get more concrete about what you believe by coming up with a hypothetical test that could be performed to prove you right or wrong. For example, if you believe "Our computer servers are highly secure," a hypothetical test might be something like this: Suppose you were to hire a hacker to try to break in to your systems. If they succeed, you lose one month's salary. How confident do you feel that you would win that bet?

If you believe "I was being reasonable in that fight with my partner, and he was being unreasonable," a hypothetical test might go something like this: Suppose another person, an objective third party, is given all of the relevant details about the fight, and is asked to judge which of you two is being more reasonable. If he judges in your favor, you win $1,000; if not, you lose $1,000. How confident do you feel that you would win that bet?

# THE EQUIVALENT BET TEST

The examples of bets in the previous section are meant to generate a *qualitative* sense of your confidence in a belief. Do you feel happy to take the bet, without hesitating? Do you feel a little bit of doubt? Do you feel truly torn? Your hesitation, or lack thereof, is a proxy for your degree of confidence that your belief is true.

Contemplating a bet can also be used to pin down how sure you are *quantitatively*, helping you put a number on your degree of confidence. Sometimes I hear an ambitious technological forecast like, "Self-driving cars will be on the market within the year!" My first reaction is often to scoff, "Well, that's crazy." But how sure am I that the forecast is wrong?

To answer that question, I imagine facing a choice between two possible bets. I use a technique I adapted from decision-making expert Douglas Hubbard called an "equivalent bet test."[12] Here's how it works in this case: I can bet on self-driving cars, and get $10,000 if they're on the market in a year. Alternately, I can take the "ball bet": I'm given a box containing four balls, one of which is gray. I reach in and pull out one ball, without looking—if it's gray, I win $10,000.*

| Ball bet (1 in 4 chance of winning): | Bet on self-driving cars |
|---|---|
| Draw from a box with four balls, one of which is gray. If I draw the gray ball, I get $10,000.  | If fully self-driving cars are available for purchase in a year, I get $10,000. |

---

* To make it fair, the ball bet would have to pay out in a year as well, just like the self-driving car bet, so that my decision isn't skewed by the possibility of an immediate payoff.

Which gamble would I rather take? I hesitate for a moment, but I feel happier with the ball bet. Since the probability of winning the ball bet is 1 in 4 (or 25 percent), the fact that I feel more confident in the ball bet implies that I'm *less than 25 percent confident* in self-driving cars making it to the market in a year.

Let's try decreasing the odds of winning the ball bet. Suppose the box contains sixteen balls, only one of which is gray. Now which do I prefer: betting on drawing the gray ball or betting on self-driving cars in a year?

| Ball bet (1 in 16 chance of winning): | Bet on self-driving cars |
|---|---|
| Draw from a box with sixteen balls, one of which is gray. If I draw the gray ball, I get $10,000. | If fully self-driving cars are available for purchase in a year, I get $10,000. |

This time, I notice that I prefer my chances on self-driving cars. After all, sometimes technological progress surprises us. Maybe one of the companies working on self-driving technology is actually farther along than they've been letting on. It seems unlikely, but I'd still rather gamble on that than on being lucky enough to draw the gray ball. And since the probability of drawing a gray ball is 1 in 16 (or about 6 percent), the fact that I would prefer to bet on self-driving cars implies that I am *more than 6 percent confident* that self-driving cars will make it to the market in a year.

Okay, let's adjust the chances of winning the ball bet back upward a little bit, to one in nine. Now which do I prefer?

| Ball bet<br>(1 in 9 chance of winning): | Bet on self-driving cars |
| --- | --- |
| Draw from a box with nine balls, one of which is gray. If I draw the gray ball, I get $10,000.<br><br> | If fully self-driving cars are available for purchase in a year, I get $10,000. |

Hmm. I'm really torn. Neither seems like a clearly better bet. The bets feel *equivalent* to me—and since we know that the probability of winning the ball bet is 1 in 9 (or about 11 percent), that implies that I have roughly 11 percent confidence in self-driving cars coming out within a year. I still don't think the "Self-driving cars will be on the market in a year" forecast is *likely* to come true, but I've gone from a glib "That's crazy" to a more honest best guess.

THE CORE SKILL of the previous chapter on thought experiments was a kind of self-awareness, a sense that your judgments are *contingent*—that what seems true or reasonable or fair or desirable can change when you mentally vary some feature of the question that should have been irrelevant. The specific thought experiments we covered are all useful tools that I and other people use regularly. But the underlying shift in how you view your mind's output is even more useful.

There's a core skill in this chapter, too: being able to tell the difference between the feeling of *making a claim* and the feeling of *actually trying to guess what's true*. Making a claim feels like your press secretary is speaking. It feels pat; neat and tidy. Sometimes hurried, as if you're trying to put something past yourself. The mental motion is declaring, proclaiming, insisting, or perhaps scoffing.

Trying to guess what's true feels like being the board of directors, deciding how to bet. There's at least a second or two when you don't know what answer you're going to end up giving. It's like you're squinting at the evidence, trying to summarize what you see. The mental motions involved are estimating, predicting, weighing, and deliberating.

Quantifying your uncertainty, getting calibrated, and coming up with hypothetical bets are all valuable skills in their own right. But having the self-awareness to be able to tell whether you're describing reality honestly, to the best of your abilities, is even more valuable still.

# PART III

# Thriving Without Illusions

## Chapter 7

# Coping with Reality

WHEN STEVEN CALLAHAN'S ship capsized during a solo voyage in 1981, his prospects for survival looked grim. He had managed to escape the wreck in an inflatable raft, but he was way out in a remote part of the Atlantic Ocean, far from any shipping lanes, with little food or water. Callahan did the only thing he could do. He set course for the nearest land—the Caribbean islands, 1,800 miles away.

Life as a castaway was grueling. Sharks circled the raft, as the waves tossed it to and fro, dousing him with seawater that left him shivering and burned the sores on his body.

Fortunately, Callahan was able to sustain himself by using a spear gun to kill fish, and rigging up a device to collect rainwater for drinking. He calculated how much water he could afford to consume per day—half a pint. That was a mouthful every six hours or so. Enough to survive, just barely. As the weeks passed, he tracked the probable error in his navigation, gradually widening the error bars around his estimate of the distance he'd covered.[1]

Many times a day, he faced difficult decisions. If he stayed up at night, he had a better chance of spotting a passing ship. But it also meant he would burn through his water and energy reserves more quickly, and have a harder time staying awake during the day.

When a ship did pass by, he had to decide whether to try to signal with his flare gun. If there was a good enough chance of being spotted, then it would obviously be worth it. But if the ship was too far away, it would be a waste of one of his precious few flares.

If he didn't fish enough, he would run out of food. But each time he fished, he used up energy, and risked losing his spear or damaging his raft.

Every time he made a decision, Callahan ran through the possible results in his head, weighing the risks of one choice against another. Everything was a gamble; nothing was guaranteed. "You are doing the best you can. You can only do the best you can," he repeated to himself, like a mantra.[2]

He drifted at a speed of eight miles per hour, day after day, losing over a third of his body weight, until he was finally spotted by a fishing boat off the coast of Guadaloupe and rescued. He had been adrift for seventy-six days.

Callahan had been so disciplined about conserving water that he had five full pints remaining. Now he downed them all, one after another, quenching his thirst after eleven weeks and finally allowing himself to think the blessed thought: "I'm saved."

## KEEPING DESPAIR AT BAY

One of the most fundamental human needs is to feel like things are basically okay: that we're not failures, that the world isn't a horrible place, and that whatever life throws at us, we'll be able to handle it. In a life-or-death situation, of course, this need is especially hard to satisfy. That's why most people in an emergency resort to various

forms of motivated reasoning, like denial, wishful thinking, and ratio-
nalizing.

The cruel irony is that an emergency is when you most need to be
clear-eyed. Callahan's voyage was one difficult judgment call after
another—estimating the rate at which he could afford to consume
food and water, or the probability of being spotted by a ship, or the
priority of different risks. The more you rely on motivated reasoning,
the more you degrade your ability to make judgment calls like these.

In the wake of his shipwreck, Callahan contemplated his new reality, and realized that he could not afford to self-deceive. "I have
often hidden things from myself. I have sometimes fooled other people. But Nature is not such a dolt," he told himself. "I may be lucky
enough to be forgiven some mistakes, the ones that don't matter, but
I can't count on luck."[3]

The trait that saved Callahan wasn't an invulnerability to fear or
depression. Like anyone else in a dire situation, he struggled to keep
despair at bay. The trait that saved him was his commitment to finding ways of keeping despair at bay *without* distorting his map of reality.

He counted his blessings. At least he'd had the foresight, before his
voyage, to upgrade to a larger life raft. Being stuck in the tiny raft that
had originally come with the boat when he purchased it would have
been torturous.

He reminded himself that he was doing everything possible. ("You
are doing the best you can. You can only do the best you can.")

And he found ways to calm his fears of death, not by denying it,
but by coming to terms with it. He resolved to make good use of whatever time he had left by writing a guide for future sailors. "My writ-
ings may be found aboard the raft, even if I am dead," he reasoned.
"They might be instructive to others, especially those who sail and
might find themselves in a similar situation. It's the last service I
can render."[4]

# HONEST VS. SELF-DECEPTIVE WAYS OF COPING

Thankfully, the stakes we face in everyday life are seldom as high as that. But even though we rarely have to deal with threats to our lives, we very often have to deal with threats to our mood and self-esteem. A worry springs to mind: "Was it a mistake to quit my job?" "Did I offend him?" Someone criticizes us. We face an unpleasant choice. We fail at something. In reaction, we reach for a thought that keeps negative emotions at bay—a coping strategy.

People generally take for granted that coping requires self-deception, and experts are no exception. In the book *Mistakes Were Made (But Not by Me)*, psychologists Carol Tavris and Elliot Aronson explore self-justification, a type of motivated reasoning in which you convince yourself after the fact that you made the right choice. The book is mostly about the many downsides of self-justification—how it commits us to stick with bad decisions rather than changing course, and dooms us to repeat our mistakes instead of learning from them. Still, Tavris and Aronson conclude, we need at least some amount of self-justification for the sake of our mental health: "Without it, we would prolong the awful pangs of embarrassment. We would torture ourselves with regret over the road not taken or over how badly we navigated the road we did take."[5]

But is it really true that we *need* self-justification to prevent us from "torturing ourselves with regret"? Couldn't we just . . . learn to *not* torture ourselves with regret instead?

In *Thinking, Fast and Slow*, Nobel Prize–winning psychologist Daniel Kahneman points out an emotional benefit of motivated reasoning: resilience. It's easier to bounce back from a failure if you can blame it on anyone but yourself. He uses the example of a door-to-door salesperson, a job that involves long strings of rejection: "When one has just had a door slammed in one's face by an angry homemaker, the thought that 'she was an awful woman' is clearly superior to 'I am an inept salesperson.'"[6]

But are those really our only two options? We could instead tell ourselves, "Yes, I screwed up that sale. But everyone makes mistakes." Or "Yes, I screwed up that sale. Still, I'm improving—I used to get doors slammed in my face every day, and now it only happens every week!" Surely we can find a way to bounce back from our setbacks that doesn't require us to blame them on other people—an honest coping strategy.

Just ask Charles Darwin. He suffered from bouts of crippling anxiety, especially when his book was being attacked by critics. ("I am very poorly today & very stupid & hate everybody & everything," he moaned to a friend in one especially relatable letter.)[7] But it was important to Darwin to avoid self-deception, and not to shut his eyes to legitimate criticism or to his own mistakes. Like Callahan, Darwin drew his strength from the comforting and *true* thought that he was doing his best:

> Whenever I have found out that I have blundered, or that my work has been imperfect, and when I have been contemptuously criticized, and even when I have been overpraised, so that I have felt mortified, it has been my greatest comfort to say hundreds of times to myself that "I have worked as hard and as well as I could, and no man can do more than this."[8]

Scouts aren't invulnerable to fear, anxiety, insecurity, despair, or any of the other emotions that give rise to motivated reasoning, and they rely on coping strategies just like anyone else. They just take more care to select coping strategies that don't mess with the accuracy of their judgment.

I like to imagine all of the possible coping strategies—all of the ways we could stave off negative emotions—piled up in a giant figurative bucket. Some involve self-deception, such as denying a problem or blaming it on a scapegoat. Others involve reminding yourself of a true fact, such as "I've handled problems like this successfully in the past." Some coping strategies in the bucket don't involve making a claim at all (and are therefore not self-deceptive), such as taking a deep breath and counting to ten.

When a negative emotion strikes, it's as if we hurriedly reach into the bucket to grab something, anything, to make ourselves feel better. We don't pay much attention to the kind of coping strategy we pull out, and whether it involves self-deception or not. As long as it makes us feel better, and it's halfway plausible, it'll do.

What I'm proposing in this chapter is that there is an abundance of different coping strategies, and you don't need to be so quick to go with the first thing you happen to pull out of the bucket. You can almost always find something comforting that *doesn't* require self-deception if you rummage around in there just a bit longer. Here are a few of the most common examples.

## THE "BUCKET" OF COPING STRATEGIES

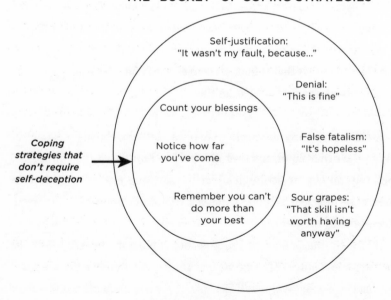

# Make a plan

In one episode of the TV show *The Office,* bumbling branch manager Michael Scott has been told by upper management that he has to lay off one of his employees before the end of the month. Michael hates doing unpopular things, so he puts it off again and again. On the last day of the month, with only a few hours left, he still hasn't decided who to lay off. One of the salesmen, Jim Halpert, drily sums up Michael's knack for denial: "I think he keeps hoping that someone's going to volunteer. Or be run over by a bus before the deadline."[9]

There are self-deceptive ways of coping with the thought of something unpleasant, such as coming up with rationalizations for why a task isn't actually necessary, or flat-out denial, in the vein of Michael Scott. But there are also honest coping strategies, like coming up with a hypothetical plan.

I once felt guilty about something inconsiderate I had done to a friend and spent a week trying to justify my behavior to myself. *Should I apologize?* "No, that's unnecessary. She probably didn't even notice," I told myself, at various times; and "She probably forgave me already anyway," at other times. Obviously, I didn't find these internally contradictory justifications fully satisfying, which is why I had to keep having the same argument with myself again and again.

Finally, I asked myself: "Okay, suppose I had to apologize. How would I do it?" It didn't take me long to draft in my head the rough contours of an apology that I felt I could deliver without too much angst. And when I imagined my friend's reaction, I realized that I expected her to be appreciative, not angry. Once the prospect of apologizing seemed tolerable, I returned to my original question: "Should I apologize?" Now the answer was much clearer: "Yes, I should."

It's striking how much the urge to conclude "That's not true" diminishes once you feel like you have a concrete plan for what you would do if the thing *were* true. It doesn't have to be elaborate. Even a simple plan, like "Here's how I would explain the failure to my team . . ." or "Here's how I would begin my search for a new job . . ." goes a long way toward making you feel like you don't need to rely on denial to cope with reality.

## Notice silver linings

Sometimes when I'm in the middle of an argument, I start to get a sneaking suspicion that I might be in the wrong. That's not exactly a comfortable prospect. It's tempting to push the thought out of my mind and focus on saving face.

Instead, I remind myself of a silver lining: Conceding an argument earns me credit. It makes me more credible in other cases, because I've demonstrated that I don't stick to my guns just for the sake of it. It's like I'm investing in my future ability to be convincing.

A silver lining to losing your job might be that now you don't have to put up with your annoying coworkers; a silver lining to a disastrous date might be that you can turn it into an entertaining story to tell later on. A silver lining to any mistake is the lesson you're going to extract from the experience, which you can use to help save you from similar mistakes in the future.

Remember, the goal isn't to convince yourself that your misfortune is actually a good thing. You're not looking for a "sweet lemons" rationalization here. You're recognizing a silver lining to the cloud, not trying to convince yourself the whole cloud is silver. But in many cases, that's all you need—noticing the silver lining is enough to make you willing to accept the reality of the cloud.

## Focus on a different goal

A friend of mine named Jon cofounded a software company, and in the early days, spent a lot of time recruiting and interviewing potential new hires. He soon noticed something disturbing: When he came across a talented engineer who was interested in the position, he should have felt delighted. High-quality engineers can make all the difference to the success of a new software company. But instead, Jon felt something closer to disappointment or bitterness. He would scrutinize the engineer's work, hoping to find an excuse to reject it.

Reflecting on his behavior, Jon realized: *I've always prided myself on being the best programmer in the room.* That's why he was motivated to denigrate his "competition," as a coping strategy to protect his self-esteem.

Jon knew that his goal of needing to be the best programmer in the room was unrealistic, not to mention very counterproductive for his fledgling company. So he decided to redirect his focus and revise his goal: Rather than priding himself on being a great programmer, he decided to start priding himself on being an *astute judge of programming talent.* That was a satisfying enough substitute for the original goal, and actually helpful for hiring instead of counterproductive.

## Things could be worse

The summer of 1993 has been called "the most disillusioning moment in AIDS treatment history."[10] For several years, desperate patients had pinned their hopes on a new drug called azidothymidine, or AZT, that was supposed to slow the onset of the disease. Early clinical trials in the United States had suggested that AZT was promising.

However, a European research group had also been running a study of AZT. When they published their results in 1993 after three years of data collection, the news was devastating: AZT didn't work any better than a placebo. Ninety-two percent of the people taking AZT had survived the study, compared to 93 percent who survived on the placebo.

To make matters worse, there were no other drugs in the pipeline. After the early trials had seemed to show AZT to be effective, the government had stopped working on alternatives. Many activists gave up, and many patients sank into depression—the false promise of AZT had been the one thing keeping them going.

But not everyone felt like giving up. In his history of the AIDS crisis, *How to Survive a Plague*, David France profiles a small group of activists called the Treatment Action Group. They had been following the drug-testing process closely and knew that the odds of finding a miracle drug right away were slim. When the bad news about AZT broke in the summer of 1993, they were disappointed—but not crushed.

Most of the activists in the Treatment Action Group were HIV-positive themselves. How had they kept up their spirits despite their realism about the chance of a cure? In part, by focusing on their gratitude for the things that could have been worse. France describes a meeting during that dispiriting summer at which one of the activists, a man named Peter Staley, said:

> Maybe that is our future, that we're gonna watch each other die. And that's going to be awful, if that's the case. It's already been awful, so there's not too much we can do about that . . . I'm just— you know, I really honestly feel glad that I've got people to be with. Not many people have that.[11]

The Treatment Action Group's ability to stay positive without denying the reality of their situation was a crucial strength—and one that would become especially valuable in the following months, as we'll see when we return to their story in Chapter 14.

## DOES RESEARCH SHOW THAT SELF-DECEIVED PEOPLE ARE HAPPIER?

Perhaps you've read one of the many books or articles that have come out in the last thirty years with titles like "Why Self-Deception Can Be Healthy for You,"[12] or *Kidding Ourselves: The Hidden Power of Self-Deception.*[13] Or "Depressed People See the World More Realistically— And Happy People Just Might Be Slightly Delusional."[14] These books and articles summarize a popular subfield in psychology arguing that our mental health depends on holding "positive illusions" about ourselves and our lives.

However, before you toss my book out the window and start trying to self-deceive your way to happiness, let's take a closer look at this research. Here's my summary of the methodology of a typical study from this field, by a psychologist at the University of Washington named Jonathon Brown—see what you think of it:[15]

1. Brown asks people to rate themselves relative to their peers on positive traits like "responsible" and "bright."
2. He finds that people with high self-esteem tend to rate themselves as being better-than-average on those positive traits.
3. Therefore, Brown concludes, psychological health is associated with "self-enhancement biases."

Do any problems jump out at you?

Well, for one thing, Brown never learns whether people's ratings of themselves are accurate or not. He simply assumes that if someone claims to be better than average, they must be under the influence of "self-enhancement biases." But of course, for any given trait, a lot of people really *are* better than average. Some people are more responsible than average, some people are brighter than average, and so on. So another way to summarize these results would simply be, "People with a lot of positive traits tend to have high self-esteem."[16] There's no need to invoke a "self-enhancement bias" in this story at all.

Calling people's beliefs "biased" or "illusions" without any objective standard of reality to compare them to is a problem that's rampant throughout the research on self-deception. One of the most widely cited papers in psychology is a summary of the case for positive illusions, a 1988 review article that Jonathon Brown coauthored with UCLA psychologist Shelley Taylor, titled "Illusion and Well-being: A Social Psychological Perspective on Mental Health." If you've read an article or book on the benefits of self-deception, chances are it cites this paper. And just from skimming its language, you can tell that the field conflates positive *illusions* and positive *beliefs*. Here's a sample paragraph:

> Positive illusions have been tied to reports of happiness. People who have high self-esteem and self-confidence, who report that they have a lot of control in their lives, and who believe that the future will bring them happiness are more likely than people who lack these perceptions to indicate that they are happy at the present.[17]

Notice the switch that occurs between the first and second sentences in that paragraph. The first sentence claims happiness is connected to "positive illusions" about your life. But the supporting second sentence merely says happiness is connected to positive *beliefs* about your life—beliefs that we have no reason to doubt are accurate.

Sometimes, researchers simply decide ahead of time what *must* be true of people and then assume that anyone who says otherwise is lying to themselves. The Self-Deception Questionnaire was developed in the 1970s by psychologists Harold Sackeim and Ruben Gur, who used it to determine that "people who were happiest, were the ones who were lying to themselves more."[18] Your score is based on how you answer a series of questions about yourself on a scale from 1 ("not at all") to 7 ("very much so").

One of the questions is "Do you ever get angry?" If you give an answer of 1 or 2 out of 7, you're classified as self-deceiving. But I have some friends whom I've known for over a decade, and I can count on one hand the number of times I've seen them get angry. If they answered this question honestly, they would be classified as self-deceivers.

And the questions get weirder from there. One is "Do you ever feel attracted to people of the same sex?" Another is "Have you ever wanted to rape or be raped by someone?" Again, if you give an answer of only 1 or 2 (out of 7) to these questions, you are assumed to be lying to yourself.[19] This research does not tell us much about self-deception . . . though it might tell us something about the researchers themselves.

OF COURSE, THE fact that the "self-deception causes happiness" research is fatally flawed doesn't prove that self-deception *can't* cause happiness. It clearly can, in many cases. It just comes with the downside of eroding your judgment. And given that there are so many ways to cope that *don't* involve self-deception, why settle?

The suggestions in this chapter such as making a plan, finding silver linings, and changing your goal are just a sample of some of the ways scouts have found to manage their emotions. Different strategies work for different people. One friend of mine copes with painful criticism by conjuring up a feeling of gratitude toward his critic. This works for him but does not work for me at all. Instead, I cope by focusing on how much better I'm going to be in the future if I can get myself to think honestly about the criticism.

With practice, you develop your own tool kit of coping strategies that work for you. Just remember: don't settle! Your ability to see clearly is precious, and you should be reluctant to sacrifice it in exchange for emotional comfort. The good news is that you don't have to.

*Chapter 8*

# Motivation Without Self-Deception

W**HEN** I **WAS** sixteen, I seriously considered moving to New York after my high school graduation to pursue a career on the stage. I knew the odds would not be in my favor. Acting is a notoriously difficult way to make a living; stage acting even more so. But I had been bitten by the theater bug, and spent my evenings singing along to my *Rent* and *Les Misérables* soundtracks on CD while daydreaming about being on Broadway.

I happened to know a successful stage actor, so I asked him what he thought I should do, given the long odds. "Screw the odds," he told me. "Everything in life is a risk, but if you want it, you should go for it. If you worry about failing, that's just going to be a self-fulfilling prophecy."

Call this the *self-belief* model of success: If you convince yourself that you will succeed, you'll be motivated to attempt hard things and persist in the face of setbacks, such that eventually your optimism will be self-fulfilling. Conversely, if you acknowledge the long odds facing you, or contemplate the possibility of failure, you'll be too discouraged to try, and your pessimism will be a self-fulfilling prophecy as well.

Browsing motivational images on Pinterest or Instagram, you'll see the self-belief model everywhere. "Whether you think you can or you think you can't—you're right," according to one popular saying attributed to Henry Ford.[1] "She believed she could, so she did," proclaim thousands of stickers, posters, and pillows.[2] Other examples from motivational authors and bloggers abound:

> Nothing grand in work or life was ever achieved by following the odds. For every rule, there is always an exception and damned if it can't be you![3]

> If you truly dedicate yourself to your goal, everything is possible. You just have to want it bad enough.[4]

> To succeed, you need an unshakeable belief in your goal and your ability to achieve it . . . By preparing for a negative outcome, you're eroding your confidence and self-belief.[5]

> You need to truly believe you will succeed with every fibre in your being.[6]

He doesn't pop up on many Pinterest boards, but one of the earliest advocates of self-belief was nineteenth-century philosopher William James. In his most famous essay, "The Will to Believe," he offers an arresting example to make his case: Imagine you're climbing a mountain. Unfortunately, you've gotten yourself stuck on a ledge with no escape—except for a daunting leap to a nearby peak. James says:

> Have faith that you can successfully make it, and your feet are nerved to its accomplishment. But mistrust yourself, and think of all the sweet things you have heard the scientists say of may-

bes, and you will hesitate so long that, at last, all unstrung and trembling, and launching yourself in a moment of despair, you roll in the abyss.[7]

Many situations in our lives are like this, he argued. Choosing to have faith in your success, irrespective of the risk or difficulty, is the only way to summon the will to succeed. Is James right? If you could press a button and become irrationally optimistic about your chances of success—should you?

## AN ACCURATE PICTURE OF YOUR ODDS HELPS YOU CHOOSE BETWEEN GOALS

As you might have guessed, I didn't take my actor friend's advice. Even at sixteen, I just couldn't get behind the idea of jumping into a career path without doing my research first.

To give you a sense of just how bad the odds are for an aspiring stage actor: Out of the 49,000 members in Actor's Equity, the national union of stage actors, only 17,000 get any acting work at all in a given year. Of those who do get work, the median annual salary is $7,500.[8] And the actors in the union are the relatively more successful ones— non-equity actors are doing even worse.

Of course, any given individual may have a better or worse chance of success than the overall odds suggest, depending on how talented, hardworking, charismatic, or well connected they are. But the overall odds are an important baseline to be aware of; the longer the odds, the better and luckier you'll have to be to beat them.

I talked to another friend of mine in show business. She gave me different advice than the first actor had. "Look, it's really tough out here," she told me. "That doesn't necessarily mean you shouldn't do it, but ask yourself: Are you sure acting is the only career you could be excited about?"

My answer to that question was "no" (to the great relief of my parents). There were other subjects I found interesting, and I was pretty sure I would discover more once I got to college. For someone else with a more singular passion for acting, or more talent than me, the long odds might be worth it. But to weigh these factors successfully, you need an accurate picture of what the odds actually are.

This is the biggest problem with the self-belief approach to motivation. Because you're not supposed to think realistically about risk, it becomes impossible to ask yourself questions like, "Is this goal desirable enough to be worth the risk?" and "Are there any other goals that would be similarly desirable but require less risk?" It implicitly assumes that you don't need to make any decisions; that you've already found the one right path, and there are no other options out there worth weighing.

In fact, notice that in William James's story of the perilous leap on the mountain—his argument for the value of irrational self-belief—he has constructed the example such that there's zero decision-making involved. You aren't given the opportunity to compare multiple options or brainstorm ideas you might have missed. The only thing you can do is try to execute the jump successfully.

In such a situation, where there is only one path available to you, maybe having a realistic picture of your odds of success on that path isn't very useful. But how often does such a situation actually occur? Even in a real-life mountain-climbing scenario, there's never literally only one choice. Instead of attempting to leap to a nearby peak, you could try climbing down the side of the mountain. Alternately, you could stay put and hope for rescue. Whether either of those options is a better bet than jumping depends on your estimate of their relative chances of success.

And even though the rhetoric around "following your dream" makes it sound like everyone has one and only one dream, most people have more than one thing they enjoy and are good at, or could at least become good at. You're doing yourself a disservice if you throw yourself into the pursuit of a goal without asking: "Is this goal worth pursuing, compared to other things I could do instead?"

AT THIS POINT, you might be thinking: "Sure, an accurate picture of the odds is important when you're choosing a path. But once you've already made your choice, *then* you should switch into irrational optimism for the execution phase."

Of course, it's not quite as simple as "switching into irrational optimism." You can't just do a thoughtful, realistic calculus of risk and then erase it from your memory. But suppose you could—should you? The following two vignettes will make it clear why my answer is still "no."

## AN ACCURATE PICTURE OF THE ODDS HELPS YOU ADAPT YOUR PLAN OVER TIME

Ever since she was in high school, Shellye Archambeau had been determined to one day become CEO of a major tech company.[9] In 2001, she felt she was finally on the brink of fulfilling that dream. She had put in fifteen years climbing the ranks at IBM, becoming the first African American woman in the company's history to hold an international executive position. After leaving IBM, she had done stints as an executive officer at two other technology companies. Shellye was ready.

Unfortunately, 2001 was also the year the dot com bubble burst. Silicon Valley was flooded with newly out-of-work executives with more experience and connections than her, all of whom would now be competing with her for CEO positions. Bad timing, indeed. Shellye figured she had two choices. She could stick to her original goal of aiming for a top-tier tech company and face even longer odds than before. Or she could amend her goal, dropping the requirement that her company be "top-tier." Instead she could aim for a fixer-upper, a company that was floundering but easier to get into, and that she might be able to turn around with strong management.

She went for option 2, and she succeeded. Shellye was hired to be CEO of Zaplet, Inc., a start-up that was almost bankrupt at the time. Over the following fourteen years, Shellye grew Zaplet into Metric-Stream, a company of 1,200 employees worth over $400 million.

The reality is that there's no clear divide between the "decision-making" and "execution" stages of pursuing a goal. Over time, your situation will change, or you'll learn new information, and you'll need to revise your estimate of the odds.

# AN ACCURATE PICTURE OF THE ODDS HELPS YOU DECIDE HOW MUCH TO STAKE ON SUCCESS

Over the course of the 1980s, entrepreneur Norm Brodsky built a $30 million messenger company called Perfect Courier. To grow even faster, he decided to acquire a competitor, an ailing messenger company called Sky Courier. He infused Sky Courier with $5 million from Perfect Courier to help turn it around. But that wasn't enough to save it. So he put another $2 million in. When that still wasn't enough, he put in some of Perfect Courier's credit as well. Brodsky knew he was effectively wagering one of his companies on his ability to fix the other, but he wasn't worried. "It never crossed my mind that I might not be able to make Sky Courier successful," he said.[10]

Unfortunately, Brodsky was soon dealt two unlucky blows, one after the other. First came the stock market crash in October 1987. That ate up a lot of his business. Second was the rapid rise of the fax machine. Who needs a courier service to send important documents when you can simply pop them into a fax machine instead?[11]

By the following autumn, Sky Courier had collapsed, taking Perfect Courier down with it. The most agonizing part, for Brodsky, was having to lay off thousands of employees. Ruefully, he realized: "I'd taken a lovely, secure, profitable business and destroyed it by exposing it to a level of risk it never should have faced."

Venture capitalist Ben Horowitz argues, in *The Hard Thing About Hard Things*, that there's no point in thinking about your odds of success when building a company. "When you are building a company, you must believe there is an answer and you cannot pay attention to your odds of finding it. You just have to find it," he writes. "It matters not whether your chances are nine in ten or one in a thousand; your task is the same."[12]

But even if your task is the same, that still leaves the question of how much you should be willing to gamble on your ability to succeed at that task. If your company has a 9 in 10 chance at success, then it might well be worth it to stake your life savings on it. If your chances are closer to 1 in 1,000, you probably want to leave that nest egg untouched.

HAVING AN ACCURATE picture of the odds doesn't ever stop being valuable. Still, that leaves us with a psychological challenge: If you have an accurate picture of the odds, how do you keep from getting discouraged? How do you motivate yourself to give it your all, while knowing there's a significant chance your "all" won't be enough in the end?

## BETS WORTH TAKING

When Elon Musk decided to start a space flight company, his friends thought he was crazy. Musk had just made over $180 million from the sale of PayPal, his second business, and he was betting most of that windfall on the company that would soon become SpaceX.

"You're going to fail," they warned him. "You'll lose all your PayPal money." One of his friends even put together a compilation of videos of rockets blowing up and begged Musk to watch it, in hopes of dissuading him from his pipe dream.[13]

This is the point in most stories about someone with a "crazy dream" that usually goes something like, *But he couldn't be deterred, because he knew in his heart that the doubters were wrong.* That is not how this story goes. When Musk's friends told him that he would probably fail, he replied: "Well, I agree. I think we probably will fail."[14] In fact, he estimated that there was only about a 10 percent chance that a SpaceX craft would ever make it into orbit.

Two years later, Musk decided to invest most of the remainder of his PayPal profits into an electric car company, Tesla. That, too, he gave a roughly 10 percent chance of success.[15]

The low odds Musk assigned to his own projects' success left many people scratching their heads. In an appearance on *60 Minutes* in 2014, interviewer Scott Pelley tried to understand Musk's logic:

> **Elon Musk:** Well, I didn't really think Tesla would be successful. I thought we would most likely fail . . .
>
> **Scott Pelley:** But you say you didn't expect the company to be successful? Then why try?
>
> **Elon Musk:** If something's important enough you should try. Even if the probable outcome is failure.[16]

Musk's low expectation of success confounds people because they assume the only reason to do something is if it's likely to succeed. But scouts aren't motivated by the thought, "This is going to succeed." They're motivated by the thought, "This is a bet worth taking."

Most people are already on board with the idea of a "bet worth taking," in at least some contexts. To give a simple example, suppose someone offered you a bet in which you roll a normal six-sided die. If it lands on a six, you win $200; if not, you lose $10. Should you take it?

Almost certainly. This is a good bet for you—and you can see exactly how good it is by calculating its *expected value*. That's the average amount a bet pays out each time, if you were to take it an infinite number of times.

| Probability | Value |
|---|---|
| 1 in 6 chance of rolling a 6 | Win $200 |
| 5 in 6 chance of rolling something else | Lose $10 |

To calculate a bet's expected value, multiply the probability of each outcome by its value and then add up those results. For this bet, the expected value would be:

$$([\text{\textonesuperior/\textsix} \text{ probability of winning}] \times \$200) + ([\text{\textfiveoldstyle/\textsix} \text{ probability of losing}] \times -\$10) = \$33.33 - \$8.33 = \$25$$

In other words, if you took this bet many times, the average amount you would win each time is about $25. Not bad money for simply rolling a die! This is a great bet to take, even though the most likely outcome is failure.

Evaluating the probabilities involved in a real-life bet, like starting a company, is a much messier, more subjective endeavor. The possible outcomes aren't well defined the way they are in the case of the die roll. Their corresponding probabilities are subjective. And their "value" involves many factors besides money: How much enjoyment would you get out of running a company? Would it leave you with useful connections and skills, even if it failed? How much of your time would it take up? How much social cachet (or stigma) would it involve?

Nevertheless, you can almost always do a rough estimate that's better than nothing. As we've seen, Elon Musk estimated a 10 percent chance of success and a 90 percent chance of failure for Tesla. But the value of success would be enormous—taking the idea of electric cars from pipe dream to mainstream reality would go a long way toward freeing society from its reliance on fossil fuels. And even in the case of failure, Musk figured there was still one worthwhile thing Tesla would accomplish: "I thought that we at least could address the false perception that people have that an electric car had to be ugly and slow and boring like a golf cart," Musk told Pelley on *60 Minutes*.

Musk's reasoning about SpaceX was similar: roughly 10 percent chance of success, 90 percent chance of failure. But the value of success would be huge. Developing a cheaper form of space flight would make it possible for humanity to one day colonize Mars, which would help safeguard our species against catastrophic risks on Earth. And even if SpaceX failed, it wouldn't have been a total waste of time if they made a little progress: "If we could just move the ball forward, even if we died, maybe some other company could pick up the baton and keep moving it forward, so that we'd still do some good," he reasoned.[17]

## MUSK'S THINKING ABOUT THE TESLA AND SPACEX BETS

| Probability | Value |
| --- | --- |
| 10% chance of success | The company makes a big dent in one of the most pressing problems facing humanity (sustainability, space travel). |
| 90% chance of failure | Musk loses his investment, but isn't personally ruined. The company probably makes a bit of progress on the problem. |

Overall, both Tesla and SpaceX seemed like good bets to him—even though the most likely outcome for each was failure.

Another way to think about whether a bet is positive expected value is to imagine taking it many times. Would the value of the expected successes outweigh the value of the expected failures? Over the course of a lifetime, someone like Elon Musk probably has the time and money to attempt at least ten companies like Tesla and SpaceX. If his best guess is that nine of those ten companies will be failures, then the key question is: Would it be worth failing nine times in exchange for one big success?

In reality, you almost never get to repeat the exact same bet many times. But you'll have the opportunity to make many different bets over the course of your life. You'll face bets at your company and in your career more broadly; bets on investment opportunities; chances to bet on trusting another person, or making a difficult ask, or pushing your comfort zone. And the more positive expected value bets you make, the more confident you can be that you'll end up ahead overall, even if each individual bet is far from a sure thing.

# ACCEPTING VARIANCE GIVES YOU EQUANIMITY

I don't usually pay much attention to sports, but my interest was piqued when I saw an interview with Trevor Bauer, a pitcher for the Cleveland Indians. Bauer had recently been pitching well against the Houston Astros, with a 6–0 streak, and when an interviewer asked him the secret to his success, Bauer replied, "Random variation. It won't continue. At some point, it will break."[18]

The answer made me grin with surprise. Almost everyone, when asked to explain their success, gives a causal explanation like, "My extra practice is finally starting to pay off" or "It's because I believed in myself." How often do you hear someone chalk their own success up to "random variation"?

Bauer was right—his streak did end. Soon after, another interviewer was grilling him about the unusually high number of home runs that players had been scoring against him recently. Bauer replied, "I know the results will match my stuff at some point . . . I can't keep having the home run per fly ball rate that is absurdly high right now, and that's how most of my runs are being scored right now."[19]

A pitcher's "home run per fly ball" rate fluctuates a lot over short periods of time, which means that the statistic is mostly capturing random variance and not skill. Bauer's point was that it therefore didn't make sense to get too worried about his current home run per fly ball rate being unusually high. Once again, he was right—by the very next season, Bauer had one of the lowest home run per fly ball rates of anyone in the game.[20]

It might be motivating to believe with absolute certainty that

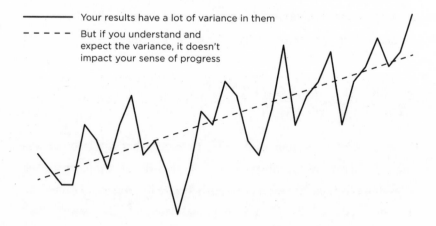

THE PSYCHOLOGICAL EFFECT OF EXPECTING VARIANCE*

---

* The emotional toll of variance is actually worse than this graph suggests. We're loss averse, meaning that the pain of a loss is greater than the pleasure of a similarly sized gain. Therefore, if you don't build variance into your expectations, the low points on the spiky line graph will feel even lower than they are.

you're going to win, but it's not realistic—there's always some element of chance involved, in any endeavor. Over time, your outcomes will fluctuate; some of your bets will turn out well, and many will turn out poorly.

But as long as you continue making positive expected value bets, that variance will mostly wash out in the long run. Building that variance into your expectations has the nice side effect of giving you equanimity. Instead of being elated when your bets pay off, and crushed when they don't, your emotions will be tied to the trend line underneath the variance.

The goal isn't to attribute everything to luck. It's to do your best to mentally separate out the role that luck plays in your results from the role that your decision-making plays, and to judge yourself based on the latter. Here's an example of Bauer doing a postmortem of his pitching in one game:

> Not a great pitch, but I defend the logic behind throwing it. Walked [Jason] Castro, not a good idea. Then, tried to get [Brian] Dozier on a fastball away, came back, good pitch, but he hit it.[21]

Notice how he gives himself credit, then blame, then credit—all based on the quality of his pitching choices, independently of how they turned out.

## COMING TO TERMS WITH THE RISK

In 1994, Jeff Bezos had a cushy and well-paying job as an investment banker in New York City. He had been increasingly considering quitting to launch a company on this exciting new thing called "The Internet."

But he wanted to make sure he had a clear view of the odds facing him. By his estimate, about 10 percent of internet start-ups grew into successful businesses. Bezos suspected that his skill level and business idea were better than average, but he also knew that wasn't a justification for ignoring the baseline odds completely. All things considered, he gave himself about a 30 percent chance of success.

How did he feel about that level of risk? Could he stomach the possibility of failure? Bezos imagined being eighty years old and looking back at his life choices. Missing out on his 1994 Wall Street bonus wasn't the kind of thing he would care about decades later. But passing up the chance to participate in the growth of the internet absolutely was. "If it failed, fine," he decided. "I would be very proud of the fact when I'm 80 that I tried."[22] That's what clinched his decision to take the plunge, quit his job, and start the company that would become Amazon.

The "self-belief" model of motivation assumes that if you acknowledge the possibility of failure, then you'll be too demoralized or afraid to take risks. In that model, people who believe that failure is unthinkable are the ones who try the hardest to succeed. Yet in practice, things often seem to work the other way around—accepting the possibility of failure in advance is liberating. It makes you bold, not timid. It's what gives you the courage to take the risks required to achieve something big.

When one interviewer praised Elon Musk for being fearless in starting companies that other people think are crazy, Musk admitted that he actually feels fear very strongly. He's just learned to manage that fear by coming to terms with the probability of failure. "Something that can be helpful is fatalism, to some degree," he explained. "If you just accept the probabilities, then that diminishes fear. So in starting SpaceX, I thought the odds of success were less than 10 percent, and I just accepted that probably I would lose everything."[23]

People working on hard projects who are conscious of their high risk of failure generally aren't dwelling on that risk on a day-to-day basis. When they get up in the morning, they're motivated by more concrete things—the pitch meeting coming up next week; the goal they've set for themselves to ship their first product next month; the challenge of putting out whatever the latest fire is; the progress they've made so far; the people who are counting on them.

But in those moments when they're deciding what risks to take or stepping back to reflect on their life choices, being able to feel satisfied with the bet they're taking—even if it fails—makes all the difference. There's a line from a blog post I read years ago that has stayed with me, and still gives me a sense of resolve when I'm taking a bet I believe is worthwhile but risky. Maybe it will do the same for you: "You want to get into a mental state where if the bad outcome comes to pass, you will only nod your head and say 'I knew this card was in the deck, and I knew the odds, and I would make the same bets again, given the same opportunities.'"[24]

IN THE PREVIOUS CHAPTER, we saw how we have a choice of coping strategies for dealing with emotions like anxiety, disappointment, regret, and fear. Some coping strategies involve self-deception, and some don't—so why settle for the former?

The same logic applies to our strategies for motivating ourselves to be ambitious, take risks, and persevere when things get tough. The soldier approach to motivation requires you to believe things that aren't true—that your odds of success don't matter as long as you believe in yourself, that failure is not an option, that "luck" is irrelevant.

Soldier morale can be effective, at least in the short term. But it's a brittle kind of morale, one that requires you to avoid or rationalize away new information that could threaten your ability to keep believing in success.

Scouts rely on a different kind of morale. Instead of being motivated by the promise of guaranteed success, a scout is motivated by the knowledge that they're making a smart bet, which they can feel good about having made whether or not it succeeds. Even if a particular bet has a low probability of success, they know that their overall probability of success in the long run is much higher, as long as they keep making good bets. They're motivated by the knowledge that downturns are inevitable, but will wash out in the long run; that although failure is possible, it's also tolerable.

The scout approach to morale doesn't ask you to sacrifice your ability to make clear-eyed decisions. And it's a robust kind of morale, one that doesn't require protection from reality, because it's rooted in truth.

*Chapter 9*

# Influence Without Overconfidence

IN THE PREVIOUS CHAPTER, we saw how Jeff Bezos, before found-ing Amazon, estimated that his business idea had about a 30 per-cent chance of success. But surely he wouldn't admit that to potential investors . . . right? Why would anyone fund an entrepreneur whose pitch was, "Just to be clear, I'm probably going to fail"?

As a matter of fact, Bezos did share his uncertainty with his po-tential investors. In every pitch, he informed his audience, "I think there's a 70 percent chance you're going to lose all your money, so don't invest unless you can afford to lose it."[1]

As his company grew, Bezos continued to speak candidly about the uncertainty surrounding its future. In a 1999 interview on CNBC, he said: "There's no guarantee that Amazon.com can be a successful company. What we're trying to do is very complicated."[2] By 2018, Amazon was on the cusp of becoming the most valuable company in the world. In a company-wide meeting that fall, Bezos told his employ-ees: "I predict one day Amazon will fail . . . If you look at large compa-nies, their life-spans tend to be thirty-plus years, not a hundred-plus years."[3]

--------

THE COMMON WISDOM is that the more confidence you can muster in your beliefs, the more influential you will be. Confidence is magnetic. It invites people to listen to you, follow you, and trust that you know what you're doing. If you look up advice on how to be influential or persuasive, you'll find lots of exhortations to believe in yourself:

> It is the person who has an unbridled sense of certainty that will always be able to persuade others.[4]

> Every successful business leader has a strong sense of self-belief.[5]

> No-one likes opinions with a "probably" in them. People want certainty.[6]

This would seem to bode poorly for scouts; if you're being intellectually honest, you're not going to have certainty about everything. Fortunately, as the example of Jeff Bezos suggests, the common wisdom isn't quite right. In this chapter, we'll bust some myths about confidence and influence, and see how successful scouts navigate that relationship.

## TWO TYPES OF CONFIDENCE

*Confidence* is one of those words that we use to mean different things without even realizing it. One is *epistemic* confidence, or certainty—how sure you are about what's true. This is the kind of confidence we explored in chapter 6. If you say, "I'm 99 percent sure he is lying," or

"I guarantee this will work," or "There's no way the Republicans can win," you're displaying a lot of epistemic confidence.

Separately, there's *social* confidence, or self-assurance: Are you at ease in social situations? Do you act like you deserve to be there, like you're secure in yourself and your role in the group? Do you speak as if you're worth listening to?

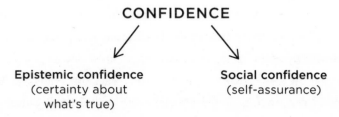

**CONFIDENCE**

**Epistemic confidence**
(certainty about
what's true)

**Social confidence**
(self-assurance)

We tend to conflate epistemic confidence and social confidence, treating them as if they're a package deal. It's easy to picture someone with both types of confidence, such as a leader pumping up his team with an inspiring pep talk about how there's no doubt in his mind that they're going to succeed. It's also easy to picture someone lacking in both types of confidence, stammering nervously, "Uh, I'm really not sure what we should do here . . ."

But epistemic confidence and social confidence don't have to be a package deal. Just look at Benjamin Franklin. He was brimming with social confidence—famously charming, witty, and ebullient, he made friends and launched new institutions his entire life. He was basically a celebrity in France, where he was constantly surrounded by adoring women who called him "Cher Papa" ("Dear Papa").[7]

Yet Franklin paired his abundance of social confidence with an intentional *lack* of epistemic confidence. It was a practice he had started when he was young, after noticing that people were more likely to reject his arguments when he used firm language like *certainly* and *undoubtedly*. So Franklin trained himself to avoid those expressions, prefacing his statements instead with caveats like "I think . . ." or "If I'm not mistaken . . ." or "It appears to me at present . . ."[8]

It was a tough habit to stick to at first. One of Franklin's favorite pastimes as a young man had been proving other people wrong, or what might nowadays be called "destroying" people in arguments. But the habit soon got easier as he started noticing how much more receptive people were to his opinions when he expressed them gently.

Over time, Franklin became one of the most influential people in American history. He codrafted the Declaration of Independence. He convinced France to back the American colonies' revolution against the British. He successfully negotiated the treaty that ended the Revolutionary War, then helped draft and ratify the US Constitution.

In his autobiography, an elderly Franklin reflects on his life and marvels at how effective his habit of speaking with "modest diffidence" turned out to be: "And to this habit (after my character of integrity) I think it principally owing that I had early so much weight with my fellow-citizens when I proposed new institutions, or alterations in the old," he concluded.[9]

In chapter 4, I described Abraham Lincoln's readiness to defer to other people's judgment on issues where he thought they knew better, and to say "You were right, I was wrong." You might expect this to make him seem unconfident, but as one of his contemporaries wrote, "No man who ever lived could be in his presence and dominate him."[10] That's because Lincoln was remarkably self-assured. He was at ease with himself, comfortable in his own skin, and when he spoke he could hold a crowd's rapt attention for hours.

# PEOPLE JUDGE YOU ON SOCIAL CONFIDENCE, NOT EPISTEMIC CONFIDENCE

Franklin's and Lincoln's experiences suggest that when it comes to the impression you make on other people, being self-assured is more important than expressing certainty—and research agrees.

In one study, university students worked together in small groups while researchers videotaped their interactions.[11] Afterward, the researchers went through the video and coded each student's behavior on various aspects of epistemic confidence (e.g., how many times did they claim to be confident in their own estimate?) and social confidence (e.g., How much did they participate in the discussion? Did they seem calm and relaxed?).

Then the researchers screened the videos for other people and asked them: "How competent does each of these students seem to you?" The competence ratings the students received were predominantly based on how much *social confidence* they displayed. The more a student participated in conversation, used an authoritative tone of

| BEHAVIORAL CUE | OBSERVER-PERCEIVED COMPETENCE |
|---|---|
| Percent of time spoke | 0.59** |
| Confident and factual vocal tone | 0.54** |
| Provided information relevant to problem | 0.51** |
| Expanded posture | 0.37** |
| Calm and relaxed demeanor | 0.34** |
| Offered an answer later | 0.24* |
| Offered an answer first | 0.21* |
| Statements of certainty in estimate | 0.21* |
| Statements about ease or difficulty of task | 0.18 |
| Statements about one's own competence | 0.09 |

Social confidence { Percent of time spoke … Offered an answer first

Epistemic confidence { Statements of certainty in estimate … Statements about one's own competence

TABLE ADAPTED FROM C. ANDERSON ET AL. (2012),

TABLE 2. PAGE 10.

\* = RESULTS SIGNIFICANT AT $p < 0.05$; \*\* = RESULTS SIGNIFICANT AT $p < 0.01$

voice, and had a relaxed demeanor, the more competent they seemed. By comparison, the students' *epistemic confidence* hardly mattered. Their statements about how certain they were in their answer, how easy the task was for them, or how competent they were at the task were barely or not at all significant.

Other researchers have investigated this same question using actresses trained to display different combinations of high versus low social confidence, and high versus low epistemic confidence, to see how much difference each factor makes.[12] Their results were similar. Whether or not participants judged an actress to be "confident" depended largely on her social cues, such as making eye contact, speaking evenly, and using decisive hand gestures. It made comparatively little difference whether she spoke with high certainty ("I'm positive that . . .") or low certainty ("I think maybe . . .").

People sometimes bemoan the fact that "superficial" things like posture and voice make such a difference in how we judge each other. But on the bright side, that means that projecting competence doesn't require self-deception. You can boost your social confidence through practice speaking up in groups, hiring a speech coach, dressing better, improving your posture—all without compromising your ability to see things clearly.

The founding of Amazon is a case in point for the precedence of social confidence over epistemic confidence. The company's big break came in the spring of 1996, when it received a visit from John Doerr, a partner at Kleiner Perkins Caufield & Byers, one of the most prestigious venture capital firms in Silicon Valley (now just Kleiner Perkins). Doerr left that meeting wowed by Amazon and ready to invest. Even better, the interest from a high-profile venture capitalist triggered a bidding war that drove Amazon's valuation up from $10 million to $60 million.

So, what exactly sold Doerr on Amazon? I'll let him explain: "I walked into the door and this guy with a boisterous laugh who was just exuding energy comes bounding down the steps. In that moment, I wanted to be in business with Jeff."[13]

# TWO KINDS OF UNCERTAINTY

How do patients react if their doctor expresses uncertainty? A handful of studies have investigated this question and come to very different conclusions. Some studies find that patients react negatively to uncertainty, seeing it as a sign of incompetence. Other studies find that patients don't appear to mind hearing uncertainty from their doctors, or even appreciate it.

These conflicting results seem mysterious until you look more closely at what each study is testing. In the studies that found that patients react negatively to hearing uncertainty from their doctors, "uncertainty" refers to statements such as these:

> I mean, I don't know really how to explain it.
> I haven't come across this before.
> I'm not quite sure what's causing your headaches.[14]

Meanwhile, in the studies that found that patients react positively to uncertainty from their doctors, "uncertainty" refers to statements such as these (from clinicians discussing risk factors for breast cancer):

> The evidence about breastfeeding is pretty weak. But one determining factor, which is a bit stronger, is age of first pregnancy. But you know, like all things, there are trade-offs. It's only a very weak determinant.

You've got two first-degree relatives and an aunt, so that does
certainly put you in a higher risk category . . . how high is not
easy to determine—probably somewhere between one in five
and one in ten.[15]

These are clearly two very different kinds of uncertainty. One can
hardly blame the patients in the first group for being put off. If a doctor says, "I'm not sure what's causing this," it's reasonable to wonder
whether a better, more experienced doctor would be able to diagnose
you. In the second group, however, the doctors sound like experts even
while they're giving an uncertain diagnosis. They're offering useful
context, such as the fact that a woman's age during her first pregnancy
is a stronger risk factor than whether or not she breastfeeds, and
they're giving informative estimates, such as "probably between one in
five and one in ten," rather than simply saying they don't know.

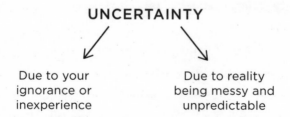

When people claim that "admitting uncertainty" makes you look
bad, they're invariably conflating these two very different kinds of
uncertainty: uncertainty "in you," caused by your own ignorance or
lack of experience, and uncertainty "in the world," caused by the fact
that reality is messy and unpredictable. The former is often taken as
a bad sign about someone's expertise, and justifiably so. But the latter is not—especially if you follow three rules for communicating uncertainty:

## 1. Show that uncertainty is justified

Sometimes your audience won't be aware of how much uncertainty exists "in the world" on the topic you're speaking about, and they'll expect you to give answers with more certainty than is actually possible. That's okay; you just need to set their expectations. Remember how Jeff Bezos warned a CNBC interviewer in 1999 that Amazon's success was not guaranteed? At the same time, he put that warning in perspective, pointing out that while it was clear that the internet revolution was going to produce some giant companies, it was very difficult to predict in advance *which* specific companies those would be. He illustrated the principle of unpredictability with an example from the recent past: "If you go back and look at the companies created by the PC revolution, in 1980, you probably wouldn't have predicted the five biggest winners."[16]

In fact, if you show that certainty is unrealistic, you can be more persuasive than someone who states everything with 100 percent certainty. When an attorney meets with a potential client for the first time, the client always asks how much money they can expect to be awarded. It's tempting for the attorney to give a confident, optimistic estimate, but the reality is that he doesn't yet have enough information to go on. Instead, here's what a prosecutor interviewed in *How Leading Lawyers Think* says in such a situation: "I tell them, 'Any attorney who answers that either is lying to you or does not know what he's doing, and you should run like hell.'" [17]

## 2. Give informed estimates

Matthew Leitch is a British consultant who used to work on risk management for PricewaterhouseCoopers. On his website *Working in Uncertainty*, he describes what he's learned about commanding respect while communicating uncertainty to clients. One lesson: Give informed estimates and explain where they came from. For example, he might tell a client, "There's no hard data to rely on for this so I've taken the average estimate from three senior marketing managers," or "A survey of 120 companies similar to ours showed that 23 percent had experienced an incident of this type."[18]

Even if reality is messy and it's impossible to know the right answer with confidence, you can at least be confident in your analysis. A venture capitalist described one of the best pitches he's ever seen, from a young entrepreneur named Mike Baker:

> Mike diagnosed the online advertising industry so thoughtfully and painted a vision for where it was heading that was grounded in his own experience and a lot of data . . . He was so articulate in describing, "If I'm right, this is going to be unbelievably valuable. I might be wrong, and that's the risk, but if I'm right, I can execute on it, I know this technology, and I have the right partners lined up to take advantage of it."[19]

Showing that you're well-informed and well prepared on a given topic doesn't require you to overstate how much certainty is possible on that topic. A few pages ago I quoted venture capitalist John Doerr saying that he wanted to invest in Amazon just based on seeing Jeff Bezos "bounding down the steps," but of course that's not the full story. He was also impressed with Bezos's technical proficiency. When he asked about Amazon's volume of daily transactions, and Bezos was able to pull up the answer with a few keystrokes, Doerr "swooned."[20]

## 3. Have a plan

One reason people don't like hearing uncertain answers is that it leaves them at a loss for how to act. You can reassure them by following up your uncertainty with a plan or recommendation.

If you're a doctor, that might mean helping your patient decide what treatment works best for him given the uncertainties, or assuring him that you'll continue closely monitoring his condition with him. If you're a consultant, having a plan might involve designing a test to pin down some crucial factor with more precision, or proposing a multi-phase plan to allow for occasional reevaluation.

And if you're an entrepreneur, having a plan means being able to make a strong case for what you are going to do to make your business a good bet—a bet that you feel confident about taking, and that other people can feel confident investing in, even though success isn't guaranteed. In his 1999 CNBC interview, after acknowledging that Amazon was a risk, Jeff Bezos went on to explain why it was nevertheless a good risk to take:

> It's very, very hard to predict. But I believe that if you can focus obsessively enough on customer experience, selection, ease of use, low prices, more information to make purchase decisions with, if you can give customers all that plus great customer service . . . I *think you have a good chance.* And that's what we're trying to do.[21]

## YOU DON'T NEED TO PROMISE SUCCESS TO BE INSPIRING

A friend of mine recently started a company developing apps to help people with depression and anxiety. He's a probabilistic thinker who strives to be well calibrated, and he's not blind to the long odds facing a new company. I asked him if his realistic outlook made it hard to get employees or investors excited. "No, you can get someone psyched up in a lot of ways," he replied. "You don't have to psych them up by lying or by being overconfident about the chance of success."

You can set ambitious goals. You can paint a vivid picture of the world you want to create. You can speak from the heart about why you personally care about this issue. When my friend is talking about his company, he likes to share real stories of people who struggled with mental health and have been helped by his app. All of those things can be inspiring, and none of them require you to make unrealistic claims.

On YouTube, there's a rare example of an early video interview with Jeff Bezos from 1997, about one year after he founded Amazon. (Early enough that the interviewer's first question for Bezos is "So, who are you?") As Bezos enthuses about his vision for the future of internet commerce, it's easy to see why investors found his excitement contagious:

> I mean, it's just incredible . . . this is day one. This is the very beginning. This is the Kitty Hawk stage of electronic commerce. We're moving forward in so many different areas, and lots of different companies are as well, in the late twentieth century. It's just a great time to be alive, you know? . . . I think a millennia from now, people are going to look back and say, "Wow, the late twentieth century was really a great time to be alive on this planet."[22]

It's a speech that communicates vision. Conviction. Passion. And it doesn't require Bezos to pretend that his start-up is a sure bet, or even that it's more than 50 percent likely to succeed.

After hearing Bezos's pitch, investor Tom Alberg discussed it with a friend before deciding to put in $50,000 of his own money. "It's very risky," he said, "but Jeff is for real. He's obviously a smart guy. He's very passionate about it."[23]

IN THIS CHAPTER, we've covered three key principles of influence without overconfidence:

First, you don't need to hold your opinions with 100 percent certainty in order to seem confident and competent. People simply aren't paying that much attention to how much epistemic confidence you express. They're paying attention to how you act, to your body language, tone, and other aspects of your social confidence, all of which are things you can cultivate without sacrificing your calibration.

Second, expressing uncertainty isn't necessarily a bad thing. It depends on whether the uncertainty is "in you" or "in the world." If you can demonstrate a strong command of the topic and speak with ease about your analysis and your plan, you'll seem like more of an expert, not less.

Third, you can be inspiring without overpromising. You can paint a picture of the world you're trying to create, or why your mission is important, or how your product has helped people, without claiming you're guaranteed to succeed. There are lots of ways to get people excited that don't require you to lie to others or to yourself.

That's the overarching theme of these last three chapters: whatever your goal, there's probably a way to get it that doesn't require you to believe false things. From now on, whenever you hear someone claim that you *need* to self-deceive in order to be happy, motivated, or influential, you should raise a skeptical eyebrow. There are multiple paths to any goal, some of which involve self-deception and some of which don't. It may take a little more care and practice to find the latter, but in the long run, it's well worth it.

Here's an analogy: Suppose a bully keeps threatening to beat you up and take your lunch money. You might think your choices are either (1) pay up or (2) take the beating. Framed that way, it might well be correct to give him the money. It's only a few dollars; surely that's better than getting a black eye, right?

But if you zoom out and look at the long run, it becomes less clear that handing over the money every time is your best option. Instead, you could learn to fight. Or you could devise a clever way to arrange for the bully to get caught red-handed. You could find a way to change classrooms or even schools. There are lots of ways to change the game board you're playing on so that you end up with better choices, instead of simply resigning yourself to picking the least-bad choice currently in front of you.

We're in a similar position with respect to the trade-off between scout mindset and soldier mindset, in which we have to sacrifice some of our ability to see clearly or else suffer a beating to our self-esteem, motivation, comfort, and more. You can accept those terms and say, "Okay, might as well pay up and sacrifice some accuracy, because it's worth it." Or you can say, "No, I don't accept those terms," and find ways to look good and feel good, while also seeing reality as accurately as possible.

# PART IV

# Changing Your Mind

*Chapter 10*

# How to Be Wrong

POLITICAL SCIENTIST PHILIP TETLOCK spent almost two decades measuring people's ability to forecast global events. The results were disappointing—even so-called experts were barely able to do better than random chance. Or, as Tetlock famously put it, the average expert was "roughly as accurate as a dart-throwing chimpanzee."[1]

Yet there were exceptions. A small subset of people turned out to have genuine skill at answering questions such as "Will the Muslim Brotherhood win the elections in Egypt?" or "Will there be a violent incident in the South China Sea in 2013 that kills at least one person?" Tetlock dubbed them the "superforecasters."

In a forecasting tournament sponsored by the Intelligence Advanced Research Projects Activity (IARPA), a branch of the United States intelligence community, the superforecasters handily beat teams of professors from top universities by margins of up to 70 percent.[2] In fact, the superforecasters did so much better than everyone else that IARPA dropped the other teams after only two years, despite originally planning to run the tournament for four.

What made the superforecasters super?

It wasn't that they were smarter than everyone else. And it wasn't that they had more knowledge or experience than everyone else. They were mostly amateurs, yet they outperformed even the CIA's professional analysts, who had the advantage of years of experience, not to mention access to classified information on the topics about which they were making forecasts. The superforecasters, armed only with Google, beat the CIA by 30 percent.

What made the superforecasters so great at being right was that they were great at being wrong.

# CHANGE YOUR MIND A LITTLE AT A TIME

The superforecasters changed their minds all the time. Not dramatic, 180-degree reversals every day, but subtle revisions as they learned new information. The highest-scoring superforecaster, a software engineer named Tim Minto, usually changed his mind at least a dozen times on a single forecast, and sometimes as much as forty or fifty times. On the following page is a graph of Minto's evolving confidence in the proposition "The number of registered Syrian refugees reported by the United Nations Refugee Agency as of 1 April 2014 will be under 2.6 million." Every dot represents a time that Minto revised his forecast over the course of three months. He's course-correcting as he goes, like a captain steering his ship.

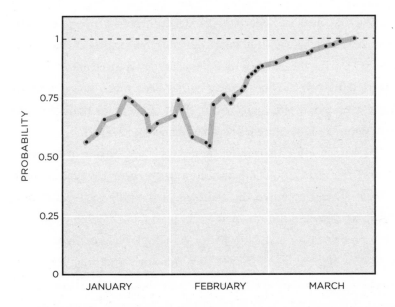

THE BELIEF-UPDATING STYLE OF A SUPERFORECASTER. ADAPTED FROM
TETLOCK AND GARDNER (2015), PAGE 167.

You're probably already comfortable with the idea of changing your mind incrementally in some contexts. When you submit a job application, you might figure you have about a 5 percent chance of ultimately getting an offer. After they call you to set up an in-person job interview, your estimate might rise to about 10 percent. During the interview, if you feel like you're hitting it out of the park, maybe your confidence in getting an offer rises to 30 percent. If you haven't heard from them for a couple of weeks after your interview, your confidence might fall back down to 20 percent.

What's much rarer is for someone to do the same thing with their opinions about politics, morality, or other charged topics. For years, Jerry Taylor was one of the top climate change skeptics in the country. He worked for the Cato Institute, a libertarian think tank, and earned a good living appearing on talk shows and reassuring the public that fears about climate change were being blown way out of proportion.

The first crack in Taylor's skepticism occurred after he participated in a televised debate with a famous climate change advocate named Joe Romm.[3] During the debate with Romm, Taylor repeated one of his standard talking points: Global warming has been much slower than the doomsayers predicted. Compared to the original projections presented to Congress in 1988, the earth hasn't warmed much at all.

Backstage after the taping, Romm accused Taylor of misrepresenting the facts, and challenged him to go check the testimony for himself. Taylor accepted the challenge, expecting to be vindicated. But to his shock, Romm turned out to be right. The 1988 projections were a much closer match to reality than Taylor had realized.

Taylor figured he must have been missing something. He had received this information from a well-respected, skeptical climate scientist. So he went back to the scientist, pointed out the problem, and asked, "What's going on here?" To Taylor's dismay, the scientist didn't have a good answer ready. He hemmed and hawed for twenty minutes, until finally Taylor realized that this person whom he had trusted was "purposely and consciously skewing the debate." It shook him.

From then on, whenever a fellow climate skeptic cited something, Taylor would follow up on the reference. Again and again, he found himself disappointed in the quality of the research. He still considered the skeptic narrative more plausible than the activist narrative overall, but bit by bit, Taylor was becoming less confident about that.

Changing your mind frequently, especially about important beliefs, might sound mentally and emotionally taxing. But, in a way, it's less stressful than the alternative. If you see the world in binary black-and-white terms, then what happens when you encounter evidence against one of your beliefs? The stakes are high: you have to find a way to dismiss the evidence, because if you can't, your entire belief is in jeopardy.

If instead you see the world in shades of gray, and you think of "changing your mind" as an incremental shift, then the experience of encountering evidence against one of your beliefs is very different. If you're 80 percent sure that immigration is good for the economy, and a study comes out showing that immigration lowers wages, you can adjust your confidence in your belief down to 70 percent.

It may later turn out that study was flawed, or further evidence may come out showing that immigration boosts the economy in other ways, and your confidence in your belief may go back up to 80 percent or even higher. Or you may find additional evidence about the downsides of immigration, which could gradually lower your confidence even further below 70 percent. Either way, each adjustment is comparatively low stakes.

# RECOGNIZING YOU WERE WRONG MAKES YOU BETTER AT BEING RIGHT

The way most people react when the world violates their expectations is to ask themselves, *"Can I believe I'm still right?"* Most of the time, the answer is "Yes, easily."

Since beginning his study of forecasting in the 1980s, Tetlock has heard hundreds of justifications for failed forecasts, which he has catalogued into seven belief system defenses. One of them he calls "I Was Almost Right."[4] After George W. Bush won the 2000 U.S. presidential election, many people who had confidently predicted a win for his opponent Al Gore insisted that they *would have been* right if conditions had been slightly different: *If Gore had been a better debater. If the election had been held a few days later. If the third-party candidate had been less stubborn.**

The superforecasters had a very different relationship with their

---

* Of course, as we saw in chapter 6, even a well-calibrated forecaster will get their confident predictions wrong sometimes. But the typical forecaster is overconfident, meaning that they're wrong much more often than they think they will be.

mistakes. When their predictions missed the mark by a lot—if they predicted something was very likely and it didn't happen or if they predicted something was very *unlikely* and it *did* happen—they would go back and reevaluate their process, asking, "What does this teach me about how to make better forecasts?" Here's an example:

The Yasukuni Shrine in Japan is a controversial spot. On the one hand, it holds many of Japan's military heroes; on the other hand, it also holds over a thousand of Japan's war criminals. When a political figure visits Yasukuni, it's considered a diplomatic faux pas, a slap in the face to other countries like China and Korea that have suffered at the hands of the Japanese armies in the past.

One of IARPA's forecasting questions in 2013 was "Will Japan's prime minister, Shinzo Abe, visit Yasukuni this year?" There had been a rumor that Abe was planning a visit, but a superforecaster named Bill Flack didn't buy it. It just didn't make sense for Abe to shoot himself in the foot, diplomatically speaking, for no real gain. But the rumor turned out to be true. Flack asked himself why he got that one wrong and realized: "I think that the question I was really answering wasn't 'Will Abe visit Yasukuni?' but 'If I were PM of Japan, would I visit Yasukuni?'"[5]

This is another reason superforecasters are much happier to think about what they got wrong—they know that analyzing their errors is an opportunity to hone their technique. Lessons like "Don't assume world leaders would react the same way as you" are like power-ups, upgrades to your mental arsenal that make you smarter going forward.

The superforecasters had started the tournament with greater accuracy than everyone else, and as the months went on, their lead increased. Each year, the superforecasters' average accuracy improved by roughly 25 percent. Meanwhile, the other forecasters didn't improve at all.[6]

# LEARNING DOMAIN-GENERAL LESSONS

Remember Bethany Brookshire? She's the journalist we met in chapter 4 who tweeted that male scientists were more likely to call her "Ms.," while female scientists were more likely to call her "Dr.," but then fact-checked her own claim and realized she was wrong. Brookshire's decision to check her claim, even though she could easily have gotten away with not doing so, was commendable. But was it useful?

When a forecaster recognizes he was wrong, it helps him make better forecasts. When an investor recognizes he was wrong, it helps him make better investments. In Brookshire's case, however, her error doesn't seem relevant to any particular domain in which she would benefit from improved judgment. So, at first glance, the answer to the question "Was it useful for Brookshire to notice her error?" might seem to be "no."

But that would be missing one of the biggest benefits of noticing your errors: the opportunity to improve your judgment in general. When Brookshire realized she had been wrong, she asked herself why, and pinpointed two likely culprits.[7] One was *confirmation bias*: "I had a preexisting belief that men wouldn't respect me as much in email as women," Brookshire realized, "and I most remembered the observations that confirmed this belief, forgetting entirely the evidence that showed me my belief was wrong." The other was *recency bias*: "I was giving more weight to things that I had observed recently, forgetting things I had observed in the past," she concluded.

Those lessons aren't just relevant to estimating gender bias in emails. They're *domain-general*, meaning that they apply to a wide variety of different domains, as opposed to *domain-specific* lessons that apply only to a single domain, like political forecasting or investing. Domain-general lessons are about how the world works, or how your own brain works, and about the kinds of biases that tend to influence your judgment. For example:

> It's easy to be fooled by cherry-picked evidence.
> If it seems like someone is saying something dumb, I might be misunderstanding them.
> Even when I feel certain, there's still a chance I'm wrong.

You might think these principles sound obvious and that you know them already. But "knowing" a principle, in the sense that you read it and say, "Yes, I know that," is different from having internalized it in a way that actually changes how you think. Brookshire already knew about confirmation bias and recency bias before her viral post. She was a science journalist. She had read about biases and knew that she was vulnerable to them, as all humans are. But such knowledge doesn't really become part of you until you've derived it for yourself by going through the experience of realizing you were wrong, asking yourself why, and seeing the effect of the bias at work.

Even when you're wrong about something random or trivial, there are still generally useful lessons to be had. When I was a teenager, I watched a few episodes of *Batman*, a TV show that aired in the United States in the late 1960s. It's a campy, over-the-top show in which grown men wearing leotards run around shouting things like, "Holy ravioli, Batman!" Yet I thought it had been intended as a serious adventure show for audiences of the sixties, who I figured were simply too unsophisticated to realize how silly it all was. When I later found out that I was wrong, and *Batman* was always considered camp, I was taken aback. My domain-general lesson was one that has stuck with me ever since: "Huh . . . Maybe I'm too quick to assume that other people are simpletons."

- - - - - - - -

So FAR IN this chapter we've explored two ways in which scouts think about error differently from most people. First, they revise their opinions incrementally over time, which makes it easier to be open to evidence against their beliefs. Second, they view errors as opportunities to hone their skill at getting things right, which makes the experience of realizing "I was wrong" feel valuable, rather than just painful.

There's one more lens on error worth noting—a fundamentally different way of thinking about what it means to be wrong.

## "ADMITTING A MISTAKE" VS. "UPDATING"

A friend of mine named Andrew was surprised when one of his colleagues accused him of never admitting he was wrong. In response, Andrew pointed out two recent occasions on which he had been wrong and readily acknowledged it—in the company of that very same colleague.

The colleague, whom I'll call Mark, was surprised in turn. He replied, "I guess that's right. Why did I have the opposite impression?" Mark was silent for a minute, reflecting. Then he said, "You know . . . I think it's because you never seem embarrassed about it. You're so matter-of-fact, it almost doesn't register to me that you're admitting you were wrong."

It's true. I've seen Andrew acknowledge he was wrong many times, and it usually sounds something like this: "Ah, yup, you're correct. Scratch what I said earlier, I don't believe it anymore." It's cheerful, straightforward, nonchalant.

Mark's implicit assumption was that changing your mind is *humbling*. That saying "I was wrong" is equivalent to saying "I screwed up"—something you confess with contrition or sheepishness. Indeed, that's the standard way of thinking about being wrong. Even my fellow cheerleaders for changing one's mind tend to say things like, "It's okay to admit you were wrong!" While I appreciate the intentions behind this advice, I'm not sure it makes things much better. The word *admit* makes it sound like you screwed up but that you deserve to be forgiven because you're only human. It doesn't question the premise that being wrong means you screwed up.

Scouts reject that premise. You've learned new information and come to a new conclusion, but that doesn't mean you were wrong to believe differently in the past. The only reason to be contrite is if you were negligent in some way. Did you get something wrong because you followed a process you should have known was bad? Were you willfully blind or stubborn or careless?

Sometimes the answer to these questions is yes. I once defended a public figure when I thought his critics were taking his words out of context to make him look bad. When I finally got around to watching the interview people were complaining about, I realized: "Oh, wait . . . His critics represented his words accurately after all." I had to walk back my defense, and I felt a little sheepish because I do in fact know better than to defend someone without checking first. I was just being sloppy.

But most of the time, *being* wrong doesn't mean you *did* something wrong. It's not something you need to apologize for, and the appropriate attitude to have about it is neither defensive nor humbly self-flagellating, but matter-of-fact.

Even the language scouts use to describe being wrong reflects this attitude. Instead of "admitting a mistake," scouts will sometimes talk about "updating." That's a reference to *Bayesian updating,* a technical term from probability theory for the correct way to revise a probability after learning new information. The way people use the word *updating* colloquially isn't nearly so precise, but it still gestures at the spirit of revising one's beliefs in response to new evidence and arguments. Here are some examples from bloggers of what this sounds like (emphasis mine):

- In a post titled "Preschool: I Was Wrong," psychiatrist Scott Alexander says he's become more bullish about the long-term benefits of preschool programs such as Head Start after reading the evidence: "I can't remember ever making a post about how Head Start was useless, but I definitely thought that, and to learn otherwise is a big update for me."[8]
- Researcher Buck Shlegeris describes an experience of receiving some harsh criticism, and says, "I updated initially quite far in the direction of their criticism, only to update 70% of the way back towards my initial views after I spent ten more hours thinking and talking to people about it."[9]
- Software engineer and product manager Devon Zuegel encourages readers to view her blog posts not as her permanent opinions, but instead as "a stream of thoughts, caught in the middle of updates."[10]

You don't necessarily need to speak this way. But if you at least start to *think* in terms of "updating" instead of "admitting you were wrong," you may find that it takes a lot of friction out of the process. An update is routine. Low-key. It's the opposite of an overwrought confession of sin. An update makes something better or more current without implying that its previous form was a failure.

Emmett Shear is the CEO and cofounder of Twitch, the world's largest live-streaming platform. He used to struggle a lot with acknowledging he was wrong; it felt like a painful blow to his ego. Over time, he's gotten a lot better at it, not by becoming meek and humble, but by realizing that being wrong isn't inherently a failure. "As I've gotten older, it's gotten easier to be wrong," he told me. "Not even to be *wrong*. It's just an update: *I learned this new thing . . . what's the issue?*"

# IF YOU'RE NOT CHANGING YOUR MIND, YOU'RE DOING SOMETHING WRONG

David Coman-Hidy is the head of the Humane League, an organization that's been called one of America's most important animal rights groups.[11] One thing that makes the Humane League unusual is their commitment to the premise that they're always at least a little bit wrong. Whenever a new employee joins the organization, Coman-Hidy tells them that the Humane League isn't defined by any particular "type" of activism. They're not committed to any particular battle or project or tactical approach. Their mandate is to follow the evidence and do whatever it suggests is most effective at helping animals. "If we're not doing something totally different in five years than what we're doing now, then we failed," Coman-Hidy says. "There has to be something better than what we're doing right now, and our goal is to find it."

Sometimes that means switching from one type of strategy or cause to another. In its early years, the Humane League concentrated on flashy demonstrations like picketing the homes of scientists involved in animal testing. But they found that this strategy was too alienating to be effective, and the number of animals it could save even in a best-case scenario wasn't very high. That's why they ultimately shifted their focus from lab animals to farm animals, and persuaded Unilever, which supplies 95 percent of the United States' eggs, to agree to stop killing male chicks. (The standard practice in the industry is to toss newborn male chicks into a grinder, since they won't be able to lay eggs.) That's billions of chickens saved from a painful death.

Sometimes the Humane League's commitment to following the evidence means abandoning an initiative that isn't working, even if they've already poured a lot of effort into it. In 2014, they saw some exciting preliminary results from a program called "Meatless Mondays," in which large schools give up meat on their cafeteria menus one day per week. Based on those initial results, they spent four months pouring most of their organizational resources into convincing schools across the country to sign up for Meatless Mondays. Unfortunately, their follow-up research revealed that the program didn't stick, at least not without a lot of ongoing support (hiring chefs, running training programs, and so on) that they weren't equipped to provide. Realizing it wasn't a cost-effective strategy for them after all, the Humane League had to say, "Okay, everyone, great job—but stop what you're doing. We're going back to what we were doing before."

Knowing that you're fallible doesn't magically prevent you from being wrong. But it does allow you to set expectations early and often, which can make it easier to accept when you *are* wrong. Coman-Hidy says, "My intuition is that if you bring up these biases a lot—that we are always going to think that we're right, that we're always thinking what we're doing is the best and most important thing to be doing . . . it makes it an easier pill to swallow when inevitably something better comes along. Because you've kind of inoculated yourself against the 'horror' of having been suboptimal for some period of time."

HOPEFULLY THIS CHAPTER has helped inoculate you against the "horror" of being wrong, and left you with a new attitude toward error. Discovering you were wrong is an update, not a failure, and your worldview is a living document meant to be revised. In the next chapter we'll explore another key facet of changing your mind. Now that you've gotten good at being wrong, it's time to get good at being confused.

RACCOONS ON A HILLSIDE

*Chapter 11*

# Lean In to Confusion

TAKE A MOMENT to look at the photograph on the opposite page. Go ahead, I'll wait.

. . . Now that you've returned, I have a question: Does that scene make sense to you? If you have no idea why I'm asking you that, then go back and look again, a little closer.*

Perhaps you had something akin to the experience that I and many other people had when we first saw this photo: *Okay, it's two raccoons on a hillside, with the sky above them,* you think at first. But then something catches your eye, on the right-hand side of the image. *Is that a . . . rock? In the sky?*

*I guess someone threw a rock, and it hasn't hit the ground yet,* you think. But in the back of your mind, you don't feel completely satisfied with that explanation. It doesn't quite fit. But what else could it be? A moment later, you notice another odd detail, this one much subtler. *What is that thin white line on the side of the rock?*

Then, suddenly, everything clicks into place: *That's not the sky. It's water, reflecting the sky.* The rock isn't suspended in midair, it's poking

---

* The fact that the raccoon on the left is "maskless" is unrelated to the thing I'm hinting at here. Masklessness is just a trait that pops up in raccoons occasionally.

up out of the water. And we're not looking up the hill at the raccoons, we're looking down at them.

OUR ABILITY TO change our minds depends on how we react when the world confounds your expectations. Sometimes, like in the case of the raccoon photo, we get curious and start reconsidering our perception of what's going on.

More often, however, we react to observations that conflict with our worldview by explaining them away. Someone who believes "Nobody likes me" might shrug off social invitations from coworkers with the explanation, "They only invited me out of pity." Someone who believes "I'm a great teacher" might explain away their poor teacher ratings by saying, "My students are just mad that I'm a tough grader."

To some extent, this kind of sense-making is unavoidable. We couldn't function in the world if we were constantly questioning our perception of reality. But especially when motivated reasoning is in play, we take it too far, shoehorning conflicting evidence into a narrative well past the point where we should have taken a step back and said, "Wait, am I misinterpreting what's going on here?"

An especially tragic example of this phenomenon occurred during World War II. California governor Earl Warren was convinced that Japanese American citizens were plotting to sabotage the American war effort against Japan. When it was pointed out to him that there had so far been no evidence of a Japanese American conspiracy, he found a way to interpret the absence of evidence as further confirmation of his suspicions: "I take the view that this lack [of evidence] is the most ominous sign in our whole situation," he said. "I believe we are just being lulled into a false sense of security."[1]

This chapter is about how to resist the urge to dismiss details that don't fit your theories, and instead, allow yourself to be confused and intrigued by them, to see them as puzzles to be solved, like the mysterious floating rock in the raccoon photograph. Over the next few pages, we'll look at a series of case studies in which the world didn't behave as someone expected, and see what a difference curiosity can make.

## THE PUZZLE OF THE PEACOCK'S TAIL

"The sight of a feather in a peacock's tail, whenever I gaze at it, makes me sick!"[2]

Charles Darwin penned this line in a letter to a friend in 1860. It had been one year since he had published *On the Origin of Species*, and he was now immersed in a heated international debate over his theory of evolution. He was only half joking about feeling sick at the sight of a peacock's tail. Those feathers, beautiful though they were, seemed to pose a direct threat to the theory he had spent decades developing and on which he had staked his professional reputation.

Darwin's theory of evolution by natural selection held that features that helped an animal survive would get passed down to subsequent generations, and features that didn't help with survival would gradually get weeded out of existence. The peacock's tail was gaudy and enormous, reaching heights of up to five feet. Such a tail would only weigh the bird down and make it harder to escape predators, so why would it have evolved?

Darwin didn't consider himself a quick or highly analytical thinker. His memory was poor, and he couldn't follow long mathematical arguments. Nevertheless, Darwin felt that he made up for those shortcomings with a crucial strength: his urge to figure out how reality worked. Ever since he could remember, he had been driven to make sense of the world around him. He followed what he called a "golden rule" to fight against motivated reasoning:

... whenever a published fact, a new observation or thought came across me, which was opposed to my general results, to make a memorandum of it without fail and at once; for I had found by experience that such facts and thoughts were far more apt to escape from the memory than favourable ones.[3]

Therefore, even though the peacock's tail made him anxious, Darwin couldn't stop puzzling over it. How could it possibly be consistent with natural selection?

Within a few years, he had figured out the beginnings of a compelling answer. Natural selection wasn't the only force shaping evolution. *Sexual* selection was just as important. Some features, like a big, gaudy tail, were especially attractive to members of the opposite sex. Those features could therefore become common in a species over time, because even though they might hurt the animal's odds of surviving, they helped the animal's odds of reproducing. The latter could outweigh the former.

Ironically, the feathers that made Darwin sick with worry only wound up making his theory stronger in the end. It wasn't the first time. As Darwin was researching *On the Origin of Species*, he followed up on every observation he could find that contradicted his theory, puzzling over them and revising his theory in response. By the time he was done, his account of natural selection was so solid and well evidenced that despite the fierce resistance it initially sparked, within a decade the majority of the scientific establishment had become convinced Darwin was right.

## THE UNEXPECTED ALIEN ATTACK

In the sixteenth episode of *Star Trek: The Original Series*'s first season, the starship *Enterprise*'s shuttle has just crash-landed on a hostile alien planet. Spock is in command, and he decides on a plan: the *Enterprise* crew will fire off a few warning shots to show off their superior weaponry, and the aliens will realize they're outmatched and retreat.

That's not how things play out. Instead, the aliens are angered by the *Enterprise*'s display of aggression, and they attack, killing two crew members. The ship's doctor, McCoy, berates Spock for his failed plan:

> **McCoy:** Well, Mr. Spock, they didn't stay frightened very long, did they?
>
> **Spock:** Most illogical reaction. When we demonstrated our superior weapons, they should have fled.
>
> **McCoy:** You mean they should have respected us?
>
> **Spock:** Of course!
>
> **McCoy:** Mr. Spock, respect is a rational process. Did it ever occur to you that they might react emotionally, with anger?
>
> **Spock:** Doctor, I'm not responsible for their unpredictability.
>
> **McCoy:** They were perfectly predictable. To anyone with feeling. You might as well admit it, Mr. Spock. Your precious logic brought them down on us![4]

There, see what happens when you try to be logical? *People die.*

Just kidding. Spock wasn't actually being logical. He was too attached to his model of how people "should" think, according to him, to pay attention to how they actually *do* think. Presumably Spock has had many interactions with other non-Vulcans in the years before this event, and many opportunities to notice that their behavior follows different rules than he expects. Why hasn't he learned from those experiences and improved his ability to predict how people will behave? Because when someone's behavior violates his expectations, he shrugs and says, "Well, that was illogical of them," and doesn't try to understand what he's missing.

Spock's reaction is a textbook example of one of Tetlock's seven belief system defenses we learned about in chapter 10. Previously, we examined the "I Was Almost Right" defense. Here, Spock is employing what Tetlock calls the "Politics Is Hopelessly Cloudlike" defense: when a forecaster's confident prediction doesn't come true, they shrug and say something like, "Well, this stuff is unpredictable."[5] If this represented a lasting update toward agnosticism, that would be one thing. But somehow, when it comes time to make the next forecast, the forecaster is once again confident in their ability to predict global politics.

If you want to become better at predicting people's behavior, then shrugging off the times when they violate your expectations is exactly the wrong response. Spock should have leaned in to his confusion about the aliens' decision to attack: "What am I missing? Why might this behavior make sense to them?"

In fact, there are many reasons why a nation might choose to attack despite being outmatched, and academics and military strategists have thought long and hard about why. Political scientist Bruce Bueno de Mesquita catalogued conflicts between nation-states between 1816 and 1974, and found that 22 percent of the conflicts were cases in which a weaker nation attacked a stronger one.[6] In some cases, the weaker side simply had more at stake; in other cases, they were counting on allies to back them up. There's even the "madman" strategy: show yourself to be an unpredictable actor, with no instinct for self-preservation, and hope that the enemy decides it's too risky to tussle with you. Understanding factors like these can make the difference between being prepared for a future attack or caught dangerously off guard.

# THE MYSTERY OF THE IRRATIONAL NEGOTIATOR

I didn't tell that story as an excuse to pick on Spock again. (Well, not *just* for that reason.) The instinct to judge other people's behavior as stupid, irrational, or crazy is very common, and it's also a sign that there's something you're missing. This is a point that top negotiators all emphasize: don't write off the other side as crazy. When their behavior confuses you, lean in to that confusion. Treat it as a clue. You'll often find that it leads you to the information you need to resolve the negotiation.

Negotiation experts Max Bazerman and Deepak Malhotra at Harvard Business School describe in their book *Negotiation Genius* the case of an executive whose company was being sued by a disgruntled former employee. The ex-employee claimed the company owed him $130,000 in commissions he had earned before he was fired. The company did the math, and found that the employee was mistaken. They sent him their analysis showing that he was not owed any money, but he still refused to abandon his lawsuit.

The executive, who was a client of Deepak Malhotra's, thought the ex-employee was being completely irrational, since he had no chance of winning in court. Malhotra suggested: "Is it possible that he doesn't trust your accountant?" He urged the executive to try hiring an objective, third-party accounting firm to do the analysis and send the results directly to the ex-employee. Sure enough, the suit was dropped.[7]

Chris Voss used to be the FBI's lead international kidnapping negotiator. In his bestselling book on negotiation, *Never Split the Difference*, he stresses the importance of leaning in to confusion. "It is when we hear or see something that doesn't make sense—something 'crazy'—that a crucial fork in the road is presented," he writes. "[Push] forward, even more forcefully, into that which we initially can't process; or take the other path, the one to guaranteed failure, in which we tell ourselves that negotiating was useless anyway."[8]

## THE CASE OF THE AWKWARD CONVERSATION

Imagine you're having a conversation with someone and it's not going well. In fact, it's downright awkward. You're not getting each other's jokes or references. There are uncomfortably long pauses before either of you thinks of another thing to say. The rhythm of the conversation is just . . . off. Eventually, your conversation partner comments, "Well, this is kind of awkward!"

In your opinion, does their comment make things better or worse?

To me, the answer is obvious: When someone says, "This is awkward," it makes things *more* awkward, and therefore worse. So when an acquaintance of mine called attention to the awkwardness of one of our interactions, I was incredulous. "Why would anyone *do* that?" I thought. "Doesn't he realize that he's just making it worse?"

I decided to pose the question to my Facebook friends. I described the scenario, and asked, "Does someone calling attention to the awkwardness of a conversation make you feel better or worse?" (I removed identifying information and phrased my question as neutrally as possible so people wouldn't be able to guess what my own opinion was.)

I was sure most people would agree with me—but I was wrong. To my surprise, thirty-two people said pointing out awkwardness made things better, compared to only sixteen people who said it made things worse.

Still, my initial reaction to the poll results was dismissive. "People who answered 'better' don't really mean that," I thought. "They're probably not actually picturing the situation."

I wasn't quite satisfied with that explanation. It felt like a stretch, much the way "The rock is flying through the sky" didn't quite work as an explanation of what was going on in the raccoon photo. Was it really plausible that so many people were claiming to feel a certain way, yet didn't mean it?

I ended up chatting about it with one of the thirty-two people who had replied "better" to my poll. He was as surprised by my answer as I was by his. I tried to explain: "Look, when someone points out awkwardness, it forces me to find a way to smooth things out immediately. But I was *already* trying to find a way to smooth things out—so by bringing it up, he's just increasing the time pressure on me."

"Wait, you feel like it's your responsibility to make conversations go smoothly?" he asked incredulously.

"Wait, you *don't*?" I replied with equal incredulity.

I realized that I had underestimated how wildly different people's internal experiences of social situations can be. That's changed the way I react in general when someone's behavior strikes me as rude, inconsiderate, or unreasonable. Whereas previously my train of thought would have stopped there, with my feeling irritated at them, I'm now more open to the possibility that we're simply perceiving the social situation differently, and I get curious about how.

# THE MYSTERY OF THE HOMEOPATHIC HOSPITAL

London in the 1850s was a frightening place to live. Every few years, a new outbreak of cholera racked the city, killing hundreds or thousands at a time. Otherwise healthy people would notice a slightly upset stomach, then be found dead within days—or even hours.

The government commissioned a council of scientists to survey the city's hospitals, record what methods they were using to treat the disease, and figure out which treatments seemed to be more effective. The results weren't encouraging. The mortality rate among the hospitals' cholera patients was 46 percent, no better than the mortality rate among untreated cholera sufferers. None of the standard "cures," which included opium, chalk, and castor oil, seemed to make a difference.

But there was one hospital that was intentionally excluded from the survey. The London Homeopathic Hospital was a small institution established a few years earlier, funded by wealthy donors who were fans of a trendy new approach to medicine called "homeopathy." Homeopathy drove mainstream doctors in the nineteenth century up the wall, very much as it does today. Its central theory completely flouts scientific sense that if you dilute medicine until it's physically indistinguishable from pure water, it will still retain the "spiritual force" of the drug it once was, and it will have become more potent, not less.

To the council's surprise and annoyance, the London Homeopathic Hospital reported a cholera mortality rate of only 18 percent, less than half the mortality rate at mainstream hospitals. The council resolved to leave the London Homeopathic Hospital's data out of the survey.[9] After all, homeopathy was nonsense! Their data would only muddle the survey's conclusions. Even worse, it would be an insult to science and to reason itself.

It's too bad. If the council had investigated the surprising result instead of suppressing it, the history of medicine might have been forever changed for the better. That's because the homeopaths' success was real—it just didn't have anything to do with homeopathy. It turns out that the leaders of the homeopathic movement had, somewhat by accident, hit on two keys to treating cholera. One key was the importance of good hygiene—they urged their doctors to sterilize the blankets of the sick before reusing them. Second, they recommended that cholera patients drink whey, which helped replenish the patients' fluids and electrolytes. That's essentially an early version of what we now call oral rehydration therapy, something that didn't become a standardized treatment for cholera until the 1960s.

Neither of those recommendations was derived from the central theory of homeopathy. They were just based on good and lucky hunches about how to help people get better. If the council had gotten curious about the homeopaths' surprising results, those hunches might have become medical orthodoxy decades earlier than they actually did, saving millions of lives as a result.

That's the thing about surprising and confusing observations. You don't know in advance what they'll teach you. All too often, we assume the only two possibilities are "I'm right" or "The other guy is right"— and since the latter seems absurd, we default to the former. But in many cases, there's an unknown unknown, a hidden "option C," that enriches our picture of the world in a way we wouldn't have been able to anticipate.

ALL OF THESE examples have been about how a single puzzling observation can change your worldview. But more often than not, it's the accumulation of many puzzling observations over time that changes your mind—a paradigm shift. By now the phrase *paradigm shift* has become an overused buzzword in business, referring to a big change of approach (or, more often, to a small change that someone is trying to spin as a big change). Originally, however, it referred to a specific way in which science makes progress, described by the philosopher Thomas Kuhn in *The Structure of Scientific Revolutions*.

A paradigm shift starts with a core belief, or paradigm, that everyone assumes is true. Gradually, some people observe anomalies, things that don't seem to fit with that paradigm. At first, scientists shrug off those anomalies as exceptions or mistakes, or they modify their paradigm a little bit at a time to accommodate the new observations. But the more anomalies accumulate, the more confused the scientists become, until someone eventually develops a new paradigm that makes everything make sense again.

The rule for paradigm shifts in life is the same as it is in science. Acknowledge anomalies, even if you don't yet know how to explain them, and even if the old paradigm still seems correct overall. Maybe they'll add up to nothing in particular. Maybe they just mean that reality is messy. But maybe they're laying the groundwork for a big change of view.

## ANOMALIES PILE UP AND CAUSE A PARADIGM SHIFT

Donna was in her early twenties and working in a restaurant when she got a message from a recruiter with Rodan + Fields, a skincare company, asking if she would like to become an independent sales representative for them. It was just what Donna needed to hear at that juncture in her life. She had been feeling frustrated and demoralized in her current job, with no clear sense of what to do instead. There weren't any promising opportunities in the small town where she lived. The idea of being an entrepreneur, working for herself for once, sounded wonderful. She signed a contract and paid Rodan + Fields close to $1,000 for the "how to sell" start-up kit, which they strongly recommended she buy.

What Donna didn't know at the time was that Rodan + Fields is a multilevel marketing company, or MLM, like Amway and Herbalife. The way to achieve success in an MLM is to recruit more salespeople to work under you, getting a cut of their profits in turn. By the very nature of the game, the only way for one person to win is for many other people to lose. The math is brutal; a study by the Federal Trade Commission calculated that over 99 percent of people who sign up for an MLM end up with less money than they started with (in addition to losing all the time they put into it).

But as I said, Donna didn't know this, and she threw herself into her new job. She contacted hundreds of her acquaintances and tried to sell them lotions and creams. She posted ads on Facebook. She bought more instructional videos from Rodan + Fields that promised to teach her the secrets of successful salesmanship. But her sales still weren't enough to recoup the cost of the products she was buying from the company, especially after her "upline"—the woman who had recruited her—took her cut.

Donna was confused. The promotional materials had made it sound so easy and liberating, but it didn't feel that way at all. "Wasn't this supposed to make me feel independent?" she thought in consternation.[10] There were other confusing aspects to her experience, too. When she watched the instructional videos, they didn't seem to contain useful information. Then there was the jarring disconnect between the way her fellow saleswomen talked and the reality of her own experience. Some Rodan + Fields saleswomen who had newborn babies gushed about how they were still working and making money. Donna had taken care of a newborn before, and she couldn't fathom how anyone could manage to do both at once.

Her upline assured her that the system worked, and that if she was failing, it was because she wasn't trying hard enough. So Donna tried to force the accumulating anomalies into the paradigm "This system works." After all, Rodan + Fields was endorsed by lots of prominent people. It must be legit, right? She felt miserable, but blamed herself. "I reasoned that the 'whys' I didn't understand would be clear once I learned more or leveled up," she said.

Then the paradigm shift happened.

Donna was browsing Netflix and spotted a show titled *Scientology and the Aftermath*, a documentary series produced by and featuring actress Leah Remini. In the series, Remini talks about her experience of abuse and harassment while she was a member of the Church of Scientology and interviews other former Scientologists about their own experiences. When Donna read the description of the series, she thought, "Oh, this will be fun, such a crazy cult-like organization." But as she watched, she felt a growing sense of recognition. The way the Scientologist leaders spoke...the pyramid structure of the organization... it felt like watching the last year of her own life play out on the screen.

Donna thought back on the various things that had confused her about her experience with Rodan + Fields. The discrepancy between the "easy and fun" job she had been promised and the reality in which she was struggling to earn any profit at all. The lack of support she had perceived from her fellow salespeople. The hard-to-swallow claims about earning a profit while taking care of a newborn. All those anomalies made a lot more sense when viewed through a new paradigm: "This organization is exploiting me."

Once Donna's suspicions had been triggered, it didn't take her long to go online and find the facts about MLMs, along with many accounts from people just like her who had worked diligently for an MLM for years, only to end up in debt. When she realized what had happened, Donna began to cry. But at least she had only lost $2,000 and one year of her life. From the stories she read, she knew it could have been much worse.

To a casual observer, it might look like Donna's mind change was sudden; one day she was a true believer, and the next she realized it was all a lie. But the groundwork for her "sudden" mind change had been developing for months. Even as she continued to believe overall in the paradigm "The system works," she was simultaneously noticing anomalies, observations that were difficult to explain under that paradigm—"the 'whys' I didn't understand," as she put it.

That's a key determinant of whether someone manages to escape an MLM after just a few months or whether they end up entrenched for years. Do they notice the anomalies, the aspects of their experience that aren't what they expected? Do they notice when their attempts to explain the anomalies feel forced? Do they allow themselves to feel confused?

Instead, many people in MLMs actively suppress their doubts, often because they've been warned by the MLM leadership that negative thinking will make them fail. Each month, when they fail to turn a profit, they don't say to themselves, "Huh, it's weird that I'm losing money even though I'm working full-time." They say, "I guess I'm not trying hard enough." Signs of a problem accumulate, but each time, they are explained away without trouble.

In his book *Sources of Power*, decision researcher Gary Klein cites this as one of the top three causes of bad decisions. He calls it a "de minimus error," an attempt to minimize the inconsistency between observations and theory.[11] Each new piece of evidence that doesn't fit a doctor's medical diagnosis can be explained away or dismissed as a fluke, so the doctor never realizes her initial diagnosis was wrong. Each new development in a battle can be made consistent with the paradigm "The enemy is on the run," so the general never realizes that the enemy has actually regrouped until it's too late. If the decision-maker had been able to step back and see all the anomalies at once, it would have been clear to them that their paradigm was wrong. But because they were explaining away one single anomaly at a time, their confusion never got the chance to build up sufficiently.

That doesn't mean you should go to the other extreme and abandon a paradigm as soon as you notice the slightest bit of conflicting evidence. What the best decision-makers do is look for ways to make sense of conflicting evidence under their existing theory but simultaneously take a mental note: *This evidence stretches my theory by a little (or a lot)*. If your theory gets stretched too many times, then you admit to yourself that you're no longer sure what's happening, and you consider alternate explanations. Marvin Cohen, a researcher who collaborates with Klein, uses the analogy of a spring: "Each time the decision maker explains a piece of conflicting evidence, it is like stretching a spring. Eventually, the spring resists any further efforts in that direction, and snaps back."[12]

It's a tricky skill. It forces you to act without clarity, to operate under one paradigm while being aware of its flaws and inconsistencies, knowing that it might be wrong and that you might end up abandoning it. You have to resist the temptation to resolve inconsistency prematurely by forcing all of your observations into one paradigm, and instead be willing to remain confused—for days, weeks, or even years.

# BE WILLING TO STAY CONFUSED

If you were a Christian teenager in the United States in the late 1990s or early 2000s, chances are good that you had a certain book on your shelf: *I Kissed Dating Goodbye*. Written by a twenty-one-year-old pastor's son named Joshua Harris, it encouraged Christians to avoid dating before marriage, in order to keep themselves pure for their future spouse.

*I Kissed Dating Goodbye* sold well over a million copies and catapulted Harris to fame. But by the 2010s, Harris—who was now a pastor himself—began to hear from a growing number of people who had read his book as teenagers and taken it to heart, but now felt it had screwed up their lives. "Your book was used as a weapon against me," one woman told him on Twitter.[13] "I feel the only man I deserve is one who is broken like me," another woman said. "Because of the shameful purity movement rhetoric we learned from your book, sex became tainted," wrote a male reader who's now married. "To this day, I cannot be intimate with my wife without feeling like I'm doing something wrong."

At first Harris found it easy to dismiss these online critics as haters. But then he began to hear similar stories from classmates of his, who confessed that they also felt the book's impact on their lives had been negative. That brought him up short. He couldn't write off his real-life friends as haters or angry trolls. Their testimonies were anomalies, difficult to explain under the "nothing wrong with my book" paradigm.

In 2016, Harris began to publicly share his doubts about *I Kissed Dating Goodbye*. But when journalists pressed him for a definitive conclusion—was he officially disavowing his book?—he demurred. "I just need to listen to where people are before I come out with my own thoughts," Harris said. "I don't have all the answers yet."

We'll return to Harris later to see how his journey turns out. But for now, we'll leave him suspended in confusion—as we all should learn to be.

LEANING IN TO confusion is about inverting the way you're used to seeing the world. Instead of dismissing observations that contradict your theories, get curious about them. Instead of writing people off as irrational when they don't behave the way you think they should, ask yourself why their behavior might be rational. Instead of trying to fit confusing observations into your preexisting theories, treat them as clues to a new theory.

Scouts view anomalies as puzzle pieces to collect as you go through the world. You probably won't know what to do with them at first. But if you hang on to them, you may find that they add up to a richer picture of the world than you had before. As Isaac Asimov reportedly said: "The most exciting phrase to hear in science, the one that heralds new discoveries, is not 'Eureka' but 'That's funny . . .'"

*Chapter 12*

# Escape Your
# Echo Chamber

Y OU'VE PROBABLY HEARD some version of the following speech
before: "It's important to listen to people on the other side of the
aisle! Escape your echo chamber! Get outside of your filter bubble!
That's how you broaden your perspective and change your mind."

It's the kind of advice that sounds good; the kind of advice that
well-intentioned people repeat and that other well-intentioned people
nod along to enthusiastically.

The dirty little secret is that it doesn't work.

## HOW *NOT* TO LEARN FROM
## DISAGREEMENT

I suspect even the well-intentioned people passing around that advice already know, on some level, that it doesn't work. We've all had
the experience of receiving strongly worded disagreement on Facebook, maybe from an old classmate or a second cousin who has a totally different worldview from us. And when they explain to us how

our views on abortion are immoral or why our political party is incompetent, we don't usually come away from those interactions feeling enlightened.

Still, it's so common for articles and books to decry the echo chambers and filter bubbles making us closed-minded that many people have taken that warning to heart and tried to listen to the "other side." Usually, they find the experience frustrating.

Rachael Previti is a liberal journalist who in 2019 resolved to watch only Fox News for one week. Her postmortem is representative of most accounts I've seen: "I wanted to look for the bright side in some of the things conservatives had to say instead of being like, 'Oh my god look at all of these things conservatives think!'" Previti said. "But honestly, it was hard to find what was really stood for besides bashing liberals."[1]

In 2017, a Michigan magazine attempted a two-sided version of the "escape your echo chamber" experiment.[2] It recruited one couple and one individual with very different views from each other who agreed to exchange media diets for one week. On the liberal side were Aric Knuth and Jim Leija, who live in Ann Arbor and who both work for the University of Michigan. They're fans of NPR and avid readers of the *New York Times* and the feminist website *Jezebel*. On the conservative side was Tom Herbon, a retired engineer and enthusiastic supporter of Donald Trump living in a suburb of Detroit. Herbon is a daily reader of the *Drudge Report* online, and keeps his radio tuned to The Patriot, a talk radio station featuring conservative personalities like Sean Hannity.

Knuth and Leija agreed to read the *Drudge Report* and listen to The Patriot. In exchange, Herbon agreed to read the *New York Times* and *Jezebel*, and leave his radio tuned to NPR while he was at home. After a week, the magazine checked in with its three guinea pigs. Had they learned anything?

Indeed they had: Everyone had learned that the "other side" was *even more* biased, inaccurate, and grating than they previously believed. Leija had never listened to The Patriot talk radio before, and found it shocking. He said, about Herbon, "It made me really sad that there is this person who listens to this radio station all day long that is filled with people who are exactly like him, that say exactly the things he wants to hear." Herbon, meanwhile, had loathed *Jezebel* and the *New York Times* so much that he gave up on them halfway through the experiment (although he did manage to stick with NPR for the full week). He said, "I was immediately turned off by inaccuracies of what I know to be fact. If people don't know what a fact is, we have a huge problem."

If those experiments aren't formal enough for you, there was also a large-scale study in 2018 on the effects of listening to the "other side."[3] Researchers offered people on Twitter eleven dollars to follow an automated Twitter account (a "bot") that would expose them to tweets from the other side of the political spectrum. For liberals, the bot would show them twenty-four tweets per day from conservative figures such as politicians, media outlets, nonprofits, and pundits. For conservatives, the bot would show them twenty-four tweets per day from liberal figures. The researchers made sure participants were actually reading the bot's tweets by giving everyone weekly quizzes on its content.

One month later, researchers measured the political attitudes of their participants. Had their views been moderated by the foray outside their echo chambers? Quite the contrary. Conservatives who spent a month reading liberal tweets became dramatically more conservative. Liberals who spent a month reading conservative tweets became slightly more liberal (though the effect wasn't statistically significant).

Results like these might seem to repudiate the whole idea of listening to the other side. But the situation isn't quite that grim. The right takeaway from these failed experiments isn't that learning from disagreement is hopeless—it's that we're going about it all wrong.

Our mistake lies in how we select the sources we listen to. By default, we end up listening to people who initiate disagreements with us, as well as the public figures and media outlets who are the most popular representatives of the other side. Those are not very promising selection criteria. First of all, what kind of person is most likely to initiate a disagreement? A disagreeable person. ("This article you shared on Facebook is complete bullshit—let me educate you . . .") Second, what kind of people or media are likely to become popular representatives of an ideology? The ones who do things like cheering for their side and mocking or caricaturing the other side—i.e., you.

To give yourself the best chance of learning from disagreement, you should be listening to people who make it *easier* to be open to their arguments, not harder. People you like or respect, even if you don't agree with them. People with whom you have some common ground—intellectual premises, or a core value that you share—even though you disagree with them on other issues. People whom you consider reasonable, who acknowledge nuance and areas of uncertainty, and who argue in good faith.

# LISTEN TO PEOPLE YOU FIND REASONABLE

When you picture a debate on Reddit between a bunch of feminists and a bunch of antifeminists, what descriptors come to mind? "Frustrating"? "Terrible"? "Dumpster fire," perhaps?

As a rule, that would be accurate. But for several years, r/FeMRADebates was a shining exception to the rule.[4] It was created in 2014 as a space for feminists and men's rights activists (MRAs) to discuss questions that divide them.* What made r/FeMRADebates unique

---

* Men's rights is a movement that believes society discriminates against men; its members are frequently hostile to feminism.

was the care the moderators took in setting norms of conduct from the beginning: Don't insult other members or use epithets like *feminazi* or *neckbeard*. Don't generalize. Disagree with specific people or specific views, rather than talking about what "feminists" believe as if they're a monolith.

Thanks to these rules, and the positive influence of the forum's founding members, r/FeMRADebates managed to avoid the "dumpster fire" problem to an unusual degree. How often do you see comments like this in a typical online debate?

> I glanced over your article and yes, actually, I am in the wrong here.[5]
>
> I don't fault people for 'not getting it' anymore. I think they have a reasonable position.[6]
>
> I don't always agree with [another commenter] . . . but if anyone was ever to convince me to be a feminist, it would be her for sure.[7]

Both feminists and MRAs who came to the subreddit with a dismal view of the other side frequently changed their minds over time. One member named Rashid told me that he used to be skeptical of the feminist claim that female rape victims are often blamed and their rape trivialized. After talking to a number of the feminists on r/FeMRADebates, he's concluded that it happens a lot more often than he realized.

Rashid had considered himself an "antifeminist" when he first joined the subreddit, but he has since dropped that label. What changed his mind? Talking with feminists who were arguing in good faith, he told me. "I used to spend a lot of time being exposed to the worst 'takes' from the feminist side that were being shared by other antifeminists to showcase how ridiculous feminists were," Rashid said. As a result, he had been under the impression that the worst examples of feminism were far more common than they actually were.

On the other side of the aisle, one of the group's feminist founders began to see some flaws in concepts from feminist theory, such as "patriarchy." She also came to care much more about some problems MRAs emphasize, like the sexual assault of men. In a heartfelt message to some of her frequent debate partners, she wrote: "You've seen me change my stance on more issues than I can count . . . You've made me much more accepting of the MRM [men's rights movement] in general, and made me realize the importance of many men's issues."[8]

## LISTEN TO PEOPLE YOU SHARE INTELLECTUAL COMMON GROUND WITH

When last we left climate change skeptic Jerry Taylor in chapter 10, he was in a state of uncertainty. He had been alarmed to discover that a scientist on his side had misrepresented the facts and disturbed that the sources he had been citing were shakier than he realized. He still thought the basic arguments for climate change skepticism were correct . . . but he had become much less certain of his position than he once was.

Taylor remained in that state of uncertainty for several years, until a friend set up a meeting for him with a climate activist named Bob Litterman.[9] When you hear "activist," you might picture someone sporting hemp and tie-dye who has chained themselves to a tree in an act of protest. But Litterman wasn't a typical activist. His day job was running Kepos Capital, an investment advisory firm, which he founded after spending more than two decades at Goldman Sachs.

Litterman was a prestigious figure in the field of risk management, having developed one of the most popular models used by investors to allocate their portfolios optimally.

In their meeting, held at the Cato Institute in 2014, Litterman made an argument for taking action on climate change that Taylor hadn't heard before. Catastrophic climate change is a *nondiversifiable* risk, Litterman said. That means there's nothing you can invest in that could hedge against the possibility of it happening. In normal circumstances, investors are willing to pay huge sums of money to avoid nondiversifiable risks. And by that same logic, Litterman argued, we as a society should be willing to invest a large amount of money in preventing the possibility of catastrophic climate change.

Litterman, Taylor, and one of Taylor's colleagues argued for an hour and a half. After Litterman left, Taylor turned to his colleague and said: "It looks like our position just got shredded to pieces." Shortly after that conversation, Taylor left the Cato Institute and became an activist for climate action—the only professional climate change skeptic, to date, who has switched sides.

Why was that disagreement so productive? Because even though Litterman was on the other side of the climate change issue, he was nevertheless someone with "instant credibility with people like me," Taylor said later. "He is from Wall Street. He is kind of a soft Libertarian."[10]

Knowing that you have intellectual common ground with someone makes you more receptive to their arguments right off the bat. It also makes it possible for them to explain their side in your "language." Litterman's case for climate action relied on economics and uncertainty, a language Taylor already found compelling. To someone like Taylor, one conversation with a climate activist who can make their case in those terms is going to be far more valuable than one hundred conversations with activists who talk about humanity's moral responsibility to Mother Earth.

# LISTEN TO PEOPLE WHO SHARE YOUR GOALS

My friend Kelsey Piper is a journalist for Vox, where she covers developments in philanthropy, technology, politics, and other issues affecting global well-being. Kelsey is also an atheist. And one of her good friends, whom I'll call Jen, is a practicing Catholic. That's a large difference in beliefs, one that often makes disagreements intractable, especially on issues like homosexuality, birth control, premarital sex, or euthanasia. When one person's moral positions stem from religious premises that another person doesn't share, it's hard to know how to make progress.

But one thing Kelsey and Jen do share is a desire to make the world a better place as effectively as possible. They're both part of the effective altruism movement, which is devoted to finding high-impact, evidence-based ways of doing good. That shared goal creates a sense of camaraderie and trust between them, making Kelsey more willing to listen open-mindedly to Jen's perspective than she might otherwise have been.

One topic on which Kelsey's views have shifted as a result of those conversations is abortion. At first, she had been unconflictedly pro-choice. Her view was that a fetus isn't sentient enough to count as a "person" in the morally relevant sense, the sense that would make an abortion wrong.

Now, after many conversations with Jen, Kelsey is somewhat more sympathetic to the pro-life position. Even though she considers it *unlikely* that a fetus could be sentient, "it seems possible that if I had a full understanding of the experience of being a fetus, that I would end up going, 'Oh, yeah, this is the kind of mind where something tragic has occurred when this dies,'" she told me. Kelsey is still strongly in favor of legal abortion. But she now takes more seriously the possibility that abortions are a bad outcome, one that we should be trying harder to prevent.

That shift wouldn't have happened if Kelsey hadn't made a genuine effort to understand Jen's perspective—and that wouldn't have happened if Kelsey hadn't felt like Jen was her ally in a fight to make the world better, someone who cares about many of the same things as Kelsey does. Feeling like you're on the same team in some important way can make it possible to learn from each other, even when your worldviews are otherwise very different.

# THE PROBLEM WITH A "TEAM OF RIVALS"

When Abraham Lincoln won the presidency in 1860, he reached out to the men who had been his main opponents for the Republican nomination—Simon Cameron, Edward Bates, Salmon Chase, and William Seward—and offered them all positions in his cabinet. That story was immortalized by historian Doris Kearns Goodwin in her bestselling 2005 book *Team of Rivals: The Political Genius of Abraham Lincoln.*[11]

Lincoln's "team of rivals" is now a standard example cited in books and articles urging people to expose themselves to diverse opinions. "Lincoln self-consciously chose diverse people who could challenge his inclinations and test one another's arguments in the interest of producing the most sensible judgments," wrote Harvard Law professor Cass Sunstein in his book *Going to Extremes.*[12] Barack Obama cited *Team of Rivals* as inspiration for his own presidency, praising Lincoln for being "confident enough to be willing to have these dissenting voices" in his cabinet.[13]

This is the account I had heard as well, before I began researching this book. But it turns out that the full story yields a more complicated moral. Out of the four "rivals" Lincoln invited into his cabinet—Cameron, Bates, Chase, and Seward—three left early, after an unsuccessful tenure.

Cameron was removed from his office after less than a year, for being corrupt. (A contemporary of Cameron's said about him that he "wouldn't steal a hot stove.")

Bates resigned after becoming increasingly detached from his work. He had little influence in the administration; Lincoln didn't request his counsel very often, and Bates didn't offer it.[14]

Chase was convinced that he deserved the presidency more than Lincoln, whom he considered his inferior. He clashed with Lincoln repeatedly and, more than once, threatened to resign unless his demands were met. Eventually Lincoln called Chase's bluff and accepted his resignation, telling a friend later, "I could not stand it any longer."[15]

Seward was a partial exception to this pattern. He stuck around for Lincoln's entire time in office and became a trusted friend and advisor. On more than one occasion, he changed Lincoln's mind about something important. But Seward came around only after months of undermining Lincoln's authority behind his back and trying to wrest political power for himself.

It's a testament to Lincoln's equanimity that he was able to work with his rivals at all, and it may well have been a sensible move for him politically. But it's not a great example of the value of exposing yourself to dissenting views. Dissent isn't all that useful from people you don't respect or from people who don't even share enough common ground with you to agree that you're supposed to be on the same team.

## IT'S HARDER THAN YOU THINK

One of the biggest reasons we fail to learn from disagreements is that we expect it to be easier than it actually is. We assume that if both people are basically reasonable and arguing in good faith, then getting to the bottom of a disagreement should be straightforward: Each person explains what they believe, and if one person can support their position with logic and evidence, then the other says, "Oh, you're right," and changes their mind. Simple!

When things don't play out that way—when one side refuses to change their mind, even after hearing what the other side considers to be a knock-down argument—everyone gets frustrated and concludes the others must be irrational.

We need to lower our expectations, by a lot. Even under ideal conditions in which everyone is well-informed, reasonable, and making a good-faith effort to explain their views and understand the other side, learning from disagreements is still hard (and conditions are almost never ideal). Here are three reasons why:

## 1. We misunderstand each other's views

While on a trip to Cairo, blogger Scott Alexander got into a pleasant conversation with a Muslim girl in a café. When she mentioned something about crazy people who believe in evolution, Alexander admitted that he was one of those "crazy people."

The girl was shocked. She replied, "But . . . monkeys don't change into humans. What on Earth makes you think monkeys can change into humans?"[16] Alexander tried to explain that the change from ape to human was a very gradual one, which occurred over many generations, and he recommended some books that might do a better job explaining the process than he could. But it was clear that she was still not buying it.

If you're already familiar with the theory of evolution, it's obvious to you that the girl in the café was misunderstanding it. But are you sure that none of the absurd-sounding ideas you've dismissed in the past aren't also misunderstandings of the real thing? Even correct ideas often sound wrong when you first hear them. The thirty-second version of an explanation is inevitably simplistic, leaving out important clarifications and nuance. There's background context you're missing, words being used in different ways than you're used to, and more.

## 2. Bad arguments inoculate us against good arguments

When we do encounter a good argument that's new to us, we often mistake it for a bad argument we're already familiar with. For example, in the previous chapter I cited cognitive psychologist Gary Klein, who studies how people change their minds in high-stakes contexts like firefighting or nursing. Klein's work has been very helpful to me in understanding how real-world decision-making works, and in recognizing some of the shortcomings in academic studies of decision-making.

Yet I ignored Klein's work for years after I first heard of him. That's because he talks about the "power of intuition," which made me associate him with the kind of people who exalt intuition as a pseudo-mystical sixth sense that deserves precedence over all other forms of evidence, including science. That's not Klein's view. By "intuition" he's simply referring to our brains' built-in pattern-matching abilities. But because I had encountered so many people saying things like "I don't care what science says—my intuition tells me ghosts are real," I automatically lumped Klein in with them.

# 3. Our beliefs are interdependent—changing one requires changing others

Suppose that Alice believes that climate change is a serious problem, and she's talking to Kevin, who disagrees. Alice could show Kevin an article saying that climate science models have made accurate predictions, but that's not likely to change Kevin's mind—even if Kevin is in scout mindset.

That's because our beliefs are all interconnected, like a web. The belief "climate change isn't real" is supported by other beliefs Kevin holds about how the world works and which sources are trustworthy. For Kevin to significantly update the belief "climate change isn't real," he'll have to also update a few of his associated beliefs, such as "Climate change skeptic media outlets are more trustworthy than the mainstream media," or "Smart people don't buy the climate science consensus." That can happen, but it will take a lot more evidence than a single article from a news source Kevin doesn't currently trust.

At the end of the previous chapter, we met Joshua Harris, the

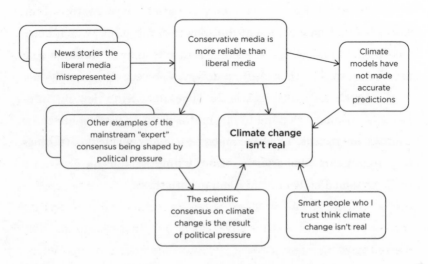

AN EXAMPLE OF INTERDEPENDENT BELIEFS

author of *I Kissed Dating Goodbye,* who began to hear from readers claiming his book had messed up their lives. The first time it began to dawn on him that his critics might have a point was in 2015. That's when it came out that several members of his church, the Covenant Life Church in Gaithersburg, Maryland, were guilty of sexually abusing minors in the congregation. Harris wasn't personally involved in the abuse, but he had known about it, and had not encouraged the victims to speak to the police.

The upsetting realization that he had mishandled that crisis rippled through Harris's web of beliefs. "That was the first time that I started realizing, you know what? You can have good intentions, and think you're making good decisions, but the effect in people's lives can be very different than you'd planned," Harris said later. That realization, in turn, sparked the thought, "Maybe there are problems with my book."[17]

During all of those years in which Harris had listened to disagreement about his book, his ability to change his mind had been bottlenecked by an unstated premise: *It's not possible to cause harm if you're well-intentioned.* Maybe he wouldn't have endorsed that belief explicitly if someone had asked, but it was there in the background all the same. And until that belief was changed, even a steady stream of complaints about his book wouldn't be enough to change the associated belief in his web: *My book isn't harmful.*

THESE THREE CHAPTERS have each presented an inversion of the way we typically think about changing our minds.

In chapter 10 ("How to Be Wrong"), we saw how most people implicitly assume that their "map" of reality is supposed to be already correct. If they have to make any changes to it, that's a sign that they messed up somewhere along the way. Scouts have the opposite assumption. We all start out with wildly incorrect maps, and over time, as we get more information, we make them somewhat more accurate. Revising your map is a sign you're doing things right.

Chapter 11 ("Lean In to Confusion") was about what to do when the world violates your theories, when other people are behaving "irrationally," or when you aren't getting the results you expected or you're surprised that someone disagrees with you. Instead of trying to smooth out the details that don't fit your worldview, like snags in a fabric, tug on them to see what they unravel.

And in this chapter, we saw how people expect it to be easy to understand disagreements and are unpleasantly surprised when they fail. But the reality is that it's hard even under the best conditions, and you should be pleasantly surprised when you actually succeed. Listening to views you disagree with, and taking them seriously enough to have a shot at changing your mind, requires mental effort, emotional effort, and, above all, patience. You have to be willing to say to yourself, "It *seems* like this person is wrong, but maybe I'm misunderstanding him—let me check," or "I still don't agree, but maybe over time I'll start to see examples of what she's talking about."

Why make a difficult task even more difficult by hearing those views from people who are unreasonable, who mock your views, and with whom you don't share any common ground? Why not give yourself the best possible shot of changing your mind, or at least being able to appreciate how a reasonable person could disagree with you? As Kelsey (the atheist journalist with the Catholic friend) put it: "If reading someone does not make me feel more compassion towards their perspective, then I keep looking."

PART V

# Rethinking
# Identity

*Chapter 13*

# How Beliefs Become Identities

O NE EVENING WHEN professor Courtney Jung was about five months pregnant, she attended a cocktail party. Sober and bored, Jung was relieved when another party guest approached her to say hello and offer congratulations on her pregnancy.[1]

However, the woman's "congratulations" quickly segued into a pitch. She was on a mission to convince Jung to breastfeed, rather than formula-feed, her upcoming baby. "Yes, well, I'll probably breastfeed," Jung said, although she hadn't yet given the matter much thought.

That response apparently lacked sufficient conviction for the breastfeeding advocate, who continued listing the many medical and emotional benefits of breastfeeding. As she pressed her case, she leaned toward Jung, out of fervor; Jung edged away, uncomfortably; and so they inched across the room throughout the night, until Jung found herself backed into a corner—literally and figuratively.

## THE "MOMMY WARS"

If you're surprised at the image of a zealot for breastfeeding, you've probably never heard of the (rather disparagingly named) "mommy wars," between mothers who believe it's vital to feed babies breast milk, and mothers who believe it's fine to feed babies formula from a bottle.

In theory, the disagreement over how much benefit an infant gets from breast milk is a straightforward scientific one. But in practice, the language of the disagreement sounds like it's describing a terrifying holy war. Bottle-feeding mothers complain of being "brainwashed by pro-breastfeeding propaganda"[2] and "bullied into losing the ability to think critically"[3] by the "Breastapo." One new mother who attended a seminar on breastfeeding said later, "I felt like I was in a North Korea indoctrination session."[4] Meanwhile, bloggers in the pro-breastfeeding camp dismiss such complaints and refer to articles questioning the merits of breast milk as a "preemptive strike on breastfeeding"[5] by "formula apologists."

After she escaped from that corner at the party that she'd been backed into, Courtney Jung started thinking about the passion and anger that people feel around breastfeeding—and how, for many people, their views on the topic have become part of their identity. That experience planted the seed of her book, *Lactivism*, in which she wrote, "The truth is that in the United States, breastfeeding has become much more than simply a way to feed a baby. It is a way of showing the world who you are and what you believe in."[6]

# WHAT IT MEANS FOR SOMETHING TO BE PART OF YOUR IDENTITY

It's an age-old rule of etiquette that you're not supposed to make conversation about politics or religion. That's because we all know that people's political and religious views are often part of their *identities*. When someone criticizes a belief that's part of your identity, it's antagonizing. It's like someone insulting your family or stomping on your country's flag. Even just discovering that someone disagrees with you about an identity-laden belief is like finding out they're on a rival team: "Oh, so you're one of *them*."

But politics and religion are merely the most well-known examples. Your decision to breastfeed or bottle-feed, your choice of programming language, and your attitude toward capitalism can all be part of your identity. They may not come with official labels like "Democrat" or "Southern Baptist," but they can spark the same passionate, combative, and defensive reactions all the same.

Agreeing with a belief isn't the same thing as identifying with it. Many people are pro-science in the sense that they would agree with the statement "Science is the best way of learning how the world works, and it deserves a lot of funding and respect." But only a fraction of those people have science as part of their identity, to the point of feeling hostile toward people who don't appreciate science, or wearing T-shirts emblazoned with popular pro-science slogans such as "Science doesn't care about your beliefs" or "Science: It works, bitches."

Anything can become part of our identity. Yet some issues seem more susceptible than others. Why is that? Why are debates over the health risks of baby formula so much more heated than debates over the health risks of air pollution? Why are there many options if you want to buy a "Proud Introvert" T-shirt, but not a single "Proud Extrovert" T-shirt to be found?

The science on identity is still evolving, but I've observed two things that turn a belief into an identity: Feeling embattled, and feeling proud.


## FEELING EMBATTLED

Beliefs crystallize into identities through the feeling of being under siege from a hostile world, much the way prolonged pressure bonds carbon atoms together to form a diamond. Think of minority religious sects or oft-mocked subcultures like "preppers," who believe it's worth preparing for a natural disaster or societal collapse. Being mocked, persecuted, or otherwise stigmatized for our beliefs makes us want to stand up for them all the more, and gives us a sense of solidarity with the other people standing with us.

It might seem like every issue must have a dominant majority and an embattled minority. But both sides of an issue can genuinely view their side as the embattled one. That's what's happening in the "mommy wars." Formula-feeders feel like they're constantly on the defensive, forced to explain why they're not breastfeeding and feeling judged as bad mothers, silently or openly. (It's not just their imagination. One 2001 poll found that two-thirds of breastfeeding mothers "feel sorry for" the children of mothers who don't breastfeed.⁷)

Breastfeeders feel embattled, too, for different reasons. They complain about a society set up to make life difficult for them, in which most workplaces lack a comfortable place to pump breast milk, and in which an exposed breast in public draws offended stares and whispers. Some argue that this is a more significant form of oppression than that faced by the other side. "Because let's face it," one breastfeeding mother wrote to bottle-feeders, "while you may feel some mom guilt when you hear 'breast is best,' no one has ever been kicked out of a restaurant for bottle feeding their baby."⁸

Or take atheists and Christians. Atheists feel embattled because of the amount of discrimination they face in the United States. Many have been told they are immoral. They often talk about "coming out" as atheists, after having spent a long time feeling obliged to hide their stigmatized views. The most recent Gallup poll in 2019 found that 40 percent of Americans would not vote for a well-qualified member of their own party if that person was an atheist. (For comparison, the corresponding percentages of people who said they would not vote for a Jewish candidate and a Catholic candidate were 7 percent and 5 percent, respectively.)[9]

Unlike atheists, evangelical Christians are more likely to live in families and communities who share their faith, so they aren't embattled in the same sense. Nevertheless, they feel increasingly alienated by the legal and cultural changes in America over the last fifty years, such as legal abortion, gay marriage, and sexualized content in the media. "The culture war is over—and we lost," one Christian leader lamented in a book titled *Prepare: Living Your Faith in an Increasingly Hostile Culture.*[10]

## FEELING PROUD

Beliefs also become part of your identity when they come to represent some virtue you take pride in. For example, for many women, the belief that breastfeeding is important signals their connection to their baby and their willingness to sacrifice for motherhood. Breastfeeding is the "ultimate representation of mother, connection and love," as one poster put it at a pro-breastfeeding conference.[11] Conversely, for many women who reject the imperative to breastfeed, that's a refusal to be shackled to the constraints of biology, constraints that tend to impose much more harshly on a new mother's freedom than a father's. "On a more ideological level, we're eschewing the nipple because of how breastfeeding stymies the progress of feminism," one journalist wrote of her and her partner's choice not to breastfeed.[12]

Or consider cryptocurrency. For many true believers, the appeal was never just about getting rich. It was about changing the world. To believe in the potential of crypto was to be a rebel, to fight for humanity's freedom from the tyranny of powerful centralized institutions. As one early Bitcoin enthusiast put it: "You're helping usher in a whole new financial era! You're depriving the big banks of their unearned power over the masses by helping build a currency controlled by everyone!"

Both self-identified optimists and pessimists take pride in their way of seeing the world. Optimists often talk as if holding positive beliefs is a sign of virtue: "Despite how easy it would be to choose cynicism, I choose to believe in humanity's inherent goodness," one optimist declared.[13] Meanwhile, pessimists see themselves as savvy and sophisticated, unlike those insipid optimists: "In investing, a bull sounds like a reckless cheerleader, while a bear sounds like a sharp mind who has dug past the headlines," one investor observed.[14]

Feeling proud and feeling embattled often feed into each other. For example, polyamorous people can sound smug or superior about their lifestyle choice, acknowledged one polyamorous blogger named Eli Heina Dadabhoy. But that's an understandable reaction to the hostility that polyamorous people are constantly barraged with. "When the world around you is constantly shouting about how wrong you are, declaring your superiority can feel like a legitimate response, the only way to oppose such strong negative messaging," Dadabhoy said.[15]

## THE "PROBABILITY WARS"

No question is so dry or esoteric that it's immune to the forces of identity. Don't believe me? Allow me to introduce you to the long-running debate between the frequentists and the Bayesians, two camps of statisticians who analyze data differently. At the root of the debate is a simple philosophical disagreement.

Frequentists define the probability of an event objectively, in terms of how frequently it would occur in a long series of trials. A frequentist would say that the probability of a coin flip coming up heads is one-half, because if you could flip the coin an infinite number of times, half of the outcomes would be heads.

Bayesianism is based around a theorem called Bayes's rule, named after the Reverend Thomas Bayes, the eighteenth-century philosopher and statistician who first came up with it. Bayesians define the probability of an event subjectively, in terms of how confident someone is that an event will occur. Remember the exercises we did in chapter 6, in which we learned to quantify our confidence in a claim by thinking about what bets we would be willing to take on it? A Bayesian would call those "probabilities"; a frequentist would not.

You might expect these debates to play out exclusively in technical language buried in academic journal articles. But for decades, there was an annual Bayesian conference where attendees sang songs cheering for Bayesianism and booing frequentism. Here's a sample stanza, meant to be sung to the tune of "The Battle Hymn of the Republic":

*Mine eyes have seen the glory of the Reverend Thomas Bayes*
*He is stamping out frequentists and their incoherent ways . . .*
*Glory, glory, probability!*
*Glory, glory, subjectivity!*
*His troops are marching on.*[16]

Obviously, this song is tongue-in-cheek. But like all good observational humor, it's based on a seed of truth. If you browse the statistics blogosphere, you'll find Bayesians and frequentists accusing each other of irrational prejudice, complaining about fundamentalist frequentists, orthodox frequentists, anti-Bayesian prejudice, smug Bayesians, angry anti-Bayesians, Bayesian cheerleaders, and die-hard Bayesians. One statistician even renounced Bayesianism and wrote a blog post titled "Breathing Some Fresh Air Outside of the Bayesian Church."[17]

Like many identity battles, the probability wars began with Bayesians feeling embattled back in the 1980s. They had to be careful not to mention the "B-word" very often, lest they be seen as troublemakers. At least one professor who favored Bayesian methods was pushed out of his department for his dissent. "We were always an oppressed minority, trying to get some recognition,"[18] remembered Alan Gelfand, one of the early adopters of Bayesianism. Now the tables have turned. In the last fifteen years, Bayesianism has become popular, and frequentists are the ones feeling marginalized—so much so that one frequentist statistician titled her blog post "Frequentists in Exile."[19]

The probability wars have even spilled out of academia and into the nerdier parts of the internet. In 2012, the webcomic *XKCD* published a strip on the difference between frequentist and Bayesian approaches that poked fun at the former.[20] The reaction was so heated that one commenter joked, "Next time make it Israelis and Palestinians, it'll be less controversial."[21]

## SIGNS A BELIEF MIGHT BE AN IDENTITY

Sometimes it's obvious when a belief has become an identity. If you have "proud vegan" in the first line of your Instagram bio, all your friends are vegan, you go to vegan rallies, and you wear vegan buttons and T-shirts, then that's a pretty open-and-shut case. But for every obvious case like that one, there are many subtler ones, beliefs that may not come with a label or official membership in a group, but that we nevertheless take personally. To notice them, be on the lookout for any of the following signs:

## 1. Using the phrase "I believe"

Prefacing a claim with the phrase "I believe" is a tip-off that it's important to your identity. Think of statements like "I believe in optimism," or "I believe that people are more good than bad," or "I believe that women are changing the world." That seemingly redundant phrase—shouldn't it go without saying that you believe your own statements?—signals that you're not simply describing the world, you're defining yourself. "People can change" is a statement about how you think the world works. But *"I believe people can change"* is a statement about *you*, about what kind of person you are—generous, forgiving, compassionate.

## 2. Getting annoyed when an ideology is criticized

"I F*cking Love Science" (IFLS) is a popular Facebook page that shares pro-science memes, cartoons, and slogans such as "Got polio? Me neither. Thanks, science." In a discussion on the "I F*cking Love Science" Facebook page, one commenter named Jessica mentioned that even scientists are often resistant to facts that contradict their beliefs. "Humans are humans," she said.

As criticisms of science go, this was pretty mild (and undeniably true). But another commenter named Warren bristled at this insult to the honor of science. He retorted: "Uh, no. A thousand times no. That's not how science works. Ever."[22]

When you feel the urge to step in and defend a group or belief system against perceived criticism, chances are good that your identity is involved. I recently spotted an article titled "Why Atheists Are Not as Rational as Some Like to Think." I felt a spike of defensiveness, and readied myself to rebut the article's claims, even before opening it. The irony is that I've made this exact same point myself—that some self-identified atheists incorrectly think their atheism proves that they're "rational." But the fact that the argument was coming from an outsider, and seemed intended to discredit atheists, automatically raised my hackles.

## 3. Defiant language

People who have science as a big part of their identity sometimes wear T-shirts or display signs that say "Proud Nerd" or "Stand up for science." Mothers who feed their babies formula write blog posts with titles like "The Unapologetic Case for Formula-Feeding,"[23] or "Standing Up for Formula Feeders," or refer to themselves as a "Fearless Formula Feeder."[24] Meanwhile, breastfeeding mothers say things like, "Woe betide any breastfeeding mother who openly admits to having preference, knowledge and even *gasp* pride in nursing her child."

Proud, standing up, unapologetic, fearless—defiant language like this is a sign that you see yourself as an embattled minority viewpoint facing off against a society that is trying to silence, oppress, or shame you.

## 4. A righteous tone

You may have noticed the righteous flourishes we sometimes add to the ends of our statements: *Period. Full Stop. End of story. End of discussion. It's that simple.* Or how about the currently popular practice of breaking up a sentence with an emphatic period after every word? *You don't support this policy? You. Are. Part. Of. The. Problem.*

Economics columnist Megan McArdle came up with the perfect analogy for what the righteous tone of voice is meant to convey. "The messages that make you feel great about yourself (and of course, your like-minded friends) are the ones that suggest you're a moral giant striding boldly across the landscape, wielding your inescapable ethical logic," she wrote.[25]

## 5. Gatekeeping

If you search online for the phrase "You can't call yourself a feminist," you'll find a wide variety of conditions people have unilaterally imposed on the use of that label, such as "You can't call yourself a feminist if you're not intersectional,"[26] and "You can't call yourself a feminist if you don't believe in the right to abortion."[27]

When a label is more than just a practical description of your beliefs—when it feels like a status symbol or a source of pride—then the question of who else gets to wear that label actually matters. It becomes important to police the identity's boundaries.

As "I F*cking Love Science" (IFLS) became increasingly popular, and its follower count reached the tens of millions, some other pro-science people started to get annoyed. "The IFLS view of 'science' is so shallow—it's just a bunch of memes and photos of galaxies! That's not what it means to love science!" they grumbled to each other. The most famous rant against IFLS fans came from a cartoonist named Kris Wilson: "People who truly love science spend their lives studying the tedious little bits as well as the big flashy facts," he wrote. "You don't love science. You're looking at its butt when it walks by."[28]

## 6. Schadenfreude

Imagine seeing an article that begins with the following sentence: "The [group name] conference this weekend fell apart spectacularly due to bickering and poor planning." Is there an ideological group's name that could go in that sentence that would cause you to grin in anticipation of the sweet pleasure of schadenfreude awaiting you in the article?

Deriving pleasure from news that humiliates some ideological group you disagree with is a sign of an "oppositional identity"—an identity defined by what it opposes. It's easy to overlook these because they often don't involve labels of their own, but they can distort your judgment all the same. If you love to hate hippies, techies, libertarians, fundamentalists, or any other ideological group, that gives you a motive to believe anything that seems to discredit their worldview. Find vegans annoying? You'll welcome any news that a vegan diet is unhealthy. Enjoy sneering at "techbros"? You're probably not going to look too critically at any hit pieces about tech companies.

## 7. Epithets

You've heard the standard epithets in political and cultural "discourse": social justice warriors, feminazis, neckbeards, snowflakes, Woke Brigade, libtards, and more. The "mommy wars" have epithets like "lactivists, "Breastapo," and "defensive formula feeders (DFFs)." Child-free people sometimes refer to people with children as "breeders" or to children as "spawn." Then there are the all-purpose epithets: idiots, loonies, morons, crazies . . .

If you use epithets like these in talking about a particular issue, that's a sign you're viewing it as a fight between people, not ideas. That doesn't necessarily mean your position on the issue is wrong or that the other side is right, but it does mean that your identity is probably coloring your judgment.

## 8. Having to defend your view

The more you've argued a position to other people, especially in public, the more it's become linked to your ego and reputation, and the harder it is to abandon that position later.

If you're known at work for being a proponent of growing fast instead of growing slow, or for being bearish instead of bullish on a certain project, or for being an advocate of "data-driven" policies instead of gut judgments, those positions can feel like part of your identity. Same thing if you're the one in your group of friends who's known for being a proponent of CrossFit, or alternative medicine, or homeschooling.

The problem is compounded if you've had to defend your view against unfair or aggressive criticism. Now, changing your mind feels like letting the enemy win. One woman who used to identify as child-free then decided to have children after all confessed that changing her mind had been especially hard: "Because people kept saying 'Oh you'll change your mind!' and it felt so invalidating. So then it really pissed me off to prove them right."[29]

THE PROBLEM WITH our tendency to turn beliefs into identities isn't that it pits us against each other. At least, that's not the problem I'm concerned with here. (Getting along with each other is important, too—it's just outside the scope of this book.)

The problem with identity is that it wrecks your ability to think clearly. Identifying with a belief makes you feel like you have to be ready to defend it, which motivates you to focus your attention on collecting evidence in its favor. Identity makes you reflexively reject arguments that feel like attacks on you or the status of your group. It turns empirical questions such as "How large are the health benefits of breastfeeding?" into questions that are much more emotionally fraught and difficult to think clearly about: "Am I a good mother? Am I a good feminist? Will my friends judge me? Was 'my side' vindicated or humiliated?"

And when a belief is part of your identity, it becomes far harder to change your mind, even when the facts change dramatically. In the 1980s, evidence began to accumulate that HIV can be transmitted in breast milk. The Centers for Disease Control and Prevention (CDC) quickly issued a recommendation that mothers with HIV should avoid breastfeeding. But breastfeeding advocates rejected the warning.[30] Breast milk was inherently good, wholesome, and natural; it *couldn't* be dangerous. Plus, they were suspicious of the motives of the CDC, with whom they had been butting heads for years. The CDC was probably under the thrall of the pro-formula lobby, they figured.

It took until 1998, and the accumulation of a mountain of additional evidence, for the leading pro-breastfeeding organizations to accept that HIV can be transmitted through breast milk, and to acknowledge that fact to new mothers in their advocacy for breastfeeding. By that time, many babies had already contracted the disease unnecessarily. Allowing beliefs to turn into identities can be literally deadly.

*Chapter 14*

# Hold Your Identity Lightly

I WAS ALARMED WHEN I first started noticing how much power our identities have over our thinking. That was about ten years ago, around the time a popular essay on this topic came out titled "Keep Your Identity Small," by tech investor Paul Graham. In it, Graham pointed to the problem I described in the previous chapter and warned, "The more labels you have for yourself, the dumber they make you."[1] Inspired in part by Graham's essay, I resolved to avoid identifying myself with any ideology, movement, or group.

This plan of mine quickly ran into problems.

For starters, avoiding labels proved awkward. At the time I followed a more or less vegan diet; when someone was planning a dinner party and asked me about my dietary restrictions, it was a lot easier and less confusing to just say "I'm a vegan" than to say "Well, I don't eat eggs, or dairy, or meat . . ." Plus, having a restricted diet was already enough of an imposition on my friends and family. When other people referred to me as "a vegan," I sure as hell wasn't going to jump in and correct them: "Actually, I prefer to be called a *person who eats a vegan diet.*"

More seriously, there were causes I wanted to help, groups and movements I genuinely believed were doing good, like effective altruism.* If I wasn't willing to identify myself publicly with a movement, it was going to be hard to help spread its ideas.

I did end up with a few lasting changes from my foray into identitylessness. For example, I stopped referring to myself as a Democrat, even though I'm officially registered to vote as a Democrat. But I ultimately accepted that there's a limit to how far you can take this process. What you need to be able to do is keep those identities from colonizing your thoughts and values. I call this "holding your identity lightly."

## WHAT IT MEANS TO HOLD YOUR IDENTITY LIGHTLY

Holding an identity lightly means thinking of it in a matter-of-fact way, rather than as a central source of pride and meaning in your life. It's a description, not a flag to be waved proudly.

For example, a friend of mine named Ben used to identify as a feminist. When he heard arguments against feminism, he felt like his tribe was under attack; he frequently found himself getting defensive, and felt unable to resist jumping into arguments to respond to feminism's critics.

So Ben decided to hold his identity more lightly. He'll still usually answer "yes" when people ask him if he's a feminist, because that label is still a basically accurate description of his views. But internally, he now thinks of himself more as a "person who agrees with most ideas that are part of the feminist consensus."

That might sound like a minor distinction, but it feels very different from the inside. "I have an easier time approaching these debates

---

* This is the movement I mentioned in chapter 12, which uses reason and evidence to find the most effective ways of doing good.

on their merits, so I've changed my mind on a small number of issues," Ben says. Even more importantly, it's squashed what he calls the "Someone is wrong on the internet!" impulse, the urge to jump into unproductive online arguments about feminism.

Someone who holds her political identity lightly is happy when her party wins an election. But she's happy because she expects her party to do a better job leading the country, not because the other side suffered a humiliating defeat. She's not tempted to taunt the losers, the way some Democrats gloated over "right-wing temper tantrums"[2] after Obama's 2012 win or the way some Republicans relished "liberal tears" after Donald Trump's 2016 win.

Holding an identity lightly means treating that identity as *contingent*, saying to yourself, "I'm a liberal, for as long as it continues to seem to me that liberalism is just." Or "I'm a feminist, but I would abandon the movement if for some reason I came to believe it was causing net harm." It means maintaining a sense of your own beliefs and values, independent of the tribe's beliefs and values, and acknowledging—at least in the privacy of your own head—the places where those two things diverge.

## "I'M NOT A ME-TOO REPUBLICAN"

During his life, Barry Goldwater was called "Mr. Republican," a "GOP Hero," "the father of modern American conservativism," and "the hero of America's conservative movement." In one sense, the label was accurate—Goldwater was a fervent anticommunist who believed in small government and states' rights. But Goldwater held his Republican identity unusually lightly. At his very first rally for his Senate campaign, he announced, "I'm not a me-too Republican," warning his audience that he wouldn't fall in line if he didn't agree with the party.[3]

It was a campaign promise he would keep for his whole career.

In the 1970s, when Republican president Richard Nixon fell under scrutiny for illegal wiretapping and other crimes, Goldwater publicly urged him to be honest. When the White House tried to portray the investigation as a partisan effort by the Democrats to smear the president, Goldwater defended the integrity of the Democratic senator leading the investigation ("I haven't detected a partisan statement yet from him").[4] And when Nixon continued to stonewall as the evidence against him mounted, it was Goldwater who led a delegation to the White House to inform Nixon that he had lost the support of both the House and the Senate, and should count on being convicted. Nixon resigned the next day.[5]

In the 1980s, when Republican president Ronald Reagan claimed he had been unaware of the Iran-Contra Affair, Goldwater was skeptical and said so. A journalist who covered the Goldwater beat during that time remembered, "That was typical Goldwater—letting his perception of the truth prevail over partisanship or friendship."[6]

Although Goldwater never abandoned his core conservative principles, his views on specific issues did occasionally change. He came to see gay rights as logically entailed by his own principles: "You don't have to agree with it, but they have a constitutional right to be gay," Goldwater said.[7] That did not endear him to his fellow conservatives. Neither did his decision to support abortion in the 1980s, when he voted to defend the Supreme Court's pro-choice ruling in *Roe v. Wade*.

In 1994, Democratic president Bill Clinton was under investigation for suspicious investments in the Whitewater Development Corporation. Republicans charged that he and his wife, Hillary Clinton, had been involved in serious crimes, including fraud. By this point Goldwater was an eighty-five-year-old with a head of white hair who leaned on a cane for support. He was no great fan of the president. He once told a reporter that Clinton didn't know a "goddamn thing" about foreign policy, and added, "The best thing Clinton could do—I think I wrote him a letter about this, but I'm not sure—is to shut up."[8]

Nevertheless, he spent a night poring over the details of the Whitewater accusations, wanting to form a fair take. The next day, he summoned reporters to his house so he could share his conclusion: the Republicans didn't have a case against Clinton. "I haven't heard anything yet that says this is all that big of a deal," he announced.[9] Other Republicans were less than pleased. Angry calls poured into GOP headquarters and radio shows, and one conservative talk show host groused, "Goldwater should know that when your party is hot on the trail and barking up the tree, you don't call off the dogs."[10]

Goldwater's response to the criticism was characteristically blunt. "You know something?" he said. "I don't give a damn."

# COULD YOU PASS AN IDEOLOGICAL TURING TEST?

In 1950, pioneering computer scientist Alan Turing proposed a test that could be used to decide if an artificial intelligence is really conscious: Could it pass as human? If a series of judges were to converse with both an artificial intelligence and a real human, would they be able to tell reliably which was which?

That's now called the Turing test. The *ideological* Turing test, suggested by economist Bryan Caplan, is based on similar logic.[11] It's a way to determine if you really understand an ideology: Can you explain it *as a believer would*, convincingly enough that other people couldn't tell the difference between you and a genuine believer?

If you think Haskell is the best programming language, can you explain why someone might hate it?

If you're in favor of legal abortion, can you explain why someone wouldn't be?

If you think it's clear that climate change is a serious problem, can you explain why someone might be skeptical?

In theory, you would consult believers from the other side to see if you passed the test. But that's not always feasible. It's time-consuming, and you may not be able to easily find an audience on the other side whom you trust to give your attempt a good-faith listen. Most of the time, I treat the ideological Turing test as a kind of "North Star," an ideal to guide my thinking: Does my characterization of the other side at least sound like something they *might* actually say or endorse?

Measured against that standard, most attempts fall obviously short.* For a case in point, consider one liberal blogger's attempt at modeling the conservative worldview. She begins, "If I can say anything at this bleak hour, with the world splitting at its seams, it's this: conservatives, I understand you. It may not be something you expect to hear from a liberal, but I do. I understand you."[12] An earnest start, but her attempt to empathize with conservatives quickly devolves into caricature. Here's her impression of the conservative take on various subjects:

> *On capitalism*: "Those at the top should have as much as possible. That's the natural order ... It's not a secret; just don't be lazy. Why is everyone so poor and lazy?"
>
> *On feminists*: "Those women make noise, make demands, take up space ... Who do they think they are?"
>
> *On abortion*: "What a travesty ... women making these kinds of radical decisions for themselves."
>
> *On queer and transgender people*: "They shouldn't exist. They're mistakes. They must be. But wait, no. God doesn't make mistakes ... Oh dear. You don't know what's happening anymore, and you don't like it. It makes you feel dizzy. Out of control."

---

* That includes many attempts by the test's advocates themselves. I once saw someone talk about how important it is to be able to pass an ideological Turing test, and then add, "Of course, people often don't want to do this, because they're afraid they'll change their minds." Does that sound like a reason that someone who didn't want to do the ideological Turing test would actually give? Not to me.

It's hardly necessary to run this text by an audience of conservatives to be able to predict that it would flunk their ideological Turing test. Her "conservative" take on capitalism sounds like a cartoon villain. The language about women taking up space and making decisions for themselves is how liberals frame these issues, not conservatives. And her impression of a conservative suddenly realizing his views on transgender and queer people are internally inconsistent ("They're mistakes . . . But wait, no. God doesn't make mistakes.") just looks like a potshot she couldn't resist taking.

She can't help but slip back into her own voice as a liberal-who-hates-conservativism, even while trying to speak as a conservative. The overall effect is reminiscent of that joke about the schoolboy who handed his teacher a note from his "mother": *Dear Teacher, Please excuse Billy from school today because he is sick. Sincerely, My mom.*

The ideological Turing test is typically seen as a test of your knowledge: How thoroughly do you understand the other side's beliefs? But it also serves as an emotional test: Do you hold your identity lightly enough to be able to avoid caricaturing your ideological opponents?

Even being willing to attempt the ideological Turing test at all is significant. People who hold their identity strongly often recoil at the idea of trying to "understand" a viewpoint they find disgustingly wrong or harmful. It feels like you're giving aid and comfort to the enemy. But if you want to have a shot at actually changing people's point of view rather than merely being disgusted at how wrong they are, understanding those views is a must.

# A STRONGLY HELD IDENTITY PREVENTS YOU FROM PERSUADING OTHERS

In March 2014, television actress Kristin Cavallari announced that she and her husband had decided not to vaccinate their child. They had done a lot of research, read a lot of books, and they felt the risks were not worth it. In response, a journalist sneered, "Oh, books—you read *books*, you say?" He then addressed his audience: "For the last time, stop listening to bubble-headed TV stars and start listening to doctors. Vaccinate your f*cking kids or you're a shitty parent. Period."[13]

But who, exactly, is his audience? What hypothetical person will be won over by being sneered at and called a shitty parent, without even being given any convincing reasons their fears are unfounded?

Another journalist reacted to Cavallari's announcement by writing an educational guide to vaccines.[14] Sounds like a promising step, at first pass—but the guide's language drips with scorn for vaccine skepticism ("anti-scientific gibberish") and condescension to its readers ("Vaccines are safe. Yes, read that again.").

It also completely misses the point. To make the case for the safety of vaccines, the journalist cites the Department of Health and refers to "scientific testing" that has proven vaccines to be safe. But a vaccine skeptic already *knows* that mainstream medical institutions claim vaccines are safe. The problem is that she doesn't trust those institutions. Citing them as authorities won't do anything other than confirm her suspicion that you don't get it.

Bottom line: it's hard to change someone's mind when you feel morally and intellectually superior to them. As Megan McArdle memorably put it: "It took me years of writing on the Internet to learn what is nearly an iron law of commentary: The better your message makes you feel about yourself, the less likely it is that you are convincing anyone else."[15]

## UNDERSTANDING THE OTHER SIDE MAKES IT POSSIBLE TO CHANGE MINDS

Adam Mongrain is a journalist who once felt nothing but contempt for vaccine skeptics. "It wasn't that I knew they were wrong about vaccines," he said. "It was more than that. I believed myself intellectually and morally superior to those people . . . I mastered a face, a kind of appalled, disapproving look for any time anybody even broached the subject of vaccine skepticism."[16]

Mongrain's attitude began shifting after he became friends with, and later married, a single mother who was staunchly opposed to vaccinating her child. He couldn't dismiss her as an idiot. Before the subject of vaccines ever came up, he had already gotten to know her and respect her as an intelligent and caring person. Instead, Mongrain started trying to wrap his mind around *how* an intelligent and caring person could be a vaccine skeptic. As their relationship progressed, he realized several things.

First, it's not crazy for someone to be skeptical of the expert consensus on vaccines. There are tragic precedents for caution—lead paint, tobacco, and bloodletting are all things the public was once assured were safe. So when experts say confidently, "Trust us, vaccines are completely safe," can you really blame anyone for being skeptical? Mongrain's wife had personal reasons to mistrust doctors as well. When she was a teenager, she had suffered a bad drug trip, and worried about lingering side effects of the drugs on her brain. When she went to see a doctor, she left frustrated at the way he dismissed her concerns without listening to her.

Once you're already primed to be suspicious of vaccines and mainstream medicine, it's easy to find evidence confirming those suspicions. There's a huge alternative medicine industry churning out articles about children becoming autistic after getting their shots. In fact, Mongrain's sister-in-law was part of that industry. She was a self-described "naturopath" who had studied vaccines extensively and believed they were toxic. When Mongrain's wife felt torn about vaccination, she would talk to her sister, and come away with her vaccine skepticism renewed.

None of this behavior is unique to vaccine skeptics, Mongrain realized. Reading sources that confirm your beliefs, trusting people whom you're close to—everyone does that. It's just an unfortunate fact that this universal tendency sometimes yields harmful results.

Once he felt like he could understand the antivaccine position, Mongrain looked for opportunities to broach the subject with his wife without being a condescending jerk. He found one in the summer of 2015. That's when he learned that a vaccine called Pandemrix had been found to trigger narcolepsy in children—a fact that the medical community and the mainstream media had been slow to acknowledge out of a fear of giving ammunition to the antivaxxers.

The medical ship didn't take too long to right itself, fortunately, but Mongrain felt that the story was still a legitimate concession he could make to his wife's concerns. "A story like Pandemrix allowed me to engage her in good faith, to admit that sometimes medicine makes bad calls and that the media can be complicit," he said. "I brought it up to my wife to show that I care about her worries, that I don't think they are beyond the pale."[17]

Acknowledging the weaknesses in your "side" can go a long way toward showing someone from the other side that you're not just a zealot parroting dogma, and that you might be worth listening to. After several such low-stakes, nonconfrontational, good-faith conversations with Mongrain about vaccines, his wife decided of her own accord to sign her daughter up for vaccinations later that year.

# IS HOLDING YOUR IDENTITY LIGHTLY COMPATIBLE WITH ACTIVISM?

We've seen how a strongly held identity distorts your ability to think. The sense of absolute moral clarity, of being on the side of good, battling evil—those are ideal conditions for soldier mindset.

But what if those are also the ideal conditions for activism? Changing the world requires passion. Dedication. Sacrifice. The soldier may have a biased, black-and-white worldview, but at least he's full of the kind of passion that moves mountains. Whereas the scout, while an admirably fair-minded thinker, is just too dispassionate and tangled up in nuances to ever take action.

Or so the common wisdom goes. Let's see how it holds up to scrutiny.

First, notice that not all ways of "taking action" are equal. Some actions are more impactful than others, and some actions are better at affirming your identity (filling you up with that satisfying "fighting for the righteous side" glow). Occasionally, there's an action that scores well on both dimensions. Picture a passionate Democrat, working on the campaign of the Democratic candidate for office in a swing state. His days and nights spent fighting for victory are both identity-affirming and impactful—in a close race for an important seat, the campaign team's efforts really can make a difference.

Usually, however, activists face trade-offs between identity and impact—and the more lightly you hold your identity, the more you can focus exclusively on actions with the highest impact. In chapter 10, I described how the Humane League pivoted away from their original approach of confrontational protests on behalf of lab animals to a strategy of negotiating with major corporations for more humane treatment of farm animals. That pivot boosted their impact by a factor of millions in terms of the number of animals affected—but through an identity lens, making nice with an "evil corporation" isn't all that appealing.

Many identity-affirming actions, in turn, have little real-world impact. Think of someone putting bumper stickers on their car or yelling at strangers online for holding the wrong views. Some identity-affirming actions even have *negative* impact—they're counterproductive for your goals. You've probably known activists who spend the bulk of their energy fighting with other activists they're already 95 percent in agreement with over that remaining 5 percent sliver of disagreement. Sigmund Freud called it the "narcissism of small differences"—for the purposes of affirming your identity, the most tempting fight is often the one that helps distinguish you from your ideological neighbors.

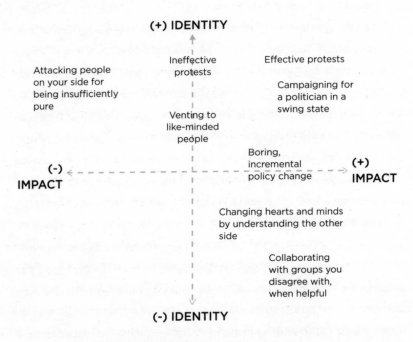

EXAMPLES OF HOW VARIOUS TYPES OF ACTIVISM SCORE
ON THE "IDENTITY" AND "IMPACT" DIMENSIONS

An effective activist must hold their identity lightly enough to be able to make clear-eyed assessments of the best ways to achieve their goals while still being able to work passionately toward those goals. For a shining example of what that can look like, consider the story of a small group of scouts whose efforts turned the tide of AIDS: the citizen scientists.

# THE CITIZEN SCIENTISTS AND THE AIDS CRISIS

In chapter 7, we met a band of AIDS activists in New York in the 1990s called the Treatment Action Group. They lived their lives against the background of a ticking clock; their friends and lovers were dying around them at a devastating rate, and most of them had the virus themselves.

When the depressing news hit in 1993 that the drug AZT was no more effective than a placebo, it sparked an important update for the activists. Previously, they had been pressuring the government to release new drugs that seemed promising right away, instead of going through the standard testing pipeline, which can take years. They now realized that had been a mistake born of desperation. "I felt I learned an important lesson," said member David Barr, "which is that as a treatment activist, to the greatest extent possible, let study results determine the policy positions I support and for which I advocate. My hopes and dreams and fears should not guide that which I advocate for."[18] Moving forward, their mandate became: *Get the science right.*

None of them were scientists themselves. Barr was a lawyer; other activists worked in finance or photography or screenwriting. But they were extremely motivated learners. They started with Immunology 101 textbooks, meeting up every week for what they dubbed "science club," giving each other assignments and maintaining a glossary of all the jargon they were unfamiliar with.

They also dove into the politics of government research, familiarizing themselves with how funding was structured and how the drug trials were conducted. The disorganization they discovered alarmed them. "It sort of felt like reaching the Wizard of Oz," said one activist named Mark Harrington. "You've gotten to the center of the whole system and there's just this schmuck behind a curtain."[19]

The more they learned, the more they realized this fight couldn't be won with their current brand of activism. They had been focused on attention-grabbing protests, like blocking traffic and chaining themselves to politicians' desks. One night, they even snuck over to the home of conservative senator Jesse Helms and, under the cover of darkness, enveloped his house in a giant condom.

But to improve the way drugs were being developed and tested, they would need to be on the inside, working with bureaucrats and scientists at the National Institutes of Health (NIH). That decision was not popular with their fellow activists, most of whom were still furious at the government for its sluggish and, at times, apathetic response to the AIDS crisis. "There was this sort of pseudo-analogy that the NIH was like the Pentagon or something—that we shouldn't meet with them and that they were bad or evil," Harrington recalled.[20]

To tell the truth, it was a bittersweet shift for the Treatment Action Group, too. They were "crossing over" from being outside the structures of power, to inside—and in the process, sacrificing some of their ideological purity. "I knew that we would never be so pure and fervent in our belief that we were right, because we were actually going to be engaged and, therefore, be more responsible for some of the things that actually happened," Harrington said.[21]

That willingness to relinquish ideological purity paid off. The "citizen scientists" were so knowledgeable about the cutting edge of AIDS research that it didn't take long for the scientists at NIH to start taking their proposals seriously. One of those proposals was for a new kind of study called a "large simple trial," which one of the activists named Spencer Cox had discovered while teaching himself study design. With a sufficiently large number of patients, the study could give them answers about a drug's effectiveness much more quickly—in just months, instead of years—without sacrificing rigor.

Because they now had the Food and Drug Administration's ear, they were able to convince the FDA commissioner to take their study design plan to the drug companies, which in turn agreed to use a modified version of Cox's design to test the latest batch of AIDS drugs.

The results were announced at a medical conference in January 1996. They were dramatic. One drug kept patients' viral load below detectable levels for up to two years. Another reduced mortality by half. In combination, they represented a stay of execution for AIDS patients.

As Spencer Cox sat in the audience staring at those results on the slide, his eyes welled up with tears. "We did it," he said. "We're going to live."[22] Over the next two years, mortality from AIDS in the United States plummeted by 60 percent. It wasn't over, not by a long shot, but the tide had finally turned.

COOPERATION WITH GOVERNMENT scientists was what ultimately reversed the spread of AIDS. But holding your identity lightly doesn't mean always choosing cooperation over disruption. Those early, disruptive protests played a crucial role in making the public aware of AIDS and pressuring the government to put more resources into fighting it. To be an effective activist you need to be able to perceive when it will be most impactful to cooperate, and when it will be most impactful to disrupt, on a case-by-case basis.

Holding your identity lightly is what allows you to make those judgment calls as well as possible. It's not a favor you do for other people, for the sake of being nice or civil. Holding your identity lightly is a favor to yourself—a way to keep your mind flexible, unconstrained by identity, and free to follow the evidence wherever it leads.

*Chapter 15*

# A Scout Identity

ONE NIGHT IN 1970, Susan Blackmore found herself on the ceiling looking down at her own body.

Blackmore was a freshman at Oxford University, studying psychology and physiology. Like many freshmen in college, she had begun experimenting with drugs and found them mind-opening. But it was that particular trip, during which Blackmore experienced her consciousness leaving her body, floating up to the ceiling, and then soaring around the world, that changed her life.

It had to be paranormal, Blackmore reasoned, proof that there was more to the universe and to human consciousness than mainstream scientists knew. She decided to switch her academic focus to parapsychology in order to obtain scientific evidence of the paranormal phenomena she now believed were real.[1]

Blackmore began pursuing a PhD and spent years running experiments. She tested people for telepathy, for precognition, for clairvoyance. She tried running her experiments with other graduate students; with pairs of twins; with young children. She trained herself in tarot card reading. But nearly every experiment she ran yielded nothing more than chance results.

On the rare occasions when her experiments did yield significant results, she got excited. But then, "as a scientist must," Blackmore recalls, "I repeated the experiment, checked for errors, redid the statistics, and varied the conditions, and every time either I found the error or got chance results again." Eventually, she had to face the truth: that she might have been wrong all along, and that perhaps paranormal phenomena weren't real.

It was a tough truth to face, especially because by that point Blackmore's whole identity was built around belief in the paranormal. She had trained as a witch and attended Spiritualist churches, wore New Age clothing, used tarot, hunted ghosts. Her friends were incredulous that she was considering "switching sides" to join the skeptics. All the forces of tribalism were pushing her to keep believing.

"But deep down," Blackmore says, "I was a scientist and always have been. These results were telling me something very loud and clear. I was wrong!"

## FLIPPING THE SCRIPT ON IDENTITY

Blackmore's identity as a believer in paranormal phenomena made it difficult for her to change her mind, yet she ultimately managed to anyway. That's because, in addition to her identity as a paranormal believer, Blackmore had a second identity, one that was strong enough to counter the first—that of a truth-seeker. She prided herself on subjecting her conclusions to thorough scrutiny, double-checking results, and ultimately believing her data.

That's a common theme among people who are good at facing hard truths, changing their mind, taking criticism, and listening to opposing views. Scout mindset isn't a chore they carry out grudgingly; it's a deep personal value of theirs, something they take pride in.

Throughout the last two chapters, we've seen how your identity is a hindrance to scout mindset, how thinking of yourself as "a feminist" or "an optimist" can shape your thinking and behavior in invisible ways, creating pressure to believe certain things and defend certain positions regardless of whether they're true. This chapter is about a way to make that phenomenon work for us instead of against us by flipping the script and making scout mindset part of our identity.

We can return now to Joshua Harris, the pastor and author of *I Kissed Dating Goodbye*. When we last left him, Harris had begun to seriously consider the possibility that his critics were right. Maybe the pro-purity message of his book was too extreme. Maybe it really had been damaging to some of his readers' relationships and self-worth, even though that was never his intention. Still, he found it hard to stomach the thought of repudiating his own book. As he admitted to a journalist, "Part of the reason this has been so hard for me is that I have so much of my identity tied up in these books. It's what I'm known for. It's like, well, crap, is the biggest thing I've done in my life this really huge mistake?"[2]

Identity made it hard for Harris to face the truth, but in the end, identity is also the reason he succeeded. In 2015, Harris stepped down as pastor and enrolled in a graduate school of theology. At age forty, it was his first time attending a traditional school full time—he had been homeschooled as a child and, after his book made him famous at twenty-one, he had become a pastor without going to college first. The change in his role sparked a corresponding change in the way he saw himself. He was no longer the "leader with answers." He was a "student with questions," and he found that the new identity made it easier for him to entertain new perspectives, even when they pushed the limits of his comfort zone.[3]

By 2018, Harris had concluded his soul-searching and found his answer: he had decided to discontinue publication of *I Kissed Dating Goodbye*. He announced the decision on his website, explaining: "I no longer agree with its central idea that dating should be avoided. I now think dating can be a healthy part of a person developing relationally and learning the qualities that matter most in a partner."[4]

# IDENTITY MAKES HARD THINGS REWARDING

Imagine you've made a promise to yourself that every day this week, you'll get up when your alarm goes off instead of indulging in your usual habit of hitting the snooze button. On Monday morning, the alarm goes off at 5:30 a.m., but you're exhausted and sorely tempted to renege on your promise. Compare the following two things you could say to motivate yourself to get out of bed:

1. "I shouldn't break promises to myself."
2. "I'm the kind of person who follows through on their promises."

The first statement frames the situation in terms of your obligations. The word *shouldn't* suggests a figurative parent or other authority figure, wagging their finger at you. If you get out of bed, it feels grudging, like you're forcing yourself to do something. By contrast, the second statement frames the situation in terms of your identity. Getting out of bed is now an affirmation of your values, proof that you're living up to the kind of person you want to be.

The same is true of scout mindset. If you pride yourself on being a scout, it becomes easier to resist the temptation to mock someone who disagrees with you, because you can remind yourself, "I'm not the kind of person who takes cheap shots," and get a hit of pride. It becomes easier to acknowledge when you make a mistake, because you can tell yourself, "I don't make excuses for myself," and feel a rush of satisfaction. And sometimes, those hits of pride or satisfaction are enough to make the scout path more tempting than the soldier path.

Why was Jerry Taylor, the former climate change skeptic, willing to listen to the best arguments against his position and double-check his facts when informed that they were wrong? Identity. He took pride in not being a hack:

Most people who do what I do for a living are not in the business of wrestling with the strongest arguments and strongest advocates for the other side. They're in the business of being the best spokesmen for their cause within their choir. And I wanted to do something beyond that. And so because I had greater aspirations for myself, it required me to wrestle with the best arguments from the other side.[5]

You may recall how, after that momentous conversation in his office with the climate activist, Taylor turned to his colleague and said, "Our position just got shredded to pieces." But his emotional reaction wasn't despair or bitterness. Instead, this is how Taylor described that moment: "Invigorating."

Think about how you feel the day after an especially strenuous workout. Your muscles are sore. But doesn't the soreness, although uncomfortable, also feel kind of satisfying? It's a reminder that you did something hard that's going to pay off for you in the long run. If you have a scout identity, that's how it feels when you realize you have to change your mind. It's not that it's easy; it still stings a little to realize that you made a mistake or that the person you've been arguing with actually has a point. But that slight sting is a reminder that you're living up to your standards, that you're becoming stronger. And so the sensation becomes pleasurable, in the same way sore muscles can be pleasurable for someone making progress toward getting in shape.

In chapter 3, we saw how our brains have a built-in bias for short-term rewards, and that this causes us to reflexively reach for soldier mindset more often than we should. Identities are a patch for that bug. They change the landscape of emotional incentives, allowing us to feel rewarded in the short term by choices that technically pay off only in the long term.

# YOUR COMMUNITIES SHAPE YOUR IDENTITY

Bethany Brookshire has always cared about getting things right. But over the course of her life, her ability to acknowledge her errors—or even to notice them in the first place—has fluctuated depending on the community she's been embedded in.

When she was in high school, Brookshire was a member of the drama club, where imperfection was considered a normal, expected part of the learning process. Against that backdrop, she found it relatively easy to notice and talk about flaws in her own performances.

When she started working on her PhD, things changed. In the cutthroat environment of academia, her colleagues would pounce on any admission of error. Brookshire noticed her mind trying to "paper over" things she had gotten wrong, and she had to struggle to overcome the impulse.

When she quit academia ten years later to become a journalist, things changed again. Brookshire's editor was genuinely appreciative when she would call out her own mistakes, as were the vast majority of her readers online. Noticing errors became easier once more. When she followed up her claim about gender bias in emails with a correction, the reaction she got was laudatory. "Surprising and awesome follow-up," said one person. "Inspirational." "We need more of this."

I've focused almost exclusively on what you as an individual can do to change your thinking, holding the world around you constant, because I wanted this book to be useful to you right away. But in the medium-to-long term, one of the biggest things you can do to change your thinking is to change the people you surround yourself with. We humans are social creatures, and our identities are shaped by our social circles, almost without our noticing.

Suppose you told your friends or coworkers that you weren't sure you agreed 100 percent with some political view they all share. Would you expect them to be curious about your reasoning or to become hostile toward you? Suppose you're having a disagreement with someone in your social group. Do you feel free to take a moment to consider their point before replying, or do you expect any hesitation on your part to be met with a triumphant smirk from them?

You can make the effort to think honestly no matter what community you're embedded in. But your friends, coworkers, and audience can either provide a headwind or a tailwind for your efforts.

That tailwind is one of the reasons I joined the effective altruist movement. The core effective altruist organizations maintain public pages titled "Our Mistakes." Prominent individuals in the movement publish blog posts with titles like "Three Key Issues I've Changed My Mind About."[6] Some of the harshest censures I've seen from effective altruists have been directed at other people in the movement, for exaggerating or promoting effective altruism to the public in an intellectually dishonest way.

And for the most part, they welcome good criticism. In 2013, a friend of mine named Ben Kuhn published a blog post titled "A Critique of Effective Altruism."[7] It sparked a sprawling discussion in which the most upvoted comments were all from other effective altruists saying some version of the following: "Nice job, but it feels like you went too easy on us. Here are some stronger criticisms I would make . . ."

Earlier that year, Ben had applied for an internship at GiveWell, one of the most prominent effective altruist organizations, but he had been turned down. After reading Ben's critique, GiveWell got back in touch with him and offered him the position.

Like any community, effective altruism isn't perfect, and I could add my own critiques to Ben's. But overall, my experience has been that it makes a sincere effort to reward people for making the community more accurate, not for falling in line or cheering blindly for our "team." In other social groups I've belonged to, there was always an implicit threat in the back of my mind, deflecting my thoughts away from certain conclusions: *You can't believe* that *or people will hate you.* It's freeing to know that among effective altruists, disagreeing with the consensus won't cost me any social points, as long as I'm making a good-faith effort to figure things out.

# YOU CAN CHOOSE WHAT KIND OF PEOPLE YOU ATTRACT

The media has called Vitalik Buterin a "prophet," a "mastermind," a "genius," and "the blockchain movement's biggest celebrity." His star rose in 2013, when a nineteen-year-old Buterin cofounded the Ethereum blockchain and its corresponding cryptocurrency, Ether, one of the most well-known cryptocurrencies after Bitcoin. Buterin's importance in the cryptocurrency world is so great that in 2017, a false rumor that he had died in a car accident sent the price of Ether tumbling, wiping out billions of dollars of value in a few hours.

Given his reputation, you might expect Buterin to speak with the utter certainty of a guru, or even a cult leader. However, it's an odd kind of cryptocurrency cult leader who says, as Buterin has, "I've just never had 100% confidence in cryptocurrency as a sector. See my many blog posts and videos, I'm consistent in my uncertainty."[8]

Indeed he is. At the height of crypto-mania in December 2017, when the total market capitalization of cryptocurrencies hit half a trillion dollars and other crypto folks were crowing, Buterin tweeted skeptically, "But have we *earned* it?" and listed reasons the whole field was overvalued. He's warned people repeatedly that crypto is a highly volatile field that could drop to near zero at any time, and that they shouldn't invest any money they aren't prepared to lose. In fact, he cashed out 25 percent of his own holdings of Ether well before the peak. When some critics accused him of lacking confidence in his own currency, he shrugged it off, saying: "Meh, I am not going to apologize for sound financial planning."[9]

Buterin is similarly frank about the best arguments for and against his strategic decisions, and the strengths and weaknesses of Ethereum. In one online conversation about Ethereum's flaws, he dropped in uninvited and said, "IMO the most valid criticisms of Ethereum as it currently stands are . . ." and listed seven problems.[10]

That truthfulness sometimes creates headaches for him. Critics paraphrase him uncharitably ("Buterin admits he doesn't believe in Ethereum!") or chide him for not maintaining a positive attitude.

So why does he keep doing it? Because even though Buterin's style doesn't appeal to everyone, the people to whom it *does* appeal tend to be especially thoughtful, smart, and scout-like—and those are the kinds of people he wants to attract to Ethereum. "Part of that is an intrinsic taste preference: I would honestly rather keep the one thousand of my Twitter followers that I respect the most than all the others," he told me, "and part of it is because I really do think that having that culture increases Ethereum's chances of success."

Whether you're starting a company, growing an audience for your writing or networking with potential clients, you build a niche for yourself based on how you talk and act. If you strive to be a scout, it's true that you won't please everyone. However—as your parents may have told you growing up—that's impossible anyway. So you might as well aim to please the kind of people you'd most like to have around you, people who you respect and who motivate you to be a better version of yourself.

## YOU CAN CHOOSE YOUR COMMUNITIES ONLINE

For all that people complain about how toxic Twitter, Facebook, and the rest of the internet can be, they don't often seem to put in much effort to craft a better online experience for themselves. Sure, there are plenty of trolls, overconfident pundits, uncharitable talk show hosts, and intellectually dishonest influencers. But you don't have to give them your attention. You can choose to read, follow, and engage with the exceptions to the rule instead.

We visited one of those exceptions in chapter 12—r/FeMRA-Debates, the home of productive disagreements between feminists and men's rights activists. Another example is ChangeAView.com, an online community founded by a Finnish high school student named Kal Turnbull that has grown to over half a million members.

On ChangeAView, people kick off discussions by sharing a view that they're open to changing their mind about. For example, a post might begin, "Change my view: Realistically, there's nothing that can be done to prevent climate change," or "Change my view: All drugs should be legal." Other commenters reply with arguments against the view, and the original poster awards a "delta" to anyone who causes them to change their mind in some way.* That usually doesn't mean a 180-degree reversal, but a small update—an exception to their view or an interesting counterargument they hadn't heard before and aren't yet sure they buy.

People want to earn deltas. They're the currency of status in ChangeAView, with each member's cumulative delta count displayed next to their name. Over time, people develop communication styles that more reliably yield deltas, such as asking clarifying questions and trying not to outright insult people whose minds they're hoping to change.

Partly because of the explicit community rules, and partly just because of the type of person who is attracted to such a community, the tone of discussions on ChangeAView is very different from that on

---

* Delta is a Greek letter that mathematicians use to indicate an incremental change.

most of the internet. It wasn't hard to find examples of comments like the following, any of which would be outliers elsewhere:

- "This is a very interesting response which takes me in an entirely unanticipated direction. Thank you."[11]
- "That is something that I had not considered. I think you deserve a delta."[12]
- "I don't have any counterpoint. I think this is probably the most persuasive argument I've seen on here so far, but I'm not sure if it's changed my view yet. I guess I'm still processing it."[13]

The people you read, follow, and talk to online help shape your identity just like the people in your "real-life" communities do. That can reinfoce soldier mindset if you spend your time with people who make you feel angry, defensive, and contemptuous. Or it can reinforce scout mindset if you spend your time in places like ChangeAView or r/FeMRADebates. You can even create a loosely knit "community" for yourself by making connections with people you see setting a good example of scout mindset online—bloggers, authors, or just random people on social media.

You never know what might happen if you do.

One week in 2010, I was following a heated debate online over whether a particular blog post was sexist. The blogger, a man in his midtwenties named Luke, chimed in to say that he had considered his critics' arguments carefully but didn't think that there was anything wrong with his post. Still, he said, he was open to changing his mind. He even published a list titled "Why It's Plausible I'm Wrong," in which he summarized and linked to some of the best arguments against him so far, while explaining why he wasn't quite persuaded by them.

A few days later—by which point the debate spanned over 1,500 comments across multiple blogs—Luke posted again. He wanted to let everyone know that he had found an argument that had convinced him that his original post was harmful.

He had surely already alienated many readers who believed his original post to be morally wrong, Luke acknowledged. "And now, by disagreeing with those who came to my defense and said there was nothing wrong with my post, I'll probably alienate even more readers," he said. "Well, that's too bad, because I *do* think it was morally wrong."[14]

"Wow," I thought. I admired both the fact that Luke didn't change his mind in the face of strong pressure, and the fact that he *did* change his mind in response to strong arguments. I decided to message him and share my appreciation: "Hey, this is Julia Galef—just wanted to tell you how much I appreciate your thoughtful writing! It feels like you actually care what's true."

"Hey, thanks—I feel the same way about your writing," Luke replied.

Ten years after that exchange, we're engaged to be married.

## YOU CAN CHOOSE YOUR ROLE MODELS

When there's a virtue to which you aspire, you can usually name at least one role model who embodies that virtue and motivates you to embody it. An ambitious entrepreneur may remind herself of other entrepreneurs who worked eighteen-hour days, eating ramen and setting up shop in their garage, and when she's feeling demoralized, they come to mind and inspire her to keep working. A parent who strives to be patient with their children keeps in mind an example of their own parents, grandparents, teachers, or other adults who showed admirable patience toward them when they were young.

The same is true of scout mindset. When you talk to people who are unusually good at scout mindset, they'll very often credit a role model, a person they keep in mind for inspiration. In fact, this was part of my goal in choosing stories to include in this book: I've been trying to convey not just why scout mindset is useful, but why people find it exciting, meaningful, and inspiring.

Different people are inspired by different things, and you'll want to focus on people who embody one of the aspects of scout mindset that happens to be particularly compelling to you. Maybe that's the ability to hold your identity lightly and focus on impact, like the citizen scientists during the AIDS crisis. I learned their story from David Coman-Hidy, head of the Humane League, who shares it with his team as a role model for what activism should look like. "To me, that is the ultimate inspirational story," Coman-Hidy told me. "That is the spirit that I think activists should be working in—that we're going to have obstacles come up, we're going to be wrong about things, we're going to suffer defeats . . . But we just need to constantly keep a sober assessment of what can do the most good."

Maybe what inspires you is the confidence of being comfortable with uncertainty. Julian Sanchez is a writer and senior fellow at the Cato Institute in Washington, DC. When he was in college, he conducted what turned out to be the final interview with the acclaimed political philosopher Robert Nozick before Nozick's death in 2002. The conversation made a profound impression on Sanchez.

Most philosophers Sanchez had read argued for their views in an aggressive way. Their goal was to force you to accept their conclusion by raising and then thoroughly decimating all potential objections to it. Nozick's approach was different: "He would take you with him as he worked through an issue," Sanchez recalled, "making no effort to hide points of doubt or confusion, often running off on intriguing tangents or raising problems only to admit he couldn't fully resolve them."[15] It was as if Nozick were saying: *I don't need to appear certain— because if I can't be sure of the answer, no one can be.*

That self-assured attitude toward uncertainty is what Sanchez now keeps in mind as a role model for his own writing on technology, privacy, and politics. "Nozick feeds into my aesthetic sensibility—which is the sense that it's a sign of confidence, intellectually, to not need to be certain about everything," he told me.

Maybe what you find most inspiring is the idea of having the courage to stare reality in the face. In chapter 7, I told the story of Steven Callahan, whose equanimity during his weeks as a castaway helped him plan for the worst and make the best choices he could when all his options were grim. One thing that helped Callahan achieve that equanimity was a role model: another shipwreck survivor named Dougal Robertson, who had managed to keep himself and his family alive at sea for over five weeks after their ship capsized in 1972.

Robertson's memoir, *Sea Survival*, was one of the few possessions Callahan made sure to salvage from his ship as it sank. He hadn't paid much for the book. But in those weeks he spent in the life raft, *Sea Survival* was worth "a king's ransom" to Callahan, not just for its practical tips on survival, but for its emotional guidance.[16] Robertson emphasized how important it was to accept the reality of your new life as a castaway, rather than clinging to the hope of being rescued. Each time a ship would pass by Callahan's raft, achingly close but still too far to spot him, Callahan would remind himself of Robertson's maxim: *Rescue will come as a welcome interruption of your survival voyage.*

Personally, I find all those facets of scout mindset inspiring—the willingness to prioritize impact over identity; the confidence to be unconfident; the courage to face reality. But if I were to name one single facet I find most inspiring, it's the idea of being *intellectually honorable*: wanting the truth to win out, and putting that principle above your own ego.

The example of intellectual honor I find myself thinking about most often is a story related by Richard Dawkins from his years as a student in the zoology department at Oxford.[17] At the time, there was a major controversy in biology over a cellular structure called the Golgi apparatus—was it real or an illusion created by our observational methods?

One day, a young visiting scholar from the United States came to the department and gave a talk in which he presented new and compelling evidence that the Golgi apparatus was, in fact, real. Sitting in the audience of that talk was one of Oxford's most respected zoologists, an elderly professor who was known for his position that the Golgi apparatus was illusory. So of course, throughout the talk, everyone was stealing glances at the professor, wondering: *How's he taking this? What's he going to say?*

At the end of the talk, the elderly Oxford professor rose from his seat, walked up to the front of the lecture hall, and reached out to shake hands with the visiting scholar, saying, "My dear fellow, I wish to thank you. I have been wrong these fifteen years." The lecture hall burst into applause.

Dawkins says, "The memory of this incident still brings a lump to my throat." It brings a lump to my throat, too, every time I retell that story. That's the kind of person I want to be—and that's often enough to inspire me to choose scout mindset, even when the temptations of soldier mindset are strong.

# Conclusion

WHEN PEOPLE HEAR that I wrote a book about how to stop self-deceiving and view the world realistically, they assume my worldview must be dour. *Give up your happy dreams and face harsh reality!* But in fact, this is an unusually optimistic book. Not "optimistic" in the unjustified sense, where you're supposed to believe things are wonderful no matter what, but optimistic in the justified sense: I think an honest look at our situation shows that we have cause for cheer.

Most people think you have to choose between being happy and being realistic. And so they shrug, throw up their hands, and say, "Ah well, so much the worse for realism," or sometimes, "Ah well, so much the worse for happiness."

A central theme of this book is that we *don't* have to choose. With a bit of extra effort and cleverness, we can have both. We can find ways to cope with fear and insecurity. We can take bold risks and persevere in the face of setbacks. We can influence, persuade, and inspire. We can fight effectively for social change. And we can do all of this by understanding and working with what's real, not shutting our eyes to it.

Part of "understanding and working with what's real" is accepting the fact that soldier mindset is part of your wiring. That doesn't mean you can't change the way you think, of course. But it does mean you should be aiming to take *incremental steps* in the direction from soldier to scout rather than expecting yourself to be 100 percent scout overnight.

Before you close this book, consider making a plan for what those incremental steps toward scout mindset might look like for you. I recommend picking a small number of scout habits to start with, no more than two or three. Here's a list of ideas to choose from:

1. The next time you're making a decision, ask yourself what kind of bias could be affecting your judgment in that situation, and then do the relevant thought experiment (e.g., outsider test, conformity test, status quo bias test).

2. When you notice yourself making a claim with certainty ("There's no way . . ."), ask yourself how sure you really are.

3. The next time a worry pops into your head and you're tempted to rationalize it away, instead make a concrete plan for how you would deal with it if it came true.

4. Find an author, media outlet, or other opinion source who holds different views from you, but who has a better-than-average shot at changing your mind—someone you find reasonable or with whom you share some common ground.

5. The next time you notice someone else being "irrational," "crazy," or "rude," get curious about why their behavior might make sense to them.

6. Look for opportunities to update at least a little bit. Can you find a caveat or exception to one of your beliefs, or a bit of empirical evidence that should make you slightly less confident in your position?

7. Think back to a disagreement you had with someone in the past on which your perspective has since shifted and reach out to that person to let them know how you've updated.

8. Pick a belief you hold strongly and attempt an ideological Turing test of the other side. (Bonus points if you can actually find someone from the other side to judge your attempt.)

Whichever other habits you choose to focus on, here's one more that should be on your list: Keep an eye out for examples of motivated reasoning in yourself—and when you spot one, *be proud of yourself for noticing*. Remember, motivated reasoning is universal; if you never notice it, that's probably not because you're immune. Becoming more aware of motivated reasoning is an essential step on the way to reducing it, and you should feel good about taking that step.

I also think the case for justified optimism extends to humanity as a whole. Knowing how deeply soldier mindset is etched into the human brain—and how difficult it is to notice in ourselves, let alone overcome, even if we're smart and well-intentioned—becoming aware of these facts has made me much more forgiving of other people's unreasonableness. (Plus, having noticed countless examples of my own motivated reasoning by now, I don't feel like I'm in any position to judge!)

At the end of the day, we're a bunch of apes whose brains were optimized for defending ourselves and our tribes, not for doing unbiased evaluations of scientific evidence. So why get angry at humanity for not being uniformly great at something we didn't evolve to be great at? Wouldn't it make more sense to appreciate the ways in which we *do* transcend our genetic legacy?

And there are many. Jerry Taylor could easily have continued defending climate skepticism, but he cared enough about the truth to investigate the evidence against his side and change his mind. Josh

Harris could have easily kept promoting *I Kissed Dating Goodbye*, but he chose to listen to his critics, reflect on their stories, and pull the book. Bethany Brookshire didn't have to fact-check her own claim about gender bias and correct the record, but she did anyway.

You can focus on humanity's capacity for self-serving distortions of reality and feel bitter. Or you can focus on the flip side of the coin, the Picquarts of the world who are willing to spend years of their life making sure the truth wins out, and feel inspired to live up to their example.

We're not a perfect species. But we should be proud of how far we've come, not frustrated that we fall short of some ideal standard. And by choosing to become a little less like soldiers and a little more like scouts, we can be even better still.

# Acknowledgments

I AM DEEPLY INDEBTED to the good people at Portfolio who helped me craft this book and showed remarkable patience with me as I wrote, rewrote, and re-rewrote. Kaushik Viswanath, your input was always thoughtful and incisive. Nina Rodríguez-Marty, you give the best pep talks. Stephanie Frerich, thank you so much for taking a chance on me in the first place. And I can't imagine a better agent than William Callahan at Inkwell, who guided this first-time author through the process with endless support, flexibility, savvy advice, and positive energy.

I've benefited greatly from being able to spend so much time with effective altruists, a community that is rich in scout mindset and full of people whose minds and hearts I admire. I feel very lucky to have a community in which ideas are taken seriously and disagreements are approached with an attitude of "Let's work together to figure out why we're seeing this differently."

Countless people generously donated their time to this book by letting me interview them, sharing their experiences, and pushing back on my ideas in thought-provoking ways. Although this list will be woefully incomplete, I want to thank some of the individuals whose input stuck with me and ended up influencing my arguments in the book: Will MacAskill, Holden Karnofsky, Katja Grace, Morgan Davis, Ajeya Cotra, Danny Hernandez, Michael Nielson, Devon Zuegel, Patrick Collison, Jonathan Swanson, Lewis Bollard, Darragh Buckley, Julian Sanchez, Simine Vazire, Emmett Shear, Adam d'Angelo, Harjeet Taggar, Malo Bourgon, Spencer Greenberg, Stephen Zerfas, and Nate Soares.

This book might never have been finished without the help of Churchill, Whistler, Zoe, Molly, Winston, and all the other dogs of Noe Valley (and their owners who let me pet them). You kept me sane during my long lonely months of editing. Thank you; you are all the best dogs.

I'm incredibly grateful to my friends and family who supported me through the book writing process. You sent me kind messages while I was holed up like a hermit, you were understanding when I had to cancel plans, and you knew when to refrain from asking, "So, how's the writing coming?" To my brother, Jesse, and my friend Spencer: every time I talked to you about the ideas I was wrestling with, I came away with clarifying insights that made the book better. To my mom and dad: thank you for the love and encouragement, and for setting a great example of scout mindset for me growing up.

Most of all, I want to thank my fiancé, Luke, for being an invaluable pillar of support, sounding board, source of inspiration, and role model. You helped me craft the thesis of this book, made brilliant suggestions, comforted me when I was struggling, and sat patiently through so many angry rants about bad methodology in the social sciences. I couldn't ask for a better partner.

# Appendix A

## Spock's Predictions

| | |
|---|---|
| 1. | **KIRK:** You couldn't get close to the other kids?<br>**SPOCK:** Impossible. They know the area too well, like mice.<br>**KIRK:** I'm going to try.<br><br>*Kirk succeeds.*[1] |
| 2. | **SPOCK:** If Romulans are an offshoot of my Vulcan blood, and I think this likely . . .<br><br>*He is correct; Romulans are an offshoot of the Vulcan race.*[2] |
| 3. | **SPOCK:** Gentlemen, by coming after me, you may well have destroyed what slim chance you had for survival.<br><br>*Everyone survives.*[3] |
| 4. | Spock, marooned on a planet with several crew members, sends up a distress signal while claiming his own action is illogical because there is "no chance" anyone will see it.<br><br>*The* Enterprise *sees it, and rescues them.*[4] |
| 5. | Captain Kirk is on trial for negligence. Spock testifies that it is "impossible" Kirk is guilty because "I know the captain."<br><br>*He is correct; Kirk was in fact framed.*[5] |
| 6. | **KIRK:** Mr. Spock, there were one hundred and fifty men, women, and children in that colony. What are the chances of survivors?<br>**SPOCK:** Absolutely none, Captain.<br><br>*In fact, there are many survivors, who are alive and well.*[6] |

| | |
|---|---|
| **7.** | **SPOCK:** What you're describing was once known in the vernacular as a happiness pill. And you, as a scientist, should know that that's not possible.<br><br>*In fact, it is possible, and Spock is drugged with one.*[7] |
| **8.** | **SPOCK:** The odds against you and I both being killed are 2,228.7 to 1.<br>**KIRK:** 2,228.7 to 1? Those are pretty good odds, Mr. Spock.<br><br>*Indeed, they both survive.*[8] |
| **9.** | **KIRK:** Mr. Spock, can we get those two guards? What would you say the odds are on our getting out of here?<br>**SPOCK:** Difficult to be precise, Captain. I should say approximately 7,824.7 to 1.<br><br>*They both escape in the end.*[9] |
| **10.** | **KIRK:** Well, what are the odds [of a successful escape] now?<br>**SPOCK:** Less than seven thousand to one, Captain. It's remarkable we've gotten this far.<br><br>*They both escape in the end.*[10] |
| **11.** | **SPOCK:** Your chances of survival are not promising. We don't even know if the explosion will be powerful enough.<br>**KIRK:** A calculated risk, Mr. Spock.<br><br>*He survives.*[11] |
| **12.** | **KIRK:** Do you think we could create a sonic disruption with two of our communicators?<br>**SPOCK:** Only a very slight chance it would work.<br><br>*It does work.*[12] |
| **13.** | **MCCOY:** The odds [of our friends surviving] are not good.<br>**SPOCK:** No. I would say approximately four hundred—<br><br>*McCoy cuts him off, but Spock was probably going to say "four hundred to one." In fact, their friends survived after all.*[13] |
| **14.** | **CHEKOV:** Perhaps an interstellar dust cloud.<br>**SPOCK:** Not very likely, Ensign.<br><br>*Indeed, what they've spotted is not a dust cloud, but a giant space creature that drains energy.*[14] |

| | |
|---|---|
| **15.** | **KIRK:** Spock, if you reverse the circuits on McCoy's neuroanalyzer, can you set up a counter field to jam the paralysis projector?<br>**SPOCK:** I'm dubious of the possibilities of success, Captain . . .<br>**KIRK:** Is there a chance at all?<br>**SPOCK:** A small one.<br><br>*Indeed, it doesn't work.*[15] |
| **16.** | **KIRK:** Mr. Spock, is it possible there's a more evolved civilization somewhere else on this planet, one capable of building that obelisk or developing a deflector system?<br>**SPOCK:** Highly improbable, Captain. Sensor probes indicate only one type of life form here.<br><br>*Spock is correct.*[16] |
| **17.** | **SPOCK:** That ship is dead . . . Probability .997, Captain.<br><br>*In fact, the ship contains a dangerous alien life form.*[17] |
| **18.** | **KIRK:** Can the transporter be programmed to repattern us as we were?<br>**SPOCK:** Possibly. But the odds against us are 99.7 to one.<br><br>*The transporter works fine. They're fine.*[18] |
| **19.** | **KIRK:** Do you think Harry Mudd is down there, Spock?<br>**SPOCK:** The probability of his presence on Motherlode is 81 percent, plus or minus .53.<br><br>*Indeed, Mudd is there.*[19] |
| **20.** | **EM:** We'll all die here.<br>**SPOCK:** A statistical probability.<br><br>*They survive.*[20] |
| **21.** | **EM:** [The saboteur is] one of us . . . ?<br>**SPOCK:** Approximately 82.5 percent in favor of the possibility.<br><br>*Indeed, the saboteur is in their group.*[21] |
| **22.** | **KIRK:** Mr. Spock, what are our chances?<br>**SPOCK:** . . . If the density grows no worse we should be able to ride it out.<br><br>*They succeed.*[22] |
| **23.** | **SPOCK:** Captain, intercepting all three ships is an impossibility!<br><br>*Kirk succeeds.*[23] |

# Appendix B

## Calibration Practice Answers

### Round 1: Animal Facts

1. False. The blue whale, not the elephant, is the largest mammal.
2. True.
3. False. The millipede is the animal with the most legs—some have as many as 750 legs. The centipede can have up to 354 legs.
4. True. The first mammals appeared roughly 200 million years ago. Dinosaurs went extinct roughly 65 million years ago.
5. False.
6. False. Camels store fat, not water, in their humps.
7. True.
8. True. A giant panda's diet is almost entirely bamboo.
9. False. The platypus is one of two mammals that lay eggs. The other is the echidna.
10. True.

### Round 2: Historical Figures

11. Confucius (551 BC) was born before Julius Caesar (100 BC).

12. Mahatma Gandhi (1869) was born before Fidel Castro (1926).

13. Nelson Mandela (1918) was born before Anne Frank (1929).

14. Cleopatra (69 BC) was born before Muhammad (circa 570).

15. Joan of Arc (circa 1412) was born before William Shakespeare (1564).

16. Sun Tzu (544 BC) was born before George Washington (1732).

17. Genghis Khan (circa 1160) was born before Leonardo da Vinci (1452).

18. Karl Marx (1818) was born before Queen Victoria (1819).

19. Marilyn Monroe (1926) was born before Saddam Hussein (1937).

20. Albert Einstein (1879) was born before Mao Zedong (1893).


## Round 3: Country Populations as of 2019

21. Germany (84 million) has more people than France (65 million).

22. Japan (127 million) has more people than South Korea (51 million).

23. Brazil (211 million) has more people than Argentina (45 million).

24. Egypt (100 million) has more people than Botswana (2 million).

25. Mexico (128 million) has more people than Guatemala (18 million).

26. Panama (4 million) has more people than Belize (390,000).

27. Haiti (11 million) has more people than Jamaica (3 million).

28. Greece (10 million) has more people than Norway (5 million).

29. China (1.43 billion) has more people than India (1.37 billion).

30. Iran (83 million) has more people than Iraq (39 million).


## Round 4: General Science Facts

31. False. Mars has two moons, Phobos and Deimos.

32. True.

33. False. Brass is made of zinc and copper, not iron and copper.

34. True. One tablespoon of oil has roughly 120 calories, while one tablespoon of butter can contain up to 110 calories.

35. False. The lightest element is hydrogen, not helium.

36. False. The common cold is caused by viruses, not bacteria.

37. True.

38. False. Seasons are caused by the tilt of the earth's axis.

39. True.

40. True.

# Notes

### Chapter 1. Two Types of Thinking

1. Descriptions of the Dreyfus affair in this chapter are based on Jean-Denis Bredin, *The Affair: The Case of Alfred Dreyfus* (London: Sidgwick and Jackson, 1986); Guy Chapman, *The Dreyfus Trials* (London: B. T. Batsford Ltd., 1972); and Piers Paul Read, *The Dreyfus Affair: The Scandal That Tore France in Two* (London: Bloomsbury, 2012).

2. "Men of the Day.—No. DCCLIX—Captain Alfred Dreyfus," *Vanity Fair*, September 7, 1899, https://bit.ly/2LPkCsl.

3. The paper that popularized the concept of directionally motivated reasoning is Ziva Kunda, "The Case for Motivated Reasoning," *Psychological Bulletin* 108, no. 3 (1990): 480–98, https://bit.ly/2MMybM5.

4. Thomas Gilovich, *How We Know What Isn't So: The Fallibility of Human Reason in Everyday Life* (New York: The Free Press, 1991), 84.

5. Robert B. Strassler, ed., *The Landmark Thucydides* (New York: The Free Press, 2008), 282.

6. The "argument is war" metaphor in the English language was most famously pointed out in George Lakoff and Mark Johnson, *Metaphors We Live By* (Chicago: University of Chicago Press, 1980).

7. Ronald Epstein, Daniel Siegel, and Jordan Silberman, "Self-Monitoring in Clinical Practice: A Challenge for Medical Educators," *Journal of Continuing Education in the Health Professions* 28, no. 1 (Winter 2008): 5–13.

8. Randall Kiser, *How Leading Lawyers Think* (London and New York: Springer, 2011), 100.

### Chapter 2: What the Soldier Is Protecting

1. G. K. Chesterton, "The Drift from Domesticity," *The Thing* (1929), loc. 337, Kindle.

2. G. K. Chesterton, *The Collected Works of G. K. Chesterton*, vol. 3 (San Francisco, CA: Ignatius Press, 1986), 157.

3. James Simpson, *The Obstetric Memoirs and Contributions of James Y. Simpson,* vol. 2 (Philadelphia: J. B. Lippincott & Co., 1856).

4. Leon R. Kass, "The Case for Mortality," *American Scholar* 52, no. 2 (Spring 1983): 173–91.

5. Alina Tugend, "Meeting Disaster with More Than a Wing and a Prayer," *New York Times,* July 19, 2008, https://www.nytimes.com/2008/07/19/business/19shortcuts.html.

6. *Election*, directed by Alexander Payne (MTV Films in association with Bona Fide Productions, 1999).

7. R. W. Robins and J. S. Beer, "Positive Illusions About the Self: Short-term Benefits and Long-term Costs," *Journal of Personality and Social Psychology* 80, no. 2 (2001): 340–52, doi:10.1037/0022-3514.80.2.340.

8. Jesse Singal, "Why Americans Ignore the Role of Luck in Everything," *The Cut,* May 12, 2016, https://www.thecut.com/2016/05/why-americans-ignore-the-role-of-luck-in-everything.html.

9. wistfulxwaves (Reddit user), comment on "Masochistic Epistemology," Reddit, September 17, 2018, https://www.reddit.com/r/BodyDysmorphia/comments/9gntam/masochistic_epistemology/e6fwxzf/.

10. A. C. Cooper, C. Y. Woo, and W. C. Dunkelberg, "Entrepreneurs' Perceived Chances for Success," *Journal of Business Venturing* 3, no. 2 (1988): 97–108, doi:10.1016/0883-9026(88)90020-1.

11. Daniel Bean, "Never Tell Me the Odds," *Daniel Bean Films* (blog), April 29, 2012, https://danielbeanfilms.wordpress.com/2012/04/29/never-tell-me-the-odds/.

12. Nils Brunsson, "The Irrationality of Action and Action Rationality: Decisions, Ideologies and Organizational Actions," *Journal of Management Studies* 19, no. 1 (1982): 29–44.

13. The distinction between emotional and social benefits is at the heart of a debate between psychologists and evolutionary psychologists over the true function of soldier mindset. Psychologists often describe the emotional benefits of motivated reasoning as a kind of "psychological immune system" that evolved to protect our emotional health, much the way our regular immune system evolved to protect our physical health.

The idea of a psychological immune system is intuitively compelling. The only problem with it, evolutionary psychologists retort, is that it makes no sense. There's no reason for evolution to endow a mind with the capacity to make itself feel good. However, there *is* a reason for evolution to endow us with the capacity to look good. If we can convince other people that we're strong, loyal, and high-status, they'll be more inclined to submit to us and mate with us. The social benefits of motivated reasoning are why it evolved, the evolutionary psychologists argue, and the emotional benefits are just side effects.

There's also a third possibility: that in many cases, our use of soldier mindset isn't an evolved trait at all. It's simply something we do because it feels good and we can. By analogy, masturbation didn't *evolve*, per se. But our sex drive evolved, and our hands evolved . . . and we humans figured out how to combine the two.

14. Robert A. Caro, *Master of the Senate: The Years of Lyndon Johnson* III (New York: Knopf Doubleday Publishing Group, 2009), 886.

15. Z. J. Eigen and Y. Listokin, "Do Lawyers Really Believe Their Own Hype, and Should They? A Natural Experiment," *Journal of Legal Studies* 41, no. 2 (2012), 239–67, doi:10/1086/667711.

16. Caro, *Master of the Senate*, 886.

17. Randall Munroe, "Bridge," *XKCD*, https://xkcd.com/1170.

18. Peter Nauroth et al., "Social Identity Threat Motivates Science-Discrediting Online Comments," *PloS One* 10, no. 2 (2015), doi:10.1371/journal.pone.0117476.

19. Kiara Minto et al., "A Social Identity Approach to Understanding Responses to Child Sexual Abuse Allegations," *PloS One* 11 (April 25, 2016), doi:10.1371/journal.pone.0153205.

20. This result is reported in Eigen and Listokin, "Do Lawyers Really Believe Their Own Hype, and Should They?" There's a similar backfire effect in negotiations—students who are randomly assigned to one side of a case before reading the facts come to believe their side is in the right, and to demand more money in the negotiation. As a result, they are less likely to reach an agreement and come away with less money on average. See George Loewenstein, Samuel Issacharoff, Colin Camerer, and Linda Babcock, "Self-Serving Assessments of Fairness and Pretrial Bargaining," *Journal of Legal Studies* 22, no. 1 (1993): 135–59.

### Chapter 3. Why Truth Is More Valuable Than We Realize

1. Bryan Caplan, "Rational Ignorance Versus Rational Irrationality, *KYKLOS* 54, no. 1 (2001): 2–26, doi:10.1111/1467-6435.00128. In Caplan's paper, he envisions people manipulating which beliefs they adopt by applying more effort

to the questions they want accurate beliefs about, and less effort to the questions they want false beliefs about. And sometimes that's how soldier mindset works—we hear an argument, and if we are in "Can I accept it?" mode, then we simply accept it without scrutiny. But other times, soldier mindset involves applying far more effort to come up with justifications for a false belief.

2. The best discussion of how present bias and vividness bias affect our decision-making is George Ainslie's *Picoeconomics: The Strategic Interaction of Successive Motivational States Within the Person* (Cambridge, UK: Cambridge University Press, 1992).

3. Andrea Gurmankin Levy et al., "Prevalence of and Factors Associated with Patient Nondisclosure of Medically Relevant Information to Clinicians," *JAMA Network Open* 1, no. 7 (November 30, 2018): e185293, https://jamanetwork.com/journals/jamanetworkopen/fullarticle/2716996.

4. "Up to 81% of Patients Lie to Their Doctors—And There's One Big Reason Why," *The Daily Briefing*, December 10, 2018, https://www.advisory.com/daily -briefing/2018/12/10/lying-patients.

5. Joanne Black, "New Research Suggests Kiwis Are Secretly Far More Ambitious Than We Let On," *Noted*, April 4, 2019, https://www.noted.co.nz/health /psychology/ambition-new-zealanders-more-ambitious-than-we-let-on/.

6. Mark Svenvold, *Big Weather: Chasing Tornadoes in the Heart of America* (New York: Henry Holt and Co., 2005), 15.

*Chapter 4. Signs of a Scout*

1. u/AITAthrow12233 (Reddit user), "AITA if I don't want my girlfriend to bring her cat when she moves in?," Reddit, November 3, 2018, https://www .reddit.com/r/AmItheAsshole/comments/9tyc9m/aita_if_i_dont_want_my _girlfriend_to_bring_her/.

2. Alexandra Wolfe, "Katie Couric, Woody Allen: Jeffrey Epstein's Society Friends Close Ranks," *Daily Beast*, April 1, 2011, https://www.thedailybeast .com/katie-couric-woody-allen-jeffrey-epsteins-society-friends-close-ranks.

3. Isaac Asimov, "A Cult of Ignorance," *Newsweek*, January 21, 1980.

4. Richard Shenkman, *Just How Stupid Are We? Facing the Truth About the American Voter* (New York: Basic Books, 2008).

5. Dan M. Kahan, "'Ordinary Science Intelligence': A Science-Comprehension Measure for Study of Risk and Science Communication, with Notes on Evolution and Climate Change," *Journal of Risk Research* 20, no. 8 (2017): 995–1016, doi:10.1080/13669877.2016.1148067.

6. Caitlin Drummond and Baruch Fischhoff, "Individuals with Greater Science Literacy and Education Have More Polarized Beliefs on Controversial Science

Topics," *Proceedings of the National Academy of Sciences* 114, no. 36 (2017): 9587–92, doi:10.1073/pnas.1704882114.

7. Yoel Inbar and Joris Lammers, "Political Diversity in Social and Personality Psychology," *Perspectives on Psychological Science* 7 (September 2012): 496–503.

8. These items are taken from two of the most widely used metrics of "rigidity." Item 1 is from the Right-Wing Authoritarianism Scale, designed to measure the "authoritarian personality." Items 2–4 are from the Wilson Conservatism Scale, designed to capture "authoritarianism, dogmatism, fascism, and anti-scientific attitude." G. D. Wilson and J. R. Patterson, "A New Measure of Conservatism," *British Journal of Social and Clinical Psychology* 7, no. 4 (1968): 264–69, doi:10.1111/j.2044-8260.1968.tb00568.x.

9. William Farina, *Ulysses S. Grant, 1861–1864: His Rise from Obscurity to Military Greatness* (Jefferson, NC: McFarland & Company, 2014), 147.

10. Charles Carleton Coffin, *Life of Lincoln* (New York and London: Harper & Brothers, 1893), 381.

11. William Henry Herndon and Jesse William Weik, *Herndon's Informants: Letters, Interviews, and Statements About Abraham Lincoln* (Champaign, IL: University of Illinois Press, 1998), 187.

12. Bethany Brookshire (@BeeBrookshire), Twitter, January 22, 2018, https://bit.ly/2Awl8qJ.

13. Bethany Brookshire (@BeeBrookshire), Twitter, January 29, 2018, https://bit.ly/2GTkUjd.

14. Bethany Brookshire, "I went viral. I was wrong," blog post, January 29, 2018, https://bethanybrookshire.com/i-went-viral-i-was-wrong/.

15. Regina Nuzzo, "How Scientists Fool Themselves—And How They Can Stop," *Nature*, October 7, 2015, https://www.nature.com/news/how-scientists-fool-themselves-and-how-they-can-stop-1.18517.

16. Darwin Correspondence Project, "Letter no. 729," accessed on January 5, 2020, https://www.darwinproject.ac.uk/letter/DCP-LETT-729.xml.

17. Darwin Correspondence Project, "Letter no. 2791," accessed on February 7, 2020, https://www.darwinproject.ac.uk/letter/DCP-LETT-2791.xml.

18. Darwin Correspondence Project, "Letter no. 2741," accessed on January 10, 2020, https://www.darwinproject.ac.uk/letter/DCP-LETT-2741.xml.

### Chapter 5. Noticing Bias

1. Max H. Bazerman and Don Moore, *Judgment in Managerial Decision Making* (New York: John Wiley & Sons, 2008), 94.

2. u/spiff2268 (Reddit user), comment on "[Serious] Former Incels of Reddit. What brought you the ideology and what took you out?," Reddit, August

22, 2018, https://www.reddit.com/r/AskReddit/comments/99buzw/serious
_former_incels_of_reddit_what_brought_you/e4mt073/.

3.   Greendruid, comment on "Re: Democrats may maneuver around GOP on
     healthcare," Discussion World Forum, April 26, 2009, http://www.discussion
     worldforum.com/showpost.php?s=70747dd92d8fbdba12c4dd0592d72114
     &p=7517&postcount=4.

4.   Andrew S. Grove, *Only the Paranoid Survive: How to Exploit the Crisis Points
     That Challenge Every Company* (New York: Doubleday, 1999), 89.

5.   A turn of phrase borrowed from Hugh Prather, *Love and Courage* (New York:
     MJF Books, 2001), 87.

6.   Julie Bort, "Obama Describes What Being in the Situation Room Is Like—and
     It's Advice Anyone Can Use to Make Hard Decisions," *Business Insider*, May
     24, 2018, https://www.businessinsider.com/obama-describes-situation-room
     -gives-advice-for-making-hard-decisions-2018-5.

7.   A more nuanced version of the status quo bias test for policy views is de-
     scribed in Nick Bostrom and Toby Ord, "The Reversal Test: Eliminating Sta-
     tus Quo Bias in Applied Ethics," *Ethics* 116, no. 4 (July 2006): 656–79, https://
     www.nickbostrom.com/ethics/statusquo.pdf.

*Chapter 6. How Sure Are You?*

1.   *Star Trek Beyond*, directed by Justin Lin (Hollywood, CA: Paramount Pic-
     tures, 2016).

2.   *Star Trek: The Original Series*, season 2, episode 11, "Friday's Child," aired
     December 1, 1967, on NBC.

3.   *Star Trek: The Original Series*, season 1, episode 26, "Errand of Mercy," aired
     March 23, 1967, on NBC.

4.   *Star Trek: The Original Series*, season 1, episode 24, "This Side of Paradise,"
     aired March 2, 1967, on NBC.

5.   "As a percentage, how certain are you that intelligent life exists outside
     of Earth?," Reddit, October 31, 2017, https://www.reddit.com/r/Astronomy
     /comments/79up5b/as_a_percentage_how_certain_are_you_that/dp51sg2/.

6.   "How confident are you that you are going to hit your 2017 sales goals? What
     gives you that confidence?," Quora, https://www.quora.com/How-confident
     -are-you-that-you-are-going-to-hit-your-2017-sales-goals-What-gives-you
     -that-confidence.

7.   Filmfan345 (Reddit user), "How confident are you that you won't convert on
     your deathbed?," Reddit, February 3, 2020, https://www.reddit.com/r/atheism
     /comments/eycqrb/how_confident_are_you_that_you_wont_convert_on/.

8. M. Podbregar et al., "Should We Confirm Our Clinical Diagnostic Certainty by Autopsies?" *Intensive Care Medicine* 27, no. 11 (2001): 1752, doi:10.1007/s00134-001-1129-x.

9. I had to exercise some creative license to put Spock's varied predictions into these categories. For example, the category "likely" includes both the time Spock declared something a "statistical probability" and also the time he predicted an "82.5% chance." For the purposes of graphing the results, I centered "impossible" predictions at 0% chance, "very unlikely" at 10% chance, "unlikely" at 25% chance, and "likely" at 75% chance. All told, this should be taken as a rough, impressionistic depiction of Spock's calibration, rather than a literal calibration curve.

10. Douglas W. Hubbard, *How to Measure Anything: Finding the Value of "Intangibles" in Business* (Hoboken, NJ: John Wiley & Sons, 2007), 61.

11. Robert Kurzban, *Why Everyone (Else) Is a Hypocrite* (Princeton, NJ: Princeton University Press, 2010).

12. The technique in this section is adapted from Douglas W. Hubbard, *How to Measure Anything: Finding the Value of "Intangibles" in Business* (Hoboken, NJ: John Wiley & Sons, Inc., 2007), 58.

### Chapter 7. Coping with Reality

1. Steven Callahan, *Adrift: Seventy-six Days Lost at Sea* (New York: Houghton Mifflin, 1986).

2. Callahan, *Adrift,* 84.

3. Callahan, *Adrift,* 39.

4. Callahan, *Adrift,* 45.

5. Carol Tavris and Elliot Aronson, *Mistakes Were Made (But Not by Me): Why We Justify Foolish Beliefs, Bad Decisions, and Hurtful Acts* (New York: Houghton Mifflin Harcourt, 2007), 11.

6. Daniel Kahneman, *Thinking, Fast and Slow* (New York: Farrar, Straus and Giroux, 2013), 264.

7. Darwin Correspondence Project, "Letter no. 3272," accessed on December 1, 2019, https://www.darwinproject.ac.uk/letter/DCP-LETT-3272.xml.

8. Charles Darwin, *The Autobiography of Charles Darwin* (New York: W. W. Norton & Company, 1958), 126.

9. *The Office*, season 2, episode 5, "Halloween," directed by Paul Feig, written by Greg Daniels, aired October 18, 2005, on NBC.

10. Stephen Fried, *Bitter Pills: Inside the Hazardous World of Legal Drugs* (New York: Bantam Books, 1998), 358.

11. David France, *How to Survive a Plague: The Inside Story of How Citizens and Science Tamed AIDS* (New York: Knopf Doubleday Publishing Group, 2016), 478.

12. Douglas LaBier, "Why Self-Deception Can Be Healthy for You," *Psychology Today*, February 18, 2013, https://www.psychologytoday.com/us/blog/the-new -resilience/201302/why-self-deception-can-be-healthy-you.

13. Joseph T. Hallinan, *Kidding Ourselves: The Hidden Power of Self-Deception* (New York: Crown, 2014).

14. Stephanie Bucklin, "Depressed People See the World More Realistically—And Happy People Just Might Be Slightly Delusional," *Vice*, June 22, 2017, https:// www.vice.com/en_us/article/8x9j3k/depressed-people-see-the-world-more -realistically.

15. J. D. Brown, "Evaluations of Self and Others: Self-Enhancement Biases in So- cial Judgments," *Social Cognition* 4, no. 4 (1986): 353–76, http://dx.doi.org /10.1521/soco.1986.4.4.353.

16. It's true that if people on average think they are better than their peers, that's evidence that at least some people are self-deceiving. After all, the real world isn't Lake Wobegon, where "all the children are above average." But it's also presumably the case that many, perhaps most, people who think they are better than their peers in some way or another are just correctly perceiving that they are above average. And those people alone could easily be responsi- ble for the increased happiness and success we observe in the study sample.

17. Shelley Taylor and Jonathon Brown, "Illusion and Well-being: A Social Psy- chological Perspective on Mental Health," *Psychological Bulletin* 103, no. 2 (1988): 193–210, doi.org/10.1037/0033-2909.103.2.193.

18. Ruben Gur and Harold Sackeim, "Lying to Ourselves," interview by Robert Krulwich, *Radiolab*, WNYC studios, March 10, 2008, https://www.wnycstudios .org/podcasts/radiolab/segments/91618-lying-to-ourselves.

19. The Self-Deception Questionnaire appears in R. C. Gur and H. A. Sackeim, "Self-deception: A Concept in Search of a Phenomenon," *Journal of Personal- ity and Social Psychology* 37 (1979): 147–69. It's been cited as evidence of the effects of self-deception in popular books like Robin Hanson and Kevin Sim- ler's *The Elephant in the Brain*, and on popular podcasts like *Radiolab*.

### Chapter 8. Motivation Without Self-Deception

1. The earliest known reference to Ford making this statement seems to be in a 1947 issue of *Reader's Digest*, which did not provide a citation for the quote (*The Reader's Digest*, September 1947, 64; via Garson O'Toole, "Whether You

Believe You Can Do a Thing or Not, You Are Right," Quote Investigator, February 3, 2015, https://quoteinvestigator.com/2015/02/03/you-can/).

2. No source is ever given for this quote.

3. Jonathan Fields, "Odds Are for Suckers," blog post, http://www.jonathan fields.com/odds-are-for-suckers/.

4. Cris Nikolov, "10 Lies You Will Hear Before You Chase Your Dreams," MotivationGrid, December 14, 2013, https://motivationgrid.com/lies-you-will-hear -pursue-dreams/.

5. Victor Ng, *The Executive Warrior: 40 Powerful Questions to Develop Mental Toughness for Career Success* (Singapore: Marshall Cavendish International, 2018).

6. Michael Macri, "9 Disciplines of Every Successful Entrepreneur," Fearless Motivation, January 21, 2018, https://www.fearlessmotivation.com/2018/01 /21/9-disciplines-of-every-successful-entrepreneur/.

7. William James, "The Will to Believe," https://www.gutenberg.org/files/26659 /26659-h/26659-h.htm.

8. Jeff Lunden, "Equity at 100: More Than Just a Broadway Baby," *Weekend Edition Saturday*, NPR, May 25, 2013, https://www.npr.org/2013/05/25/186492136 /equity-at-100-more-than-just-a-broadway-baby.

9. Shellye Archambeau, "Take Bigger Risks," interview by Reid Hoffman, *Masters of Scale*, podcast, https://mastersofscale.com/shellye-archambeau-take -bigger-risks/.

10. Norm Brodsky, "Entrepreneurs: Leash Your Optimism," *Inc.*, December 2011, https://www.inc.com/magazine/201112/norm-brodsky-on-entrepreneurs -as-perennial-optimists.html.

11. Arguably, the growth of fax machines was a threat that Brodsky should have seen coming. Fax sales had been doubling every year for the preceding several years, according to M. David Stone, "PC to Paper: Fax Grows Up," *PC Magazine*, April 11, 1989.

12. Ben Horowitz, *The Hard Thing About Hard Things* (New York: HarperCollins, 2014).

13. Elon Musk, "Fast Cars and Rocket Ships," interview by Scott Pelley, *60 Minutes*, aired March 30, 2014, on CBS, https://www.cbsnews.com/news/tesla -and-spacex-elon-musks-industrial-empire/.

14. Catherine Clifford, "Elon Musk Always Thought SpaceX Would 'Fail' and He'd Lose His Paypal Millions," CNBC.com, March 6, 2019, https://www.cnbc.com /2019/03/06/elon-musk-on-spacex-i-always-thought-we-would-fail.html.

15. Rory Cellan-Jones, "Tesla Chief Elon Musk Says Apple Is Making an Electric Car," BBC, January 11, 2016, https://www.bbc.com/news/technology-35280633.

16. "Fast Cars and Rocket Ships," *60 Minutes*.

17. Elon Musk and Sam Altman, "Elon Musk on How to Build the Future," *Y-Combinator* (blog), September 15, 2016, https://blog.ycombinator.com/elon-musk-on-how-to-build-the-future/.

18. Paul Hoynes, "'Random Variation' Helps Trevor Bauer, Cleveland Indians Beat Houston Astros," Cleveland.com, April 27, 2017, https://www.cleveland.com/tribe/2017/04/random_variation_helps_trevor.html.

19. Alex Hooper, "Trevor Bauer's Random Variation Downs Twins Again," CBS Cleveland, May 14, 2017, https://cleveland.cbslocal.com/2017/05/14/trevor-bauers-random-variation-downs-twins-again/.

20. Merritt Rohlfing, "Trevor Bauer's Homers Have Disappeared," *SB Nation* (blog), May 26, 2018, https://bit.ly/2RCg8Lb.

21. Zack Meisel, "Trevor Bauer Continues to Wonder When Lady Luck Will Befriend Him: Zack Meisel's Musings," Cleveland.com, June 2017, https://www.cleveland.com/tribe/2017/06/cleveland_indians_minnesota_tw_138.html.

22. "Amazon CEO Jeff Bezos and Brother Mark Give a Rare Interview About Growing Up and Secrets to Success." Posted by Summit, November 14, 2017. YouTube, https://www.youtube.com/watch?v=Hq89wYzOjfs.

23. Lisa Calhoun, "When Elon Musk Is Afraid, This Is How He Handles It," *Inc.*, September 20, 2016, https://www.inc.com/lisa-calhoun/elon-musk-says-he-feels-fear-strongly-then-makes-this-move.html.

24. Nate Soares, "Come to Your Terms," Minding Our Way, October 26, 2015, http://mindingourway.com/come-to-your-terms/.

### Chapter 9. Influence Without Overconfidence

1. "Amazon's Source," *Time*, December 27, 1999.

2. "Jeff Bezos in 1999 on Amazon's Plans Before the Dotcom Crash," CNBC, https://www.youtube.com/watch?v=GltlJO56S1g.

3. Eugene Kim, "Jeff Bezos to Employees: 'One Day, Amazon Will Fail' But Our Job Is to Delay It as Long as Possible," CNBC, November 15, 2018, https://www.cnbc.com/2018/11/15/bezos-tells-employees-one-day-amazon-will-fail-and-to-stay-hungry.html.

4. Jason Nazar, "The 21 Principles of Persuasion," *Forbes*, March 26, 2013, https://www.forbes.com/sites/jasonnazar/2013/03/26/the-21-principles-of-persuasion/.

5. Mareo McCracken, "6 Simple Steps to Start Believing in Yourself (They'll Make You a Better Leader)," *Inc.*, February 5, 2018, https://www.inc.com/mareo-mccracken/having-trouble-believing-in-yourself-that-means-your-leadership-is-suffering.html.

6. Ian Dunt, "Remain Should Push for an Election," politics.co.uk, October 24, 2019, https://www.politics.co.uk/blogs/2019/10/24/remain-should-push-for-an-election.

7. Claude-Anne Lopez, *Mon Cher Papa: Franklin and the Ladies of Paris* (New Haven, CT: Yale University Press, 1966).

8. Benjamin Franklin, *The Autobiography of Benjamin Franklin* (New York: Henry Holt and Company, 1916), via https://www.gutenberg.org/files/20203/20203-h/20203-h.htm.

9. Franklin, *The Autobiography of Benjamin Franklin.*

10. Maunsell B. Field, *Memories of Many Men and of Some Women: Being Personal Recollections of Emperors, Kings, Queens, Princes, Presidents, Statesmen, Authors, and Artists, at Home and Abroad, During the Last Thirty Years* (London: Sampson Low, Marston, Low & Searle, 1874), 280.

11. C. Anderson et al., "A Status-Enhancement Account of Overconfidence," *Journal of Personality and Social Psychology* 103, no. 4 (2012): 718–35, https://doi.org/10.1037/a0029395.

12. M. B. Walker, "The Relative Importance of Verbal and Nonverbal Cues in the Expression of Confidence," *Australian Journal of Psychology* 29, no. 1 (1977): 45–57, doi:10.1080/00049537708258726.

13. Brad Stone, *The Everything Store: Jeff Bezos and the Age of Amazon* (New York: Little, Brown & Company, 2013).

14. D. C. Blanch et al., "Is It Good to Express Uncertainty to a Patient? Correlates and Consequences for Medical Students in a Standardized Patient Visit," *Patient Education and Counseling* 76, no. 3 (2009): 302, doi:10.1016/j.pec.2009.06.002.

15. E. P. Parsons et al., "Reassurance Through Surveillance in the Face of Clinical Uncertainty: The Experience of Women at Risk of Familial Breast Cancer," *Health Expectations* 3, no. 4 (2000): 263–73, doi:10.1046/j.1369-6513.2000.00097.x.

16. "Jeff Bezos in 1999 on Amazon's Plans Before the Dotcom Crash."

17. Randall Kiser, *How Leading Lawyers Think* (London and New York: Springer, 2011), 153.

18. Matthew Leitch, "How to Be Convincing When You Are Uncertain," Working in Uncertainty, http://www.workinginuncertainty.co.uk/convincing.shtml.

19. Dorie Clark, "Want Venture Capital Funding? Here's How," *Forbes*, November 24, 2012, https://www.forbes.com/sites/dorieclark/2012/11/24/want-venture-capital-funding-heres-how/#39dddb331197.

20. Stone, *The Everything Store.*

21. "Jeff Bezos in 1999 on Amazon's Plans Before the Dotcom Crash."

22. "Jeff Bezos 1997 Interview," taped June 1997 at the Special Libraries (SLA) conference in Seattle, WA. Video via Richard Wiggans, https://www.youtube .com/watch?v=rWRbTnE1PEM.

23. Dan Richman, "Why This Early Amazon Investor Bet on Jeff Bezos' Vision, and How the Tech Giant Created Its 'Flywheel,'" *Geekwire*, January 3, 2017, https://www.geekwire.com/2017/early-amazon-investor-bet-jeff-bezos -vision-tech-giant-created-flywheel/.

### Chapter 10. How to Be Wrong

1. Philip E. Tetlock and Dan Gardner, *Superforecasting: The Art and Science of Prediction* (New York: Crown, 2015), 4.

2. "GJP also beat its university-affiliated competitors, including the University of Michigan and MIT, by hefty margins, from 30% to 70%, and even outperformed professional intelligence analysts with access to classified data. After two years, GJP was doing so much better than its academic competitors that IARPA dropped the other teams," in Tetlock and Gardner, *Superforecasting*, 17–18.

3. Jerry Taylor, "A Paid Climate Skeptic Switches Sides," interview by Indre Viskontas and Stevie Lepp, *Reckonings*, October 31, 2017, http://www.reckonings .show/episodes/17.

4. Philip E. Tetlock, *Expert Political Judgment: How Good Is It? How Can We Know?* (Princeton, NJ: Princeton University Press, 2017), 132.

5. Tetlock and Gardner, *Superforecasting*.

6. The measure of error used here is the Brier score. The slope of the superforecasters' Brier scores over the course of a year (averaging together the second and third years of the tournament) was –0.26. The same figure for the regular forecasters was 0.00. (In Mellers et al., "Identifying and Cultivating Superforecasters as a Method of Improving Probabilistic Predictions," *Perspectives on Psychological Science* 10, no. 3 [2015]: 270, table 1, doi:10.1177/1745691 615577794.) Mellers et al. define the Brier score as: "The sum of squared deviations between forecasts and reality (in which reality is coded as 1 for the event and 0 otherwise), ranging from 0 (best) to 2 (worst). Suppose a question has two possible outcomes, and a forecaster predicted a probability of 0.75 for the outcome that did occur and 0.25 for the one that did not. The Brier score would be $(1 - 0.75)2 + (0 - 0.25)2 = 0.125$." ("Identifying and Cultivating Superforecasters," 269.)

7. Bethany Brookshire, "I went viral*. I was wrong," BethanyBrookshire.com (blog), January 29, 2018, https://bethanybrookshire.com/i-went-viral-i-was -wrong/.

8. Scott Alexander, "Preschool: I was wrong," Slate Star Codex, November 6, 2018, https://slatestarcodex.com/2018/11/06/preschool-i-was-wrong/.

9. Buck Shlegeris, "'Other people are wrong' vs 'I am right,'" Shlegeris.com (blog), http://shlegeris.com/2019/02/22/wrong.

10. Devon Zuegel, "What Is This thing?" DevonZuegel.com (blog), https://devonzuegel.com/page/what-is-this-thing.

11. Dylan Matthews, "This Is the Best News for America's Animals in Decades. It's About Baby Chickens," Vox, June 9, 2016, https://www.vox.com/2016/6/9/11896096/eggs-chick-culling-ended.

### Chapter 11. Lean In to Confusion

1. Earl Warren, National Defense Migration Hearings: Part 29, San Francisco Hearings, February 1942, 11011, https://archive.org/details/nationaldefensem29unit.

2. Charles Darwin, letter to Asa Gray, April 3, 1860, https://www.darwinproject.ac.uk/letter/DCP-LETT-2743.xml.

3. Charles Darwin, The Autobiography of Charles Darwin (New York: W. W. Norton & Company, 1958), 141.

4. Star Trek: The Original Series, season 1, episode 16, "The Galileo Seven," aired January 5, 1967, on NBC.

5. Philip E. Tetlock. Expert Political Judgment: How Good Is It? How Can We Know? (Princeton, NJ: Princeton University Press, 2017), 134.

6. Bruce Bueno de Mesquita, The War Trap (New Haven, CT: Yale University Press, 1983).

7. Deepak Malhotra and Max H. Bazerman, Negotiation Genius: How to Overcome Obstacles and Achieve Brilliant Results at the Bargaining Table and Beyond (New York: Bantam Books, 2008), 261.

8. Christopher Voss, Never Split the Difference: Negotiating as if Your Life Depended on It (New York: HarperCollins, 2016), 232.

9. All historical details in this section, of the council's investigation and the London Homeopathic Hospital, are taken from Michael Emmans Dean, "Selective Suppression by the Medical Establishment of Unwelcome Research Findings: The Cholera Treatment Evaluation by the General Board of Health, London 1854," Journal of the Royal Society of Medicine 109, no. 5 (2016): 200–205, doi:10.1177/0141076816645057.

10. Comment by u/donnorama, "Whoops," June 18, 2018, https://www.reddit.com/r/antiMLM/comments/8s1uua/whoops/.

11. Gary A. Klein, *Sources of Power: How People Make Decisions* (Cambridge: MIT Press, 2017), 276.

12. M. S. Cohen, J. T., Freeman, and B. Thompson, "Critical Thinking Skills in Tactical Decision Making: A Model and a Training Strategy," in *Making Decisions Under Stress: Implications for Individual and Team Training*, eds. J. A. Cannon-Bowers and E. Salas (Washington, DC: American Psychological Association, 1998), 155–89, https://doi.org/10.1037/10278-006.

13. Sophia Lee, "Hindsight and Hope," *World*, January 28, 2018, https://world.wng.org/2018/01/hindsight_and_hope.

### Chapter 12. Escape Your Echo Chamber

1. Rachael Previti, "I Watched Only Fox News for a Week and This Is What I 'Learned,'" *Tough to Tame*, May 18, 2019, https://www.toughtotame.org/i-watched-only-fox-news-for-a-week-and-heres-what-i-learned.

2. Ron French, "A Conservative and Two Liberals Swapped News Feeds. It Didn't End Well," *Bridge Magazine*, April 6, 2017, https://www.bridgemi.com/quality-life/conservative-and-two-liberals-swapped-news-feeds-it-didnt-end-well.

3. Christopher A. Bail et al., "Exposure to Opposing Views on Social Media Can Increase Political Polarization," *Proceedings of the National Academy of Sciences* 115, no. 37 (2018): 9216–21, doi:10.1073/pnas.1804840115.

4. "Discuss Gender Equality," Reddit, https://www.reddit.com/r/FeMRADebates/.

5. proud_slut (Reddit user), comment on "In Defense of Feelings and a Challenge for the MRAs," Reddit, January 19, 2015, https://www.reddit.com/r/FeMRADebates/comments/2sxlbk/in_defense_of_feelings_and_a_challenge_for_the/cntu4rq/.

6. proud_slut (Reddit user), comment on "You Don't Hate Feminism, You Just Don't Understand It," Reddit, July 24, 2014, https://www.reddit.com/r/FeMRADebates/comments/2bmtro/you_dont_hate_feminism_you_just_dont_understand_it/cj6z5er/.

7. avantvernacular (Reddit user), comment on "Who has positively changed your view of a group from the opposite side on this sub?," Reddit, May 29, 2014, https://www.reddit.com/r/FeMRADebates/comments/26t0ic/who_has_positively_changed_your_view_of_a_group/chubl5t/.

8. proud_slut (Reddit user), comment on "I'm leaving," Reddit, August 7, 2014, https://www.reddit.com/r/FeMRADebates/comments/2cx56b/im_leaving/.

9. Jerry Taylor, "A Paid Climate Skeptic Switches Sides," interview by Indre Viskontas and Stevie Lepp, *Reckonings*, October 31, 2017, http://www.reckonings.show/episodes/17.

10. Jerry Taylor, "Episode 3: A Professional Climate Denier Changes His Mind," interview by Quin Emmett and Brian Colbert Kennedy, *Important Not Important,* podcast, https://www.importantnotimportant.com/episode-3-jerry-taylor-transcript.

11. Doris Kearns Goodwin, *Team of Rivals: The Political Genius of Abraham Lincoln* (New York: Simon & Schuster, 2005).

12. Cass R. Sunstein, *Going to Extremes: How Like Minds Unite and Divide* (Oxford: Oxford University Press, 2009), 29.

13. *Bill Moyers Journal,* aired February 1, 2008, on PBS, http://www.pbs.org/moyers/journal/02012008/transcript1.html.

14. "Lincoln put him in the Cabinet and then seems to have ignored him," in T. Harry Williams, "Review of Lincoln's Attorney General: Edward Bates of Missouri," *Civil War History* 12, no. 1 (1966): 76, Project MUSE, doi:10.1353/cwh.1966.0034.

15. Brian McGinty, *Lincoln and the Court* (Cambridge: Harvard University Press, 2008), 228.

16. Scott Alexander, "Talking Snakes: A Cautionary Tale," Less Wrong, March 12, 2009, https://www.lesswrong.com/posts/atcJqdhCxTZiJSxo2/talking-snakes-a-cautionary-tale.

17. Sarah McCammon, "Evangelical Writer Kisses an Old Idea Goodbye," NPR News, December 17, 2018, https://www.npr.org/transcripts/671888011.

### Chapter 13. How Beliefs Become Identities

1. Courtney Jung, *Lactivism: How Feminists and Fundamentalists, Hippies and Yuppies, and Physicians and Politicians Made Breastfeeding Big Business and Bad Policy* (New York: Basic Books, 2015), 19.

2. Kerry Reals, "Jamie Oliver, I Branded Myself a Failure Because of Pro-Breastfeeding Propaganda. Think Before You Speak," *The Independent,* March 20, 2016, https://www.independent.co.uk/voices/jamie-oliver-i-branded-myself-a-failure-because-of-pro-breastfeeding-propaganda-think-before-you-a6942716.html.

3. Glosswitch, "Our Regressive, Insensitive, and Cultish Attitudes Toward Breastfeeding," *New Statesman,* February 11, 2013, https://www.newstatesman.com/lifestyle/2013/02/our-regressive-insensitive-and-cultish-attitude-breastfeeding.

4. Adriana1987, "Breastfeeding Propaganda," BabyCentre, March 7, 2017, https://community.babycentre.co.uk/post/a30582443/breastfeeding_propaganda.

5. Eco Child's Play, "The Preemptive Strike on Breastfeeding," March 18, 2009, https://ecochildsplay.com/2009/03/18/the-preemptive-strike-on-breastfeeding.

6. Jung, *Lactivism*, 50.

7. "Breastfeeding vs. Bottle Debate Gets Ugly," ABC News, August 21, 2001, https://abcnews.go.com/GMA/story?id=126743&page=1.

8. Lauren Lewis, "Dear 'Fed Is Best' Campaigners, Parents, and Internet Trolls," *Breastfeeding World* (blog), April 14, 2017, http://breastfeedingworld.org/2017/04/fed-up-with-fed-is-best/.

9. Justin McCarthy, "Less Than Half in U.S. Would Vote for a Socialist for President," Gallup, May 9, 2019, https://news.gallup.com/poll/254120/less-half-vote-socialist-president.aspx.

10. J. Paul Nyquist, *Prepare: Living Your Faith in an Increasingly Hostile Culture* (Chicago: Moody Publishers, 2015).

11. Haley Swenson, "Breastfeed or Don't. You Do You," *Slate*, April 30, 2018, https://slate.com/human-interest/2018/04/why-simply-giving-distressed-friends-permission-to-quit-breastfeeding-was-a-total-cop-out.html.

12. Stephanie Fairyington, "It's Time for Feminists to Stop Arguing About Breastfeeding and Fight for Better Formula," *The Observer*, September 1, 2012, https://observer.com/2012/09/time-for-feminists-to-stop-arguing-about-breastfeeding-and-fight-for-better-formula/.

13. Catskill Animal Sanctuary, "Optimism Is a Conscious Choice," https://casanctuary.org/optimism-is-a-conscious-choice/.

14. Morgan Housel, "Why Does Pessimism Sound So Smart?," *The Motley Fool*, January 21, 2016, https://www.fool.com/investing/general/2016/01/21/why-does-pessimism-sound-so-smart.aspx.

15. Eli Heina Dadabhoy, "Why Are Those Polyamorists So Damn Preachy?," Heinous Dealings (blog), *The Orbit*, September 23, 2015, https://the-orbit.net/heinous/2015/09/23/poly-preachy/.

16. P. R. Freeman and A. O'Hagan, "Thomas Bayes's Army [The Battle Hymn of Las Fuentes]," in *The Bayesian Songbook*, ed. Bradley P. Carlin (2006), 37, https://mafiadoc.com/the-bayesian-songbook-university-of-minnesota_5a0ccb291723ddeab4f385aa.html.

17. "Breathing Some Fresh Air Outside of the Bayesian Church," *The Bayesian Kitchen* (blog), http://bayesiancook.blogspot.com/2013/12/breathing-some-fresh-air-outside-of.html.

18. Sharon Bertsch McGrayne, "The Theory That Will Never Die," talk given at Bayes 250 Day, republished on Statistics Views, February 17, 2014, https://www.statisticsviews.com/details/feature/5859221/The-Theory-That-Will-Never-Die.html.

19. Deborah Mayo, "Frequentists in Exile," *Error Statistics Philosophy* (blog), https://errorstatistics.com/about-2/.

20. Randall Munroe, "Frequentists vs. Bayesians," *XKCD* #1132, https://xkcd.com /1132.

21. Phil, comment on Andrew Gelman, "I Don't Like This Cartoon," *Statistical Modeling, Causal Inference, and Social Science* (blog), November 10, 2012, https://statmodeling.stat.columbia.edu/2012/11/10/16808/#comment -109389.

22. Comment on "This is what makes science so damn wonderful," I Fucking Love Science (group), https://www.facebook.com/IFuckingLoveScience/posts /2804651909555802?comment_id=2804656062888720&reply_comment _id=2804664182887908.

23. Amy Sullivan, "The Unapologetic Case for Formula-Feeding," *New Republic*, July 31, 2012, https://newrepublic.com/article/105638/amy-sullivan -unapologetic-case-formula-feeding.

24. Suzanne Barston, *Fearless Formula Feeder,* http://www.fearlessformulafeeder .com/.

25. Megan McArdle, "How to Win Friends and Influence Refugee Policy," *Bloomberg* Opinion, November 20, 2015, https://www.bloomberg.com/opin ion/articles/2015-11-20/six-bad-arguments-for-u-s-to-take-in-syrian -refugees.

26. Stephanie Lee Demetreon, "You Aren't a Feminist If . . . ," *Odyssey*, April 3, 2017, https://www.theodysseyonline.com/youre-not-really-feminist.

27. DoubleX Staff, "Let Me Tell You What the Word Means," *Slate*, October 7, 2010, https://slate.com/human-interest/2010/10/let-me-tell-you-what-the-word -means.html.

28. Kris Wilson, *Cyanide and Happiness* #3557, May 14, 2014, http://explosm .net/comics/3557/.

29. saratiara2, post #9 on "Anyone CFBC and Change Their Mind?," Wedding-Bee, March 2014, https://boards.weddingbee.com/topic/anyone-cfbc-and -change-their-mind/.

30. Jung, *Lactivism,* Chapter 7.

### Chapter 14. Hold Your Identity Lightly

1. Paul Graham, "Keep Your Identity Small," blog post, February 2009, http:// www.paulgraham.com/identity.html.

2. Lindy West, "My Ten Favorite Kinds of Right-Wing Temper Tantrums," *Jezebel*, November 8, 2012, https://jezebel.com/my-ten-favorite-kinds-of-right -wing-temper-tantrums-5958966.

3. Jeffrey J. Volle, *The Political Legacies of Barry Goldwater and George McGovern: Shifting Party Paradigms* (New York: Palgrave Macmillan, 2010), 8.

4. Godfrey Sperling, "Goldwater's Nonpartisan Brand of Honesty," *Christian Science Monitor*, June 9, 1998, https://www.csmonitor.com/1998/0609/060998 .opin.column.1.html.

5. Peter Grier, "Richard Nixon's Resignation: The Day Before, a Moment of Truth," *Christian Science Monitor*, August 7, 2014, https://www.csmonitor .com/USA/Politics/Decoder/2014/0807/Richard-Nixon-s-resignation-the -day-before-a-moment-of-truth.

6. Godfrey Sperling, "Goldwater's Nonpartisan Brand of Honesty," *Christian Science Monitor*, June 9, 1998, https://www.csmonitor.com/1998/0609/060998 .opin.column.1.html.

7. Bart Barnes, "Barry Goldwater, GOP Hero, Dies," *Washington Post*, May 30, 1998, https://www.washingtonpost.com/wp-srv/politics/daily/may98/gold water30.htm.

8. Lloyd Grove, "Barry Goldwater's Left Turn," *Washington Post*, July 28, 1994, https://www.washingtonpost.com/wp-srv/politics/daily/may98/gold water072894.htm.

9. Timothy Egan, "Goldwater Defending Clinton; Conservatives Feeling Faint," *New York Times*, March 24, 1994, https://nyti.ms/2F7vznS.

10. Egan, "Goldwater Defending Clinton."

11. Bryan Caplan, "The Ideological Turing Test," *Library of Economics and Liberty*, June 20, 2011, https://www.econlib.org/archives/2011/06/the_ideological.html.

12. Erin K. L. G., "In Which I Tell Conservatives I Understand Them Because I Used to Be One," *Offbeat Home & Life*, January 14, 2019, https://offbeathome .com/i-used-to-be-conservative/.

13. Chez Pazienza, "Kristin Cavallari Is a Sh*tty Parent Because She Refuses to Vaccinate Her Kids," *Daily Banter*, March 14, 2014, https://thedailybanter .com/2014/03/kristin-cavallari-is-a-shtty-parent-because-she-refuses-to -vaccinate-her-kids/.

14. Ben Cohen, "A Quick Guide to Vaccines for Morons and Celebrities," *Daily Banter*, March 18, 2014, https://thedailybanter.com/2014/03/a-quick-guide -to-vaccines-for-morons-and-celebrities/.

15. Megan McArdle, "How to Win Friends and Influence Refugee Policy," *Bloomberg*, November 20, 2015, https://www.bloomberg.com/opinion/articles /2015-11-20/six-bad-arguments-for-u-s-to-take-in-syrian-refugees.

16. Adam Mongrain, "I Thought All Anti-Vaxxers Were Idiots. Then I Married One," *Vox*, September 4, 2015, https://www.vox.com/2015/9/4/9252489/anti -vaxx-wife.

17. Julia Belluz, "How Anti-Vaxxers Have Scared the Media Away from Covering Vaccine Side Effects," *Vox*, July 27, 2015, https://www.vox.com/2015/7/27 /9047819/H1N1-pandemic-narcolepsy-Pandemrix.

18. David Barr, "The Boston AIDS Conference That Never Was—And Other Grim Tales," Treatment Action Group, January/February 2003, http://www .treatmentactiongroup.org/tagline/2003/january-february/necessary -diversions.

19. David France, *How to Survive a Plague: The Inside Story of How Citizens and Science Tamed AIDS* (New York: Knopf Doubleday Publishing Group, 2016), 355–56.

20. Mark Harrington, interview by Sarah Schulman, *ActUp Oral History Project*, March 8, 2003, 46, http://www.actuporalhistory.org/interviews/images /harrington.pdf.

21. Steven Epstein, *Impure Science: AIDS, Activism, and the Politics of Knowledge* (Berkeley, CA: University of California Press, 1996).

22. France, *How to Survive a Plague*, 507.

### Chapter 15. A Scout Identity

1. Susan Blackmore, "Why I Had to Change My Mind," in *Psychology: The Science of Mind and Behaviour*, 6th ed., by Richard Gross (London: Hodder Education, 2010), 86–87. Earlier draft via https://www.susanblackmore.uk /chapters/why-i-had-to-change-my-mind/.

2. Ruth Graham, "Hello *Goodbye*," *Slate*, August 23, 2016, https://slate.com /human-interest/2016/08/i-kissed-dating-goodbye-author-is-maybe-kind -of-sorry.html.

3. Josh Harris, "3 Reasons I'm Reevaluating *I Kissed Dating Goodbye*," True LoveDates.com, August 1, 2017, https://truelovedates.com/3-reasons-im-reev aluating-i-kissed-dating-goodbye-by-joshua-harris/.

4. Jerry Taylor, "A Paid Climate Skeptic Switches Sides," interview by Indre Vis- kontas and Stevie Lepp, *Reckonings*, October 31, 2017, http:// www.reckon ings.show/episodes/17.

5. Josh Harris, "A Statement on *I Kissed Dating Goodbye*," blog post, https:// joshharris.com/statement/.

6. Holden Karnofsky, "Three Key Issues I've Changed My Mind About," Open Philanthropy Project (blog), September 6, 2016, https://www.openphilan thropy.org/blog/three-key-issues-ive-changed-my-mind-about.

7. Ben Kuhn, "A Critique of Effective Altruism," *Less Wrong* (blog), December 2, 2013, https://www.lesswrong.com/posts/E3beR7bQ723kkNHpA/a-critique -of-effective-altruism.

8. Vitalik Buterin (@vitalikButerin), on Twitter, June 21, 2017, https://twitter .com/VitalikButerin/status/877690786971754496.

9. vbuterin (Reddit user), comment on "We Need to Think of Ways to Increase ETH Adoption," Reddit, April 21, 2016, https://www.reddit.com/r/ethtrader /comments/4fql5n/we_need_to_think_of_ways_to_increase_eth_adoption /d2bh4xz/.

10. vbuterin (Reddit user), comment on "Vitalik drops the mic on r/btc," Reddit, July 5, 2017, https://www.reddit.com/r/ethtrader/comments/6lgf0l/vitalik _drops_the_mic_on_rbtc/dju1y8q/.

11. phileconomicus (Reddit user), comment on "CMV: Mass shootings are a poor justification for gun control," Reddit, August 7, 2019, https://www.reddit.com /r/changemyview/comments/cn7td1/cmv_mass_shootings_are_a_poor _justification_for/ew8b47n/?context=3.

12. pixeldigits (Reddit user), comment on "CMV: Companies having my personal data is not a big deal," Reddit, September 7, 2018, https://www.reddit.com/r /changemyview/comments/9dxxra/cmv_companies_having_my_personal _data_is_not_a/e5mkdv7/.

13. shivux (Reddit user), comment on "CMV: The U.S. is doing nothing wrong by detaining and deporting illegal immigrants," Reddit, July 24, 2019, https:// www.reddit.com/r/changemyview/comments/ch7s90/cmv_the_us_is _doing_nothing_wrong_by_detaining/eus4tj3/.

14. Luke Muehlhauser, "I apologize for my 'Sexy Scientists' post," Common Sense Atheism, July 22, 2010, http://commonsenseatheism.com/?p=10389.

15. Julian Sanchez, "Nozick," blog post, January 24, 2003, http://www.juliansan chez.com/2003/01/24/nozick/.

16. Steven Callahan, *Adrift* (New York: Houghton Mifflin, 1986), loc. 563 of 2977, Kindle.

17. Richard Dawkins, *The God Delusion* (New York: Houghton Mifflin Harcourt, 2006), 320.

*Appendix A*

1. *Star Trek: The Original Series*, season 1, episode 8, "Miri," aired October 27, 1966, on NBC.

2. *Star Trek: The Original Series*, season 1, episode 14, "Balance of Terror," aired December 15, 1966, on NBC.

3. *Star Trek: The Original Series*, season 1, episode 16, "The Galileo Seven," aired January 5, 1967, on NBC.

4. *Star Trek: The Original Series*, "The Galileo Seven."

5. *Star Trek: The Original Series*, season 1, episode 20, "Court Martial," aired February 2, 1967, on NBC.

6. *Star Trek: The Original Series*, season 1, episode 24, "This Side of Paradise," aired March 2, 1967, on NBC.

7. *Star Trek: The Original Series*, "This Side of Paradise."

8. *Star Trek: The Original Series*, season 1, episode 25, "The Devil in the Dark," aired March 9, 1967, on NBC.

9. *Star Trek: The Original Series*, season 1, episode 26, "Errand of Mercy," aired March 23, 1967, on NBC.

10. *Star Trek: The Original Series*, "Errand of Mercy."

11. *Star Trek: The Original Series*, season 2, episode 6, "The Doomsday Machine," aired October 20, 1967, on NBC.

12. *Star Trek: The Original Series*, season 2, episode 11, "Friday's Child," aired December 1, 1967, on NBC.

13. *Star Trek: The Original Series*, season 2, episode 16, "The Gamesters of Triskelion," aired January 5, 1968, on NBC.

14. *Star Trek: The Original Series*, season 2, episode 18, "The Immunity Syndrome," aired January 19, 1968, on NBC.

15. *Star Trek: The Original Series*, season 2, episode 22, "By Any Other Name," aired February 23, 1968, on NBC.

16. *Star Trek: The Original Series*, season 3, episode 3, "The Paradise Syndrome," aired October 4, 1968, on NBC.

17. *Star Trek: The Animated Series*, season 1, episode 1, "Beyond the Furthest Star," aired September 8, 1973, on NBC.

18. *Star Trek: The Animated Series*, season 1, episode 4, "The Lorelei Signal," aired September 29, 1973, on NBC.

19. *Star Trek: The Animated Series*, season 1, episode 10, "Mudd's Passion," aired November 10, 1973, on NBC.

20. *Star Trek: The Animated Series*, season 1, episode 16, "The Jihad," aired January 12, 1974, on NBC.

21. *Star Trek: The Animated Series*, "The Jihad."

22. *Star Trek: The Animated Series*, season 2, episode 3, "The Practical Joker," aired September 21, 1974, on NBC.

23. *Star Trek Beyond*, directed by Justin Lin (Hollywood, CA: Paramount Pictures, 2016).

# Index